NOT HAPPY, JOHN!

Margo Kingston is the political commentator for the *Sydney Morning Herald* online (www.smh.com.au), edits Webdiary (www.smh.com.au/webdiary) and writes a weekly column on politics in the *Sun Herald*. She was born in Maryborough, Queensland, in 1959, grew up in the north Queensland sugar city of Mackay and graduated with an Arts Law degree from the University of Queensland. She practised as a solicitor and lectured in business law before joining Brisbane's *Courier-Mail* newspaper. She has since worked for the *Times on Sunday*, the Melbourne *Age* and the *Canberra Times*, and as the political researcher for Jana Wendt on Channel Nine's *A Current Affair*. She was Phillip Adams's 'Canberra Babylon' commentator on ABC Radio's *Late Night Live* for five years. Her 1999 work *Off the Rails: The Pauline Hanson Trip* won the 2000 Dobbie award for best first book by a female writer.

www.nothappyjohn.com

NOT HAPPY, JOHN!

Defending our democracy

MARGO
KINGSTON

PENGUIN BOOKS

The author and publisher wish to thank copyright holders who gave their permission to reproduce material. If any unintended omissions have occurred, we would be pleased to hear of them and to rectify the matter in future printings.

Penguin Books

Penguin Group (Australia)
250 Camberwell Road, Camberwell, Victoria 3124, Australia
Penguin Books Ltd
80 Strand, London WC2R 0RL, England
Penguin Group (USA) Inc.
Penguin Books, a division of Pearson Canada
Penguin Group (NZ)
Penguin Books (South Africa) (Pty) Ltd
Penguin Books India (P) Ltd

First published by Penguin Group (Australia),
a division of Pearson Australia Group Pty Ltd, 2004

10 9 8 7 6 5 4 3 2 1

Cover design by Sandy Cull © Penguin Group (Australia)
Text design by Miriam Rosenbloom © Penguin Group (Australia)
Cover photograph by Stephen Jaffe/Getty Images
Author photograph by Andrew Taylor
Typeset in 10.75/16pt Janson Text by Post Pre-press Group, Brisbane, Queensland
Printed and bound in Australia by McPherson's Printing Group, Maryborough, Victoria

National Library of Australia
Cataloguing-in-Publication data:

Kingston, Margo.
    Not happy, John! : defending our democracy.

    Bibliography.
    Includes index.
    ISBN 0 14 300258 9.

    1. Howard, John, 1939-– Public opinion. 2. Liberal Party
    of Australia. 3. Public opinion – Australia. 4. Australia –
    Politics and government – 1996– . I. Title.

    320.994

www.penguin.com.au

Contents

*To my mother Jann Alcorn, my friend Jan Barham
and every Australian who gathered in cities and
towns across the nation in February 2003 to request
an alternative to invading Iraq*

Acknowledgements

Phillip Adams suggested I write this book, and Jan Barham convinced me to have a go. Lyn Tranter got the ball rolling and the enthusiasm of Bob Sessions locked me in. Lesley Dunt nursed me through a tight schedule, agreed to several unusual ideas and championed my concept. She is that rare and precious creature, an editor focused on working with her writer to draw out the best she can do. Proofreader Jane Drury was a valued voice, and the typesetters, Post Pre-Press Group, accommodated late changes with good cheer. Stephen Hutcheon was, as always, a supportive and understanding boss, and Gabrielle Hooton was, as always, a thorough and intuitive researcher.

This book is a collaboration with Webdiary columnists Harry Heidelberg, Antony Loewenstein and Jack Robertson, whose excitement for the project and generosity with their time and ideas got me through the down bits and inspired my work. To meet a dire writing deadline, on Australia Day 2004 Jack agreed to be my editor before the remaining chapters went to Penguin, and not only kept me to schedule but often found the 'story' when I got lost in the detail. Jack also came up with the titles for the book's five parts and contributed many other creative touches. Without Jack this book would not be in your hands.

Gai Stern, Kathy Rowe and others who asked not to be named due to the political sensitivities in John Howard's Australia read and commented on draft manuscripts. Four years ago the former editor of the *Sydney Morning Herald* Paul McGeough, and its managing editor Tom Burton, trusted me to create and run Webdiary. This book is a result of that experiment in 'participatory journalism' between writer and reader. Thank you to the Australians who've read and contributed to Webdiary here and abroad, some of whom are quoted in this book. Thank you to the *Sydney Morning Herald* editor Robert Whitehead for supporting Webdiary, and the *Sun Herald* editor Phil McLean for publishing a weekly column incorporating the voices of Webdiarists.

Education is not the filling of a pail, but the lighting of a fire

W.B. Yeats

Introduction

I Am, You Are,
We Are Australia

When the government changes, the country changes

Paul Keating concedes democratic defeat

I voted for John Winston Howard in 1996. Like many Australians, I was angry with Paul Keating. He may have lost me when he promised not to sell the Commonwealth Bank and then did. It may have been his scare-mongering over John Hewson's Fightback! package, to steal the 1993 election – as a voter I'd admired Hewson's plucky vision, and the 'World's Greatest Treasurer' had himself championed a consumption tax.

Keating's quick reversal of his L-A-W tax cuts and unheralded hikes to indirect taxes after beating off Hewson showed that 1993 was the bankrupt campaign of a desperate prime minister willing to do whatever it takes to keep political power. The 'True Believer' triumphalism on election night simply confirmed that this now included sheer bloody gall.

Whatever it was that turned me off him – as a voter and as a professional observer – in many ways it was a reluctant parting. After thirteen years of economic reform, Labor

under Keating had got its teeth into issues of great importance to me and to the country: Reconciliation, the Republic
(I favoured a directly elected president), our place in Asia.

But there was too much baggage. Keating's government
was exhausted, arrogant and out of touch. John Howard
had soothingly assured us he'd smoothed his more extreme
policy edges on Medicare and industrial relations, and
pledged himself to act as a torchbearer of the Menzies
Liberal tradition. I voted for what I thought was a healthy
turnover of power in our democracy. Time for a change.

Be careful what you tick for.

I'm now an outsider to the goings-on at the physical and
symbolic heart of our democracy – Parliament House,
Canberra. I left the place I loved and despised in equal parts
more than three years ago, after twelve years of breathing
its air, thinking about its thoughts, chatting to its players,
questioning its decisions, investigating its secrets. Hating it.
Loving it.

In late 2003 I returned to Canberra to watch the President of the United States pay Parliament his due respects
as a democratic envoy from Australia's friends and allies,
the American people. In the triumphant flush of Saddam Hussein's defeat, Prime Minister John Howard had
invited George W. Bush to speak on the matter that had
bitterly divided the nation. Our parliamentary representatives – every Australian we'd voted into the House of

Representatives and the Senate – would hear the leader of the American people thank the Australian people for the gravest decision any sovereign people can take: the decision to start a war against another sovereign people.

As one of many citizens who'd opposed that war, I wanted to hear what the man who had led us into it would say, especially to those elected representatives who, on behalf of Australians like me, had refused to back him.

As a reporter, I wanted to see if he'd look them in the eye as he spoke.

Instead what I experienced on 23 and 24 October last year made me fear for our democracy's future.

I saw a Parliament on its collective knees before a condescending Imperial Caesar, led by a lame provincial governor of a Prime Minister so blind to the duties of his own democratic office, so unmoved by the issues still rending his own people, that he turned what might have been a healing thank-you visit into just another vehicle for his own ambitions. I saw him do so at the expense of Westminster traditions and norms of civilised behaviour that I'd thought were above partisan politics. I saw elected politicians – elected by us, the Australian people – shouted down, physically manhandled and viciously abused.

I saw a public service in ruins, reduced to mere caterers, lackies, careerists, political stooges.

And I saw a castrated press gallery largely oblivious to what was happening to our democracy right there before their eyes, on their own professional beat. A press gallery unwilling or unable to report it to a citizenry that urgently needed to know.

I was staggered.

We, the people of Australia, are systematically being left out of the democratic equation. The finely tuned mechanisms of our Westminster system, so painstakingly developed by the people over centuries of struggle, are corroding fast. Our politicians are replacing checks-and-balances subtleties with government by unseen sledgehammer – by rigid control, populist manipulation, outright misinformation and deceit – all of it disguised in a very expensive wrapping of super-spin designed to blind us to the fact that governance is now mere salesmanship.

We're increasingly being hustled by ruthless, weak and cynical representatives on behalf of those anti-democrats in the big business community who see 'globalisation' as an excuse to cut themselves free of all accountability, and who've long come to regard us ordinary voters as no more than 'consumers'. In their world we're human commodities, which they can use up and throw away as they please, shedding the mutual obligations and civic duties that once made all Australians part of the same egalitarian country.

Dissent, accountability, scrutiny, principle, even the rule of law – these things have no place in the Darwinian worldview of anti-democratic big business. A parliament is simply an obstacle, which is why ours is quickly and quietly being dismantled.

On John Howard's democratic watch.

This book contends that John Howard is not a liberal, or a Liberal, or a conservative, or a Conservative. It seeks to show that he's part of an ideological wrecking gang made up of radical-populist economic opportunists, one which long ago decided that robust liberal democracy was an impediment to the real elites – Big Business and Big Media – that sponsor them, rather than an essential complement to and underwriter of market capitalism.

This book contends that John Howard's wrecking gang has always been plain wrong but now threatens the long-term future of Australian democracy.

Sorry, John. We're not just consumers. We're not just commodities. We're citizens. And as a citizen, what I saw during George Bush's visit scared me.

As a reporter, it confirmed that I'd been right to start breathing the Canberra air again. After all you go where the real story is.

In this book I'll take you through some of my recent journalistic experiences that illustrate why our democracy is in a lot of trouble.

I want to show you why I've come to regard John Howard – 'relaxed and comfortable' Honest John, for whom I voted – as a threat to our democracy. I want to demonstrate where I think John Howard's Australia now stands in this crucial election year, after eight years of

Howard ruthlessly changing Australia to suit *his* 'times', NOT him suiting *our* times as he often claims. I'll show you who's 'in' in Howard's democracy, who's left 'out', and how such exclusion corrodes civic life for everyone in the long run – whether we're 'in' or 'out' or totally disengaged.

I also want to show you why I no longer have any confidence that either of the two major parties is capable of addressing the problems Howard's government is increasingly normalising and how their behaviour has in fact jointly brought us to this looming crisis.

And I want to show you why I think we've now reached the stage where it's up to each of us, as Australians, to work together to save the day. You might not draw that conclusion from what I report, of course, but there are a lot of Australians out there who do.

I don't know about you, but last year I felt like opting out of trying to make a difference. The assault on the very idea of civic duty seemed irresistible: as if the god of economic globalisation had decreed we were all to lose every value of ours that wasn't an economic one, completely and irretrievably. Society really was finished and we were headed for Orwell's 1984, fast. So why not opt out? Escape. Live simply. Create a beautiful personal space. Sit back – observing what was going on outside with sadness, sure, but also with relief that I was no longer part of it.

So in this book I'll also describe when the moment of

choice arrived for me, personally and professionally, and why I decided to take the activist option and to hell with surrender. And what happened when I did so, on the one issue that it is not only my right to be politically partisan about, but also my obligation: cross-media ownership laws. And the way I was rejuvenated by that decision, and how in the subsequent fight this jaded political reporter at last grasped an essential truth about a healthy working democracy: that if a cause is sound, and openly, passionately fought for, then it can quickly become a wider, non-partisan one.

My personal fight showed me again why our 'least worst' system of governance is so precious and so worth defending: there is room enough for ALL of us in it. My 'crisis of engagement' – and the rescue of my civic faith by those politicians, journalists and fellow citizens who'd remained committed – led to a reaffirmation and a determination to keep playing my part, as journalist and citizen, in the fight to help save our messy, inclusive, brilliant democratic system from John Howard's grubby wrecking gang.

Alongside many, many other determined Australian citizens.

I've been involved in some of Australia's biggest political stories in my career, and I've watched politics up close for more than fifteen years. For the last few I've been on the outside, engaging in intense conversations with readers of my *Sydney Morning Herald* online forum, Webdiary. In that time Webdiarists have followed the issues of the moment and the ebb and flow of daily politics; talked about longer term trends in our society, good and bad; and especially canvassed – furiously, frantically, despairingly – new ideas about how more of us can help clean up the democratic system. Many are as anxious as I am about the future of their democracy, and many want to get involved in taking it back.

Webdiarists are from all walks of politics. They're One Nation and Labor supporters, small-l liberals and conservatives, Democrats and Greens. We've argued with each other, often fiercely. But we've influenced each other, too, and proved that the ugly screaming matches that pass for public debate in Australia today are not all there can be. We've got beyond the crazy idea that just because we don't agree with each other on one issue it automatically means we can't like each other as people or agree on something else.

I try to minimise simplistic divisions and cheap wedges in Webdiary discussions. We've stepped out of our partisan enclaves to engage with each other's lives and beliefs. And we've found a lot of common ground in the process – often where none was first apparent.

The common ground? All of us can agree that our democracy has served us bloody well, and that it's worth protecting no matter who we vote for.

So alongside my own stories I want to publish the citizen's stories of five Webdiary contributors: stories that reveal why they think our democracy is in strife and what they're doing about it. I've got a few ideas myself. I'm sure you do, too.

My starting-point Big Idea? The political parties have lost the power to do the job for us so we have to do it ourselves.

This book is my start. I hope it snowballs into something bigger. Penguin has agreed to set up a website, www.nothappyjohn.com, in conjunction with the book, where, if you like, you can comment on each chapter and add your own suggestions. Let others know what you're doing to make your voice heard.

We citizens only ever find out how strong we are when we finally get around to working together.

Before we kick off, let's declare. On the surface this is a politically partisan book, and I'm a political journalist. Readers have a right to know where I stand.

No, I'm not happy, John.

And, yes, I firmly believe that we citizens must throw out your wrecking gang at the next election. As a voter, I regard myself as a swinger; since 1996, John, I've thoroughly swung.

Above everything else I believe in universal human rights – the foundation principle of the United Nations. It's central to my personal value system and to my idea of what this nation stands for. So, for example, although I had voted for Labor in 1998 because I was disgusted with Howard's stance on Wik, I had no choice but to change my vote when Labor agreed to Howard's plan to excise territory to deny asylum seekers access to our laws. Instead in 2001 I supported – for the first time and to my great surprise – the Greens.

But could I envision working with One Nation, say – which supports John Howard's policy of turning the boats back – to strengthen our democratic institutions?

Too right I could. Like all of us, I have my bedrock beliefs – my democratic 'line in the sand' – but that doesn't mean I hold back from the messier pragmatics of democracy. As this book will show, I can and will happily work with anyone – conservative, Liberal, ALP supporter, National Civic Council member – who wants a cleaner, more transparent system, one that produces a parliament truly representative of the various views of our citizens. One not beholden to the powerful and the cashed-up when the 'public interest' is being decided.

One very unlike the system we have now.

The second thing I'm unashamedly partisan about is my own vocation, journalism. This is what underpins my conviction that Howard's got to go – he is now on the verge of destroying Australia's mainstream independent media.

So that's where I stand. But don't get me wrong. I'm no Labor patsy. In the end all I'm really partisan about when it comes to politics is the future vibrancy of our democracy.

It's under threat. And it's worth defending.

In my dreams I imagine ordinary Australians getting together to back strong, intelligent, trustworthy, independent-minded candidates, to put some wind up the big-brand parties.

I imagine Independent and minor party politicians holding the balance of power in the House of Representatives for once – ensuring some real debate, demanding some real democratic hard yakka from the cabinet, fostering some real engagement down where the legislative action should really be: in the people's House.

I imagine the big power-players, the real elites, for a change facing a bit of stiff competition for ministers' ears. I imagine their shocked faces when they realise they can't buy access and influence and power from *our* politicians with donations to their parties.

I imagine democratic politics as an honourable vocation, not the grubby career that John Winston Howard seems so determined to bequeath as his political legacy. I imagine ethics and honesty and decency restored to mainstream debate. I imagine real people standing on real principle. I imagine party politicians prepared to step off the party line when it offends their core beliefs or when it betrays the welfare of the people who put them there.

And I imagine transparency. Trust. Civic duty and sacrifice. Truth. Humility. Humanity.

Part One

John's Australia

1

Disclosing John Howard's Elite, by the Skin of Our Teeth

Beware of he who would deny you information,
for in his mind he dreams of being your master

Message on a computer game

John Howard personally chose the Australians invited to the Lodge for a barbecue on Thursday, 23 October 2003. We paid the bills – as we should have if this were a government function and not a private party. John Howard's guest of honour was none other than George Bush, President of the United States of America.

I was interested in John Howard's invitation list because this was the only function in George Bush's one-day stop-over where he could meet real Australians. All else was staged, choreographed, ritualised – a speech to Parliament, a wreath laying at the War Memorial – and cocooned by oppressive security and the meticulous masking from the President's eyes of any sign of protest, any indication that Australia was not united behind the war on Iraq.

It was a thank-you visit – a special treat to reward a loyal ally. So who would Howard choose to represent us? In 1996, when we chose him to lead us, he promised to govern 'For all of us'. That was his slogan. So what did that mean when it came to the nitty-gritty of choosing the Australians to meet the President?

The first big shock was that he didn't want to tell us.

Pardon? On the morning of the Bush visit to the capital, I was back in the *Sydney Morning Herald*'s Canberra bureau, where I'd worked for so long before moving to Sydney, when our political correspondent Mark Riley put down the phone.

'Howard won't release the list,' he said.

'What?' I replied. 'But this is basic public information – this is a state visit by the President of the United States. The public has a right to know.'

That's when I found out that actually this was *not* a state visit, although neither Howard nor the press gallery had bothered to tell the Australian people that. A state visit is one by a foreign government's head of state to Australia. It's above politics – a visit to all of us – and that's why our head of state, the governor-general, is host and escort. Strict protocols apply. But for this visit John Howard was host. The visit was a partisan political one dressed up as a solemn ceremonial occasion.

Still, surely the Australian people had a right to know – we were paying for it, after all. Anyway why wouldn't Howard want us to know?

'Don't worry, if we press hard they'll probably change their mind by the end of the day,' Mark said. 'It happens all the time. That's the way they play.'

'What? How long has this been going on?' I asked.

Since Howard had won a third term in 2001. Nothing without pressure. Nothing unless and until John Howard's minders believed that continued blocking would produce a story sufficiently embarrassing to necessitate disclosure. High-stakes journalism, that, for something so basic. Why get the PM's office offside over something like the barbecue list?

Clever, John. Clever.

Bush's one-day stopover was frenetic: a day of chaos, of incredible stories and unprecedented difficulties in getting them. I wondered if anyone would keep making the calls to get the guest list, or whether this information would ever reach the people. Howard's office had released the menu without a qualm – why wouldn't he want the public to know who ate the food? What possible justification could he have for secrecy?

OK, I thought, which reporters were attending the barbecue as observers to report the event to the Australian people? I'd ask them to note the faces they recognised.

Sorry, Howard had banned all Australian reporters and photographers from the event. Only American reporters would be there, and detailed arrangements had been made to ensure there would be no contact between Bush's media and our own.

What? Only Mark Riley, on 21 and 22 October, had bothered to report this unprecedented shutdown of media access, let alone the discrimination against the Australian people's reporters in our own country. The *Sydney Morning Herald*'s readers were flummoxed by Riley's revelation and started getting a bit toey over what was going on in Canberra – and the heat finally started rising among the media – so Howard gave, just a little, on the day of the visit. One photographer and one reporter for the whole press gallery, he decreed.

I had one other lead. Only one press gallery reporter, Jason Frenkel of Melbourne's *Herald Sun* newspaper, had smelt a story in the guest list, and he'd spent the day before the Canberra visit ringing around to uncover some guests. He'd scored a couple, and also reported that Sydney radio talkback host John Laws, Westfield billionaire Frank Lowy (whose companies gave the Liberals $312,300 in 2001–02), Australian cricket captain Steve Waugh and former Liberal Party treasurer Ron Walker had been invited but declined due to prior commitments.

Our media and telecommunications writer Cosima Marriner kept pushing Howard's people and finally, after deadline, they faxed a page of names listed alphabetically without titles or positions. It would have taken research to get the titles right, and it was too late for that. Nothing ran in Friday's papers. The story was gone. The parliamentary address of President Hu of China was the story of the day, a day filled with its own shocks, its own extraordinary parliamentary precedents.

Howard's tactics had worked.

Blow that, I thought. On Monday, 27 October, I asked

around about the names I couldn't place and did some internet checks, but to be sure I'd got the list right I phoned the Department of the Prime Minister and Cabinet to check a couple of mystery names and get their titles. That's what you did when I worked in Canberra – you checked with departments for the facts, and with ministers for policy and politics.

Not any more. The switchboard operator transferred me straight to the Prime Minister's office, where I discovered that one of several Howard press secretaries, former Sydney *Daily Telegraph* press gallery reporter David Luff, didn't want to help at all.

'Why don't you do a Google search?' he asked accusingly, as if I were wasting his precious time.

I put to him the names of a couple of people I thought were in the American contingent and he said he didn't know, making it clear he wouldn't try to find out either. So I asked for the name and number of a public servant who would know. He said he'd ring back. He didn't.

So Howard's press secretaries now saw their job as preventing the flow of basic information to the Australian people – as information blockers, not information providers? It had taken only two years to get to this: Australian taxpayers paying the salaries of people whose job it was to make it as difficult as possible for them to be told the truth – about just about everything, it seemed.

I was too proud to call the American Embassy to find out who went to a barbecue in our country hosted by our Prime

Minister, so I published the list on Webdiary with question marks and asked readers for help. They dived in, supplying details and weblinks. We'd cracked it.

I got a huge surge of hits on that story, and many emails from readers nonplussed that only Webdiary had published the info. To my great surprise and concern Webdiary had a scoop!

Mark Riley made good use of it. A couple of days later, when he got a little spare time, he researched the Australian Electoral Commission's donations records and found that, between them, the companies of six invited businessmen had donated more than a million dollars to the Liberal Party's 2001 election campaign.

So that's how you got an invite – you *paid* for it! Money politics.

No wonder you wanted secrecy, John.

The next twist made me feel physically ill. Mark had a page-one story, no doubt about it, but in Sydney the paper's editors decided not to run it. 'Tight for space' was their call, and that was true enough, although for quite a while many of us had noted a growing editorial reluctance regarding political news. Our bosses seemingly prefer lifestyle content and glossy supplements to sell advertising. Fairfax isn't the worst offender – the merging of news and advertising and the crunch on news space is a clear and dangerous anti-democratic trend across the media.

You ain't got democracy if the public doesn't know what's going on, but Fairfax journalists and editors have been fighting a losing battle to convince our Chief Executive Officer, Fred Hilmer, that our newspaper performs any function apart from making money by exploiting our readers through advertising. Content is king, I'd argued fruitlessly. Give readers information and they'll buy us. Think about circulation, not just advertising bucks.

Lost cause.

Fred – the mastermind behind the last Labor government's National Competition Policy – thinks of our readers as mere consumers, not citizens. He believes that newspapers are 'advertising platforms' and that journalists are 'content providers'. In two weeks in Canberra after the Bush and Hu visits I saw first-hand the large number of important stories dumped for space, never to be read. Like the Bush barbecue guest list, important records of Australian history in the making were never published.

Mark's story finally ran as a filler three days later, buried on page 13 of Saturday's paper, on 1 November. If it had run earlier and more prominently a journalist might have asked Howard a question, or a minor party or Independent senator might have taken up the cudgels.

You wouldn't have expected anything from the Opposition, of course – both Big Parties solicit Big Money from Big Corporates, and both lend their ears to those who'll pay. 'A spokeswoman for the Prime Minister said the people invited were a cross-section of the Australian community who had each made a contribution to Australia in different ways, and that the Prime Minister made no apology for inviting any of them', Mark wrote. 'Opposition Leader Simon Crean's office declined to comment. Most corporate invitees also donated large, if lesser, amounts to Labor at the last election.'

Mark pointed out that 'The presence of major party donors would not have been a surprise to George Bush. The US has a system of declaring the contributions of corporate leaders seeking "face time" with the President. A certain amount buys a plate at a White House dinner, a higher amount a sleep-over in the Lincoln Room.'

He concluded that 'The system is less formal in Australia but money can still buy access – 20 corporates paid $4000 a head for dinner with Mr Howard at a fund-raiser for Employment Services Minister Mal Brough at Brisbane's Treasury Casino on October 2.'

You can imagine the blow to morale in our Canberra bureau when bosses burn great stories. They're great journos and they're brave, too. They cop heaps from Howard's boys for asking questions he doesn't want to answer – for doing their job, in other words – and to be spiked at the other end of the story chain is not easy to take. Still, we're better off than journalists on most papers.

As is so often the case in our democracy, the Senate was the Australian people's last chance to get some information about the barbecue. This time it was through a regular Senate Estimates hearing, when politicians get the chance to question our public servants about how our money is being spent. Senate Estimates is the only real accountability there is to Australians for what the government is doing, and how and why. Any senator's got the right to ask questions, and lots do, on matters big and small, many of which affect individual constituents. But not government senators: they ask nothing, except when another senator is uncovering something awry – in which case they act as attack dogs and work with the minister sitting beside the public servants to control questions. No representation of voters there.

So on Tuesday, 4 November, I watched Labor Senate leader John Faulkner quiz the Department of Prime Minister and Cabinet about the barbecue.

I learnt a lot that day. For a start, John Howard had personally decided that while President Hu of China would get a state visit hosted by the Governor-General, Bush would come on 'a working visit' with Howard as host. His officials could recall no precedent for a foreign head of state not being hosted by our head of state.

Never believe John Howard when he says he's a conservative, a respecter of tradition.

No way. He'll bend rules, trash proprieties, even downgrade the head of state he so ardently supported in the Republic debate.

Howard wanted to meet, greet and escort Bush and make sure he was in every picture with him, come what may. This was no visit to Australia. This was a visit to John.

The downside, if it were ever reported, was that he had personal responsibility for the decisions made and the tricks pulled to suit his politics. If the media did its job Australians would get a pretty good idea of John Howard's values, priorities and style by the end of the visit. But the media didn't do its job: partly because Howard made it too hard to do so in the time available, and partly because the media has forgotten its core job in a functioning democracy.

I learnt in Senate Estimates that the official term for the barbecue was 'an informal lunch hosted by the Prime Minister'. John Howard had decided who to invite, without input from his public servants. He personally decided the seating plan.

Howard chose not to invite our head of state or to make the function bipartisan by inviting the Leader of the Opposition, Simon Crean. Indeed he did not invite any politician who represented the roughly half of Australia's voters who did not vote for the Coalition.

In Howard's public service, after long and bitter experience, public servants know not to raise queries or make suggestions about such things, or anything really. They didn't this time either, despite the expertise of the Ceremonial and Hospitality Unit on such matters. The deputy head of Howard's department, Andrew Metcalfe, explained: 'We worked on the basis that it was an informal luncheon and that the invitations were being prepared in the sense of people being identified by the Prime Minister's office. We were not asked for advice, and we gave none.'

It was a rush job – John Howard loves demanding the impossible, or else, from a public service he's slashed to the bone. The initial list of seventy-two guests landed on the department's desk less than a week before the barbecue, and the menu – personally chosen by John and Janette – even later, with a demand to get Howard's 'wine consultant' to tell him what booze to serve. The department had to call in staff from other sections to get the marquee, ramps and lighting erected, hire casual luncheon staff, print the place cards and menus, organise transport, do the flowers and decorations – all of it. And guess who paid for what the Prime Minister's office described as 'a private function' to justify not inviting Crean? The cash-strapped department, of course. It didn't even go on the Prime Minister's expenses tab.

I wasn't surprised when the department refused Faulkner's request in Senate Estimates for a copy of the guest list. Metcalfe wasn't sure if Howard had released it, and if Howard hadn't he sure wasn't going to. Liberal Senator George Brandis couldn't resist: 'It was in Margo Kingston's Webdiary in the *Sydney Morning Herald*.'

Metcalfe would say no more, so Faulkner tried Defence Minister Robert Hill, who was at the barbecue. They usually get their lines straight, Howard's loyal ministers, and Hill was no different.

'It seemed to me to be a reasonable cross-section of the Australian community,' Hill said, parroting Howard's line.

Any journos invited?

'I am not sure that they would want me to dob them in,' Hill said.

And the gift?

'A Wallaby jumper was presented to Mr Bush,' Hill replied.

Metcalfe added, 'My understanding is that it was half-Wallaby and half-American.'

After the Senate lunch break Metcalfe handed the list over. 'I have now been advised that that guest list was publicly released on the day. We have a copy with us and we are happy to make a copy available.'

Stuff-up time: it wasn't the bare-bones list Howard's office had given us, it was the official list in all its glory.

So here it is: John Howard's 'cross-section of the Australian community who had each made a contribution to Australia in different ways'. Disclosed donations from invitees to the Liberal Party's 2001 election campaign are given in square brackets, along with their disclosed donations in 2002–03.

Luncheon in honour of the Honourable George Bush, President of the United States of America, and Mrs Bush
The Lodge, Canberra
Thursday, 23 October 2003

Host
The Honourable John Howard MP
Prime Minister
Mrs Janette Howard

Guest-of-Honour

The Honourable George Bush
President of the United States of America
Mrs Bush

Official Party

Dr Condoleezza Rice
National Security Adviser
Mr Andrew Card [Jr]
Chief of Staff
Mr James Kelly
Assistant Secretary of State
Mr James Moriarty
*Special Assistant to the President and Senior Director for
Asian Affairs*
Ms Andrea Ball
Chief of Staff to the First Lady

Diplomatic Corps

His Excellency Mr J Thomas Schieffer Jr [sic]
Ambassador of the United States of America
Mrs Susanne Schieffer

Ministry

The Honourable John Anderson MP
*Deputy Prime Minister and Minister for Transport and
Regional Services*
Mrs Julia Anderson
The Honourable Peter Costello MP
Treasurer
Mrs Tanya Costello
The Honourable Mark Vaile MP
Minister for Trade

Mrs Wendy Vaile

Senator the Honourable Robert Hill
*Minister for Defence and Leader of the Government
in the Senate*
Mrs Diana Hill

The Honourable Alexander Downer MP
Minister for Foreign Affairs
Mrs Nicky Downer

Defence Chiefs [sic]

General Peter Cosgrove AC MC
Chief of the Defence Force, Department of Defence
Mrs Lynne Cosgrove

Departmental Secretaries [sic]

Dr Peter Shergold AM
Secretary, Department of the Prime Minister and Cabinet
Ms Carol Green

Australian Ambassador

Ambassador Michael Thawley
Ambassador, Australian Embassy, Washington

Business

Mr Rob Gerard AO
*Chairman and Managing Director, Gerard Industries Ltd
[Gerard Industries donated $244,806 for the 2001
election campaign and $187,000 to the Liberal Party
in 2002–03, after which the government appointed him
to the Reserve Bank board]*
Mrs Fay Gerard

Mr Mark Leibler AO
*Senior Partner, Arnold Bloch Leibler, Solicitors and
Consultants [also a director of Coles Myer, which*

donated $132,000 for the 2001 election campaign and
$133,000 in 2002–03]
Mrs Rosanna Leibler
Mr Kerry Packer AC
Chairman, Consolidated Press Holdings
Mrs Ros Packer
Mr Donald McDonald AO
Chairman, Australian Broadcasting Corporation
[an odd entry under 'Business']
Mrs Janet McDonald [AO]
Mr Harry Triguboff AO
Chairman and Managing Director, Meriton Properties Pty
Ltd [Meriton – $278,000 for the 2001 election campaign
and $150,000 in 2002–03]
Mrs Rhonda Triguboff
Mr Terry Campbell
Chairman, JB Were [JB Were – $163,000 for 2001
election campaign. JB Were is one of two contributors
to the Cormack Foundation, an 'associated entity' of the
Liberal Party, which gave $1.8 million to the Victorian
branch in 2002–03 and can be used to funnel
anonymous donations]
Mrs Christine Campbell
Mr Leon Davis
Chairman, Westpac Banking Corporation
[Westpac – $142,000 for the 2001 election campaign,
$118,000 in 2002–03]
Mrs Annette Davis
Mr Kerry Stokes AO
Executive Chairman, Seven Network Limited
Ms Christine Simpson

Academics

Professor Susan [sic] Cory AC
Professor of Medical Research, University of Melbourne
[Suzanne Cory is best known as the Director of the
Walter and Eliza Hall Institute of Medical Research]
Professor Jerry Adams

Mr Paul Ramsay AO
Vice-Chancellor, University of Sydney [sic: Ramsay should
be in the 'Business' category as head of Ramsay Health
Care (Ramsay Health Care – $275,000 for the 2001 election
campaign, $165,000 in 2002–03); the Vice-Chancellor of
Sydney University, Professor Gavin Brown, was not invited]

Professor [Emeritus] Geoffrey Blainey AO
Author and Historian
Mrs Ann Blainey

Sporting Bodies

Mr John Eales AM
Former Captain of the Australian Rugby Union Team
Mrs Lara Eales

Mr Lleyton Hewitt
Australian Tennis Player

Mr Mark Taylor
Former Captain Australian Cricket Team
Mrs Judy Taylor

Former Ambassadors [sic]

The Honourable Andrew Peacock AC
President, Boeing Australia Limited

Prime Minister's Office

Mr Arthur Sinodinos
Chief of Staff

Mr Tony Nutt
Principal Private Secretary
Mr Peter Varghese
Senior Adviser (International) [now head of ONA]
Mr Tony O'Leary
Press Secretary

Others

Mr Richard Howard
Prime Minister's relatives
Mr Timothy Howard
Prime Minister's relatives
Mr Steve Irwin
The Crocodile Man [The Crocodile Hunter]
Mrs Terri Irwin
Mr Rowan McDonald
Prime Minister's relatives
Mrs Melanie McDonald [Melanie Howard]
Brigadier Maurie McNarn AO
Director General, Personnel, Army
Mrs Richenda McNarn
Professor Fiona Stanley [AC]
*Australian of the Year, Founding Director, TVW Telethon
Institute for Child Health Research*
Professor Geoff Shellam
Dr [sic] Jackie Huggins [AM]
*Board Member, Australian Institute of Aboriginal and
Torres Strait Islander Studies*

Media

Mr Alan Jones AM
*Radio Broadcaster, Radio 2UE Sydney [sic: Jones is
at 2GB]*

Mr Malcolm Farr
President, Parliamentary Press Gallery
Mr Neil Mitchell
Radio and Television, Current Affairs Commentator

Security
President's Security

It's a cosy circle, isn't it? Howard's family and his work family are all in.

For all of us, eh? Well, how come the invited guests (minus partners) are an all-white (bar Huggins), overwhelmingly male group who predominantly live in Sydney, Melbourne and Canberra?

Howard's cross-section of Australia is Big Party, Big Business, Big Media – and Big Sport. Sports stars are greatly over-represented – that's the connection with the ordinary Australians he wants to get by association.

And, of course – representing the battler perhaps? – the millionaire 'Crocodile Man', Steve Irwin, who just happened to say publicly seven weeks before, when Howard visited his Queensland zoo, that Howard was 'the greatest leader Australia has ever had' and 'the greatest leader in the entire world'. We learnt a few days later in Senate Estimates that, months before, the government had paid Irwin $175,000 – $364 a minute – for a day's work on a quarantine TV advertisement. Back in February the government had refused to disclose to Parliament Steve's payment, despite the fact that it was our money they were spending to buy his sales job. I don't want to be snippy, but surely Howard's not venturing into buying personal endorsements with our money, is he?

Never again, though – not after John's mate Steve thought it was cool to feed a 4-metre crocodile in one hand with his baby son, Bob, in the other? We all know John doesn't want parents like that in our country, don't we?

Included in the massively over-represented Big Business and Big Media invitees – his backers or perhaps his real bosses? – are Kerry Packer, Australia's richest man, with fingers in lots of pies requiring government largesse and protection, including the Nine Network; the other important Australian TV network owner, Seven's Kerry Stokes; Alan Jones, Howard's favourite Sydney talk-show host; and Neil Mitchell, his favourite Melbourne talk-show host. Malcolm Farr, Rupert Murdoch's chief political reporter for the *Daily Telegraph*, represented the press gallery. The numbers from Big Business and Big Media overwhelm Australians from the pillars of our democracy: the Parliament (none), the law (one – Leibler is a tax expert), the public service (one), the defence force (two) and the universities.

Who specifically is excluded from John Howard's Australia? Artists – not a novelist, painter, actor, dancer or creative person apart from Blainey (the historian who invented the term 'black armband' view of history and who backed Howard in the 1980s when he wanted Asian immigration reduced). Australians from non-European 'ethnic' backgrounds. Religious representatives, although Mark Leibler is a leading figure in the Zionist movement. Women – only three are there in their own right, not as partners or Howard's relatives. There's also no non-medical scientist, farmer, small businessperson, community worker or volunteer, workers' representative, judge or university vice-chancellor.

The reality behind the perception. Us and them. With me or against me.

Kylie Russell was not on the list. By rights she should have been the first invited, for Kylie is the Australian most deeply affected by the wars we fought at the request of George Bush after September 11. She's the Australian you'd think would have been most on Howard's mind as he prepared the welcome mat for George Bush, coming to thank us for our loyalty and sacrifice in those wars. Howard had said waging war was the gravest decision a leader could make – sending Australians to possible death for their country is a big responsibility to shoulder.

Kylie's husband, Andrew, an SAS sergeant, was killed in Afghanistan in February 2002 when his truck ran over a landmine. He was 33, and the first Australian casualty in combat since Vietnam. Their only child, Leisa, was born eleven days before Andrew was killed.

John Howard didn't invite Kylie to the Bush barbecue. In fact he didn't invite her to Canberra to hear George Bush speak of the cause for which her husband died. Of all the faces in the news last year, hers is the one that haunts me, and hers is the one that most hardens my heart against John Howard.

The Australia I love would have remembered Kylie Russell. John Howard's Australia didn't.

2

Yours Not to Reason Why

Democracy has proved itself a friend of peace. No fully self-governing country has provoked a war within a century's memory . . . Democracy, being founded on the rights of the individual Citizens, concerns itself first and foremost with the domestic well-being of its people . . . In the grim struggle between guns and butter, it prefers butter. It feels in its bones that war is a destroyer, and that conqueror and conquered may be at the end 'in one red burial blent'

Robert Menzies, 'The Achievement of Democracy',
from *The Forgotten People* radio broadcasts, 1942

John Howard began 2003 by farewelling our troops, for what we all knew would be war in Iraq, with the support of only 30 per cent of the Australian people and without the prior parliamentary debate he had promised.

Imagine how those poor bloody troops must have felt. It's always a sacrifice to risk your life for your country, but to do so in a war of aggression against a nation posing no threat to your homeland is the biggest ask of all. The least you'd want is the assurance that most Australians believed the war was in their interests, because they're the ones you'd be dying for, not John Howard.

Yet Howard sent the troops off with what veteran

commentator Michelle Grattan was calling 'the big lie' – that he hadn't already decided upon war on the nod from George Bush. The troops must have sensed the lie more deeply than the rest of us because they'd been preparing for months. Invasion plans had been drawn up and Australia was inextricably linked to the US Iraq war machine.

The idea that we'd pull the plug on our closest ally if the United Nations said no was unthinkable, but still Howard pretended to our troops and to us.

> John Howard stated that we had only recently started preparing for this looming conflict. Bullshit! We, that is, 1 SAS Squadron . . . were given orders to prepare for a war with Iraq around July 2002 . . . I write this [email] because I am sick of John Howard and the Federal Government's lies about our position re Iraq, and our role within the coalition.
>
> **Webdiarist 'Brian Dabeagle', 7 March 2003 (Dabeagle also sent his pseudonymous email to Greens Senator Bob Brown)**

In June 2002, just after George Bush had begun telling the world he'd invade Iraq and 'if you're not with us you're against us', John Howard jumped to attention. Long before the intelligence agencies of what would become the 'Coalition of the Willing' pulled together their dossiers on what weapons of mass destruction Iraq had, and long before Bush went to the United Nations, Howard promised Bush an armoured brigade for invading Iraq. As well, Foreign

Minister Alexander Downer labelled Labor 'appeasers'.

But Howard had to publicly backtrack hard in the face of disapproval from Australian voters. By September 2002 he was telling Australians that 'we won't just automatically click our heels and follow the Americans', and that talk of what military assistance we might offer, and what increased risk to our security might result if we did, was 'hypothetical'.

John Howard was lying.

We now know that at the same time he was discussing with George Bush the best route to war. He told the *Australian* newspaper a year later, in September 2003:

'When Bush rang me in Brisbane in early September last year, he said some people wanted him to go back to the UN, some of his people – you can probably work out who – didn't want him to go back to the UN. He said: "What do you think?" and I said: "I think your case will be that much stronger if you're seen to have tried." I also said it would make our domestic political job easier in Australia to take public opinion with us.'

Yet for ordinary Australians the debate was just starting in September 2002, and the last ANZUS disaster was in the forefront of people's minds. In July Chief of the Defence Force General Peter Cosgrove said 'we probably shouldn't have gone' to Vietnam and that the Iraq debate was 'an important issue for the Australian people' to discuss. RSL President Major-General Peter Phillips, a fellow Vietnam veteran, responded, 'It's timely that [Vietnam] is raised now, given the possibility of an American invasion of Iraq.'

Then, on 26 September 2002, former prime ministers Malcolm Fraser, Bob Hawke and Gough Whitlam, former Liberal leader John Hewson, Major-General Phillips, former Australian Defence Force chiefs General Peter Gration and Admiral Alan Beaumont, and former Royal Australian Navy chief Admiral Michael Hudson all signed off to this: 'We put this conviction directly and unequivocally: it would constitute a failure of the duty of government to protect the integrity and ensure the security of this nation to commit any Australian forces in support of the US military offensive against Iraq without the backing of a specific United Nations resolution.'

So what were we ordinary Australians to think, John Howard, when blokes like this, who knew about these things, spoke out so forcefully?

And what were we to think when former federal Liberal Party president John Valder – your supporter, John – also said that invading Iraq without UN backing was crazy, as did former Labor defence minister Kim Beazley, both men acknowledged friends of the US?

What were we to think when no Australian expert would publicly support what you planned?

Most importantly: why didn't you give a damn what they – and we – thought?

Right up until he sent us to war in March 2003, our Prime Minister wouldn't discuss the risks for the world, or even for us, and avoided all questions by saying he wouldn't make up his mind until the United Nations had decided what to do. During all the terrible, fraught months before we invaded Iraq he never once spoke of our interests, our region, our special concerns or the impact of a United Nations refusal to ratify war. He never once gave us an assessment of the increased risks of terrorism.

Nothing. Everything was 'hypothetical'.

And Howard became an echo chamber for George Bush.

He left us to float unanchored, forced to watch Bush's speeches and close-read the President's pronouncements just to figure out where *we*, Australia, were at. We sensed, rather than were told, that sometime, somehow, our leader had endorsed America's revolutionary new security policy: the September 2002 war-cry that proclaimed that Bush's America would do whatever it liked regardless of what any other country or the UN might think, regardless of international law – including invade its enemies' territories and impose its own 'superior' values on the people it conquered.

On 24 January 2003, the day after Howard farewelled HMAS *Kanimbla* to the strains of 'I Still Call Australia Home', Neil Mitchell pressed him on Radio 3AW to explain how he would persuade Australians to his cause to avoid a divided country in wartime. The Prime Minister replied: 'People are wanting to hear from the Government as to why. I understand that, and I'll do my very best to talk to them and to explain it.'

Crap, John. You never intended to do any such thing, and you never did.

We still don't know why, even now.

The closest anyone got to piercing your contemptuous spin was on 6 February 2003 in the *Sydney Morning Herald*, via columnist Paul Sheehan, who reported 'a close adviser to Howard' saying: '"The PM is losing sleep over this. He knows this policy doesn't have the feathers to fly with the public. But he thinks it's the right thing to do. He's thinking long-term. If one day we ever have to face a militant Indonesia, we've only got one ally who can do the job".'

So you want us to believe in the old insurance policy theory, last used without question during the Vietnam War, John?

The one you touted as the 24-year-old president of the NSW Young Liberals back in 1964, when you visited university campuses advocating support for that war? You didn't trust the US to meet its obligation under the ANZUS Treaty to protect us from attack, John? You had to obey America without question and fight all its wars, just to make sure?

Did you give no thought to whether the US administration was going through a foreign policy rogue phase? After all, even George's dad's security advisers James Baker and Brent Scowcroft opposed the youngster's radical pre-emptive doctrine, picked up from the neo-conservatives after September 11. As did the CIA. As did great slabs of the US defence and foreign policy establishment.

So – no doubts about young George, John? No question of seeking to *dissuade* the US? No thought that we'd be better off out of it, given the fundamentalist tensions in our region? Or that 'softly, softly' might actually be in America's interest, too? Or that joining a non-UN invasion, despite the pleadings of Indonesia's establishment not to, might help *cause* the very crisis with Indonesia that would see us cashing in our insurance policy quick smart? Or that invading a country of no threat to us might provoke a counter-attack?

Was that all there was to it, John: the 'insurance policy for the future' line?

If so, then why not get the argument out there and let the Australian people into your secret?

Did you reckon that *that* policy wouldn't have the feathers to fly either?

On the weekend of 15–16 February 2003 Australians everywhere marched in protest, breaking records in every capital city and many regional centres. We wanted the Prime Minister – and his MPs, who'd done nothing to air our concerns or ask him our questions – to know we were concerned that what he was doing could make the world, and Australia, a more dangerous place, not a safer one, and that we expected his considered response.

Together we roared, Hey, John, this is OUR country! Convince us that you're doing the right thing, please. Lots of us are having nightmares about where this decision might lead us.

Growing up in country NSW, I once saw a huge funnel-web which scared the life out of me. Instinctively I picked up a rock, took aim and threw. I hit my target, but the rock also ripped open the spider's nest. To a 10-year-old it looked like I'd unleashed a swarm of hundreds of spiders spreading out in all directions. For years after I had nightmares [in which there were] spiders spewing out, envelop[ing] me, my family and everyone I knew. Ever since it's become clear that Bush, US Vice-President Cheney and the charming Defence Secretary Rumsfeld have decided to invade Iraq regardless of the consequences, the same horrible dreams have come back to haunt my nights again.

Webdiarist Andrew O'Connell, who marched in Edinburgh, 20 February 2003

A nun I'd just met drove me to Sydney's peace march on that historic weekend of worldwide people power. It was a day on which you'd prefer to avoid crowds – hot, airless, muggy – and I could hardly breathe, sardined in at Hyde Park. I glanced around for older protesters or parents with toddlers who might need help in the heat and caught the eyes of others doing the same. There we were, out of our enclaves, North Shore matrons and Westie skinheads side by side, holding up handmade banners and looking a little bemused that so many had taken the trouble to be there. But no one looked scared, despite the crush. Patience, and giving everyone as much space and respect as possible, created a sense of stillness. And of hope.

Everyone wanted to be able to say they were there that day: to their parents, their kids, their grandkids. It mattered.

I rummaged through the T-shirts on offer from the various political parties and interest groups, but didn't buy one. I didn't want a political brand on my statement – the issue was above politics – and I didn't want to wear an image antagonistic to Bush, America or Howard. I was there, as I guessed were the vast majority of Australians around me, because I feared the consequences for the West, for my country, and particularly for our children, of a non-UN invasion of Iraq. I wanted a T-shirt that said 'Please Explain'.

I edged towards the road where the march would begin, through more of my fellow Australians than I'd ever seen before. There I found three familiar ones: Laurie Brereton, NSW Labor Right hard man, the bloke who'd disowned Labor's East Timor policy as shadow foreign affairs minister after the 1996 election defeat; Bob Brown, the diffident small-l liberal who'd turned activist to save his beloved Tasmanian wilderness and now spearheaded Australia's most radical party, the Greens; and Peter Baume, a distinguished physician who became a Liberal senator in 1974 – one of the true Liberals who fought and lost the war for the soul of the party in the 1980s before he retired in 1991 to become a community health professor.

I watched these three tough democratic stayers – who'd embraced different political persuasions in their public life – link arms to lead Sydney's largest-ever march and shout in unison 'NO WAR!'

I peeled off back towards Hyde Park to see how many blocks the march stretched for. There was no end to it. When I rang a friend later she said she hadn't marched at all – she was still waiting to leave when those three old-timers led the marchers back into Hyde Park. As I walked I saw police officers more relaxed than any I'd ever seen at a protest. Some were smiling. This was no mob of ratbags.

It was a magic moment, a day of community for all of us.

All weekend people marched in extraordinary numbers: in Europe, Africa, Asia, South America, the United States. We, the world's ordinary people, expressed the earnest wish not to wage war against Iraq and implored our leaders to find another way to disarm Saddam Hussein. Australians across the country and the globe – most of whom had never protested before – emailed Webdiary their march reports and photos, relating the hope, even joy, they had felt.

Australians had marched in numbers too big to ignore, I wrote.

I was wrong.

John Howard's response? 'Well, I don't think the mob, to use that vernacular, has quite made up its mind on this issue, and it can't really make up its mind until we know what all the alternatives are.'

The 'mob'.

It was heartbreaking for those who'd marched. And that was before Howard's tame columnists, mostly in the Murdoch press, and his shock-jock cheerleaders on radio started

My wife and I have just returned from the anti-war march held today here in Brisbane. Ten thousand were anticipated – ten times that turned up. The crowd had come downtown from across the board – mums and dads pushing strollers, old couples shading themselves under brollies, pimply and excitable teens, Vietnam vets sporting medals of service. Perhaps the best evidence of the broad base of the protest could be seen in the numerous protest banners and placards. The slick logos and professional print-work of those 'seasoned' campaigners such as the Greens, Democrats and various unions were there, sure. More noticeable, however, were the home-made jobs – a crayon and Texta message scribbled on the flip side of a cut-up removalist's box. A recycled primary school project, turned over, nailed to a piece of dowel from the shed, and inscribed with a kid's plea for peace. A series of anti-war messages done up on the home computer and taped to the outside of a golfing umbrella. Someone had even cut up an old banner promoting Ronricco (an 80s hypnotist) in order to flip it over and daub it with a clear message to John Howard – 'NOT IN MY NAME'.

Today's march made me proud to be a human again. It was a heartening indication that despite the torrent of empty 'Get Saddam' rhetoric from our leaders and the fatuous pro-war spin from the chickenhawks in the press, we the ordinary folk are thinking with our heads and talking with our feet.

Webdiarist Jim Forbes in Brisbane, 16 February 2003

calling us worse: traitors and appeasers and supporters of Saddam's vicious regime. There was to be no engagement between John Howard and his worried citizens.

That one disdainful sneer, and the inevitability of what Howard would do in our name that it implied, sent most of us back to our homes feeling hopeless. We'd marched, we'd made our voices heard – and it had mattered not a jot. Many of us gave up, just as Howard wanted.

And so, on 18 March 2003, our Prime Minister took us to war on a long-distance phone call, after Bush reversed his pledge to put the Iraq question to a UN Security Council vote. Most member nations wanted more time for the weapons inspectors, and all his backroom bribes and threats couldn't muster a majority. So Bush didn't bother.

But a democratic country is never more 'its people' than in wartime. Its soldiers promise to die if necessary to protect its citizens. The compact is a profound one and must

SNAP!
The big eagle caught in the trap,
Feathers of failed diplomacy drifting.
Bin Laden smiling, the hapless waiting,
A swift brutal war, a fractured globe.
The terrorist wins after all.

Webdiarist John Augustus, Sydney medico, 19 March 2003

not be lightly invoked. Dictators go to war without the people's consent – they don't require it. In dictatorships neither citizen nor soldier has rights, just an obligation to obey. But according to our Constitution Australia is 'a representative democracy'. Our forebears voted in more than one referendum before finally agreeing to form a nation in accordance with the Constitution enshrined by their federation votes. In Australia we, the people, are sovereign, not the leaders we elect.

Their first duty in a war is to persuade us, their people, of its rightness; only then can they lead that war legitimately in our name. If you can't persuade, you can't lead.

There's also a pragmatic way of seeing a wartime leader's duty. None worth the title would take their tribe to war severely divided. A leader has to build an honest framework for war so that the people know the broad goals and can decide they're justified and support the fight: then when things go wrong they've already dug in for the long haul.

Howard just said yes to Bush straight away, and that was it.

He left no space for the Australian people to consider the alternatives, despite his promise to do so. Parliament didn't get a look in. Howard killed off all debate, along with a community spark, to create two awful precedents in one: Anzacs *starting* a war, and starting it without the majority support of their people.

A place in history to cherish, John.

'Why, of course, the people don't want war,' Hermann Goering told a psychologist during his trial for Nazi war crimes. 'It is the leaders of the country who determine the policy, and it is always a simple matter to drag the people along, whether it is a democracy or a fascist dictatorship or a Parliament or a Communist dictatorship.'

'There is one difference,' his questioner said. 'In a democracy the people have some say in the matter through their elected representatives, and in the United States only Congress can declare wars.'

'Oh, that is all well and good, but, voice or no voice, the people can always be brought to the bidding of the leaders. That is easy. All you have to do is tell them they are being attacked and denounce the pacifists for lack of patriotism and exposing the country to danger. It works the same way in any country.'

From *Nuremberg Diary* by Gustave Gilbert

At a Coalition parties meeting in September 2002 John Howard had soothingly explained how he'd bring the Australian people to his bidding. To a backbench to heel over Iraq in public, but privately skittish about losing their seats, he said not to worry. Patriotism, waving the troops off and all that, would do the trick with public opinion.

And we did fall in behind the war. Of course we did. We're a patriotic people. Howard's decision made (by Bush), it was time to support our troops and pray for a short war, with few casualties and no ramifications.

But Howard wasn't finished with shredding the democratic rulebook. Not by a long shot. Having diminished our traditions, pride and unity before the war, he sought to do it afterwards, too, rewriting history before our eyes, again using our troops as props.

In May 2003 he announced multiple welcome-home 'victory' parades for many of them. No matter that 850 remained in and around Iraq; that their American and British comrades continued to die there; that the Iraqi people faced mayhem and death thanks to the coalition's failure to plan the peace; or that resistance in Iraq was gaining, not losing, force.

This was now John's 'victory'. And John wanted a parade.

In truth, Howard had largely cut and run on Bush and Blair. He'd helped them win the war, then politically scarpered before they'd won the peace – the tricky part. Another awful stain on our traditions – Australian soldiers don't usually walk away from the 'heavy lifting'. They'd certainly never before paraded a 'victory' while other Australian soldiers were still trying to secure it.

I was appalled, and I think a fair few of our troops might have been, too.

To them the ticker-tape parades – presided over by a Prime Minister concerned far more with presenting the Australian people with a triumphant military image than a completed military triumph in Iraq – must have seemed surreal.

Worse: they had to stand there dutifully as he blithely

rewrote the reason they'd just fought. Sending them off, he'd stressed the urgency of finding those weapons of mass destruction. None found, he welcomed them back – as in Townsville on 22 May – thus: 'You went abroad in our name in a just cause, and you joined others in liberating an oppressed people.'

Beg pardon, sir?

You heard right, soldier. Howard used *our* troops' 'victory' homecomings to win another grubby one of his own. Safely clothed in patriotic khaki, he blatantly reset his political spin, daring the same people who'd rejected his lies before those troops left to call his bluff now in their 'victorious' presence.

At the Sydney parade, one tried: 'Where are the weapons of mass destruction!?' he shouted. Howard paused, smiled patiently and resumed his 'victory' speech.

John Howard demanded those parades. And John Howard – self-declared protector of Westminster propriety – tore up our protocols and transformed himself into Australia's de-facto generalissimo to get them. Our troops fight for our country. So our head of state, the governor-general – who is also the commander-in-chief of the Australian Defence Force – officiates at their parades, taking (and returning) their salutes on *our* behalf. R.G. Casey did so at the Sydney welcome-home parades in 1968, and Sir William Deane at the Interfet ones in 2000.

But John Howard decided that *he* would represent our country. That *he* would play commander-in-chief. That *he* would take any Anzac salutes on offer. As historian Mark McKenna noted in an essay entitled 'Howard's Warriors', 'Howard may claim to be a constitutional monarchist, but his vision of the vice-regal office is one which sees the Governor-General as little more than the noble puppet of a presidential Prime Minister.' McKenna wrote:

'[His] duplicity is clear. When the Australian forces left for Iraq Howard insisted that they went not "in the name of the government of the day", but "in the name of Australia". Speaking at welcome-home parades and ceremonies, however, he emphasised that he was "the person who, more than anybody else in Australia, of course accepts responsibility for the decision to deploy you".'

With Australia largely clear of the electorally dangerous fighting in Iraq and without a single casualty, John Howard now gleefully clutched these latest Anzacs to his political bosom and declared them his alone. 'Far from being a figure above politics,' McKenna concluded, 'the parading digger is employed by John Howard and sections of the media to increase the popularity of the conservative government.'

I didn't vote for Howard to be president or commander-in-chief. And many Australians voted to retain a governor-general appointed by the Queen precisely to prevent such seedy politicisation of unifying national functions. Yet after first politicising it via his election-winning deployments during the *Tampa* affair and Operation Relex (the naval operation to turn back the boat people), Howard, the democratic institution wrecker, was again railroading that branch of executive power that should remain above politics: our armed services.

Victory parades, indeed.

The consequences of Howard's lies, since 'plausibly denied' – the spooks 'didn't tell' him the war would increase the terrorist risk, 'didn't mention' some WMD claims were disputed, blah blah – are still to be seen.

Will Australians who once trusted our leaders, at least on such grave matters as national security, now lose *that* trust, too? What happens when we stop believing our leaders about the terrorist dangers they tell us we face? What if the next WMD wolf is a *real* one?

John Howard's 'leadership' during Iraq brought into question whether we have a real democracy in Australia. His actions demand democratic reforms to ensure that no prime minister can ever again misuse power in such a way. Not in our name. They also demonstrate why Howard must be removed from power – either by the Liberal Party or, failing that, the Australian voters.

I visited a friend after Bush declared 'mission accomplished' in Iraq, at a time when the lies, the spin, and the psychological assaults inflicted by the Coalition of the Willing's governments on any public servant who told the truth, were becoming horribly clear.

My friend said, 'Margo, we usually find out thirty years

later that they lied to us to send us to war. What happens when we find out almost instantaneously? And what happens if . . . nothing happens?'

I answered, 'I guess it would mean that we don't treasure our democracy any more. And that means it will die.'

3

Divided and – Conquered?

For all of us

John Howard's campaign slogan, 1996

By 20 June last year I'd hit rock bottom. I'd done journalism – lived it, really – for more than fifteen years, and I knew in my head and heart and gut that journalism had failed the Australian people miserably in the lead-up to war. John Howard had repelled our quest for truth with disdainful ease – with the support of the world's most powerful non-democrat.

Rupert Murdoch.

I'd been unable to watch the war on television. The printed word was hard enough to stomach without viewing the suffering of other human beings. Only a sick or infantile imagination needs a haunting sound bite like this one visually spelt out: 'Often they run into our machine guns and we shoot them down like the morons they are,' US Brigadier General John Kelly said. 'They appear willing to die – we do our best to help them out in that endeavour.'

It made me wonder what brand of 'civilisation' our ANZUS allies were defending. And what kind of Australia John Howard's cheerleaders wanted *us* to become.

Just after Saddam Hussein's statue fell, I gave a shaky and emotional speech to the Sydney Institute. It was part of a long-scheduled debate with Imre Salusinszky, *Australian* editorial writer, neo-liberal commentator and *Quadrant* editorial advisory board member.

The topic: 'The State of the Left', a favourite hobby-horse of the John Howardistas.

I was drowning in the flood of ridiculously premature post-Saddam triumphalism but determined to find some positive way ahead:

'Could we start again, please?

I guess some of you assume I'm here as a representative of the beleaguered left, taking up defensive position number 123 to ward off a rampaging member of the triumphalist right about to stick the boot in one more time.

Could we start again, please?

The world, the allied and Iraqi troops, the Iraqi people, and all of us who watched and read about this war have just been through a traumatic experience, which will continue for a long time – perhaps for my lifetime.

That experience sounded – please, God – the death knell for the traditional left–right dichotomy, which lost its utility a long time ago and now survives, it seems to me, as a convenient means by which commentators accuse each other of being disgusting, idiotic ideologues to the cheers of fans who stopped thinking because it got too hard. The labels are an excuse not to engage, to reassure adherents there is a certain truth, an instinctive escape from genuine conversation in an era of profound uncertainty.

The war debate saw the traditional left split. The traditional conservatives split. The nationalists split. The realists, in general, were against a unilateral US war. No, that's too simplistic. Australians, like peoples around the world, were in many camps.

Let's be honest here. In my view, the fundamental split was between those who thought a US invasion would make the world a safer place, and those who thought it would make it more dangerous.

We do not know who is right and who is wrong. We will not know for many years. Most importantly, the question is not predetermined, merely requiring revelation in time. It will depend on how the world's nations and the world's peoples act and react from now on.

What we've just been through, for the first time in my lifetime, is the peoples and the nations of the world engaged in a tumultuous, deeply unsatisfactory debate about the world's future through the prism of one nation.

Every sensible person knew as they watched those two planes crash into the World Trade Centre on September 11, 2001 that the world changed irrevocably at that moment. Since then, we've watched the Western world unite, then divide bitterly and destructively, as America launched a pre-emptive war without disclosure of its blueprint for peace, and proved to the world, starkly, that might is right.

Now the rules of the old security order have fallen over and with them, in my view, the supposed "inevitability" of world economic globalisation, which the World Trade Centre towers also symbolised. The globalisation of environment protection and human rights – which struggle to keep up with economic globalisation – are also at grave risk.

As the UN as we know it – and thus the forces of internationalisation, of world governance – collapsed, what the world began debating so imperfectly were the greatest, deepest and most confronting questions of all. In many types of discourses we began discussing the values and beliefs to which we – as individuals, nations and collective custodians of this world, our home – subscribe, and the costs we are prepared to pay to meet the demands of those values and beliefs.

Hard choices, each one having a terrible cost. No referee. No consistency. No level playing field. Shifting arguments. Fake evidence. And the certainty of all thinking people, surely, that the stated rationales for the war were untrue; that there were deeper, more fundamental reasons in play, reasons which those who rule us believed could not be openly discussed because they were ashamed of them; or because they were too confronting for us to face; or because we might interrogate them and they might discover (or do they already know?) that the peoples of the world just don't support them.

Then war. Scenes of horror, dismemberment, liberation, anarchy, joy, hope, unimaginable pain and loss, fear, hatred, hubris. Look at them all through the prism of the experience of the people of Iraq, blessed and cursed with its abundance of oil, torn asunder by wars of empire over thousands of years.

We stared at the human condition, blinkers removed.

And then – too quickly – many of us put the blinkers back on. The debates resumed as before, only more bitter, angrier, even more divisive.

But it can't be, can it? It doesn't matter what your walk of life, your wealth, your philosophical or political bent – an unsafe world where bombs or other mechanisms of random death can hit anyone, anywhere, any time means we're all in the same boat in a world rent by terror, aren't we? We were all able to empathise with the tragedy of the war and the fragility of hope for the Iraqi people, weren't we?

There MUST be common ground, mustn't there?

What is the value of a human life? What is the responsibility of those who decide they will sacrifice some innocent lives for a larger purpose? What place does Australia have in the world, and what place can it realistically aspire to? What values does Australia stand for? What compromises to those values must Australia accept to keep us as safe as possible?

Left and right. Black and white. Good and evil. All or nothing. These binaries are methods of escape from the need to examine who we are and where our society is failing us, with clear, honest eyes. The left–right debate in Australia reinforces prejudice on both sides, and is a dangerous tool of fanatical political tribalism. It destroys. It is hopeless. It does not reflect the diversity and nuances of the views we hold, or the extent of our common ground. It does not facilitate constructive conversation. It is an admission of the failure of public debate to achieve anything of value for society.

I suggest that those of us lucky enough to be paid to think about our nation and its values, and those interested in participating in that discourse, take a deep breath at this defining moment in Australian and world history, and make the assumption that each of us is in good faith and has the best interests of Australians and Australia at heart.

Let's then explore where we differ, and why. Let's first focus on what our core beliefs are about the individual, our society and the role of government. Then let's see what common ground we've got, both in our core beliefs and principles and in our assessment of the weaknesses in the way our society and our democracy are working.

You know, it's just possible that most of us will share more core beliefs and principles than not. Most of our disagreements may well be about the best means to fulfil our common principles, and whether we are inherently pessimistic or optimistic about the human condition.

But, pessimistic or optimistic, we must find the hope in this and nurture it for all it's worth.

So let's do what we always promise we'll do next time but never do when the time comes, and look at the history of this war from September 11, when fanatics invaded America and a group of Americans called neo-cons had the clear-eyed, bright-light, absolutist, fundamentalist vision ready to put in place in response.

And let's look back on the wreckage of the rules now gone and consider in hindsight what could have been done differently, and how, by all the players, to achieve a more satisfactory, less brutal, less uncertain result for all of us. If we all had our time again what would we do differently, and what would we have liked our leaders to have done differently?

And when we've done that let's dream about what a new world order might look like, one that gives the world a better chance to survive and to maximise human freedom, happiness and dignity.

I don't know about you, but I feel humbled by this war. It brings into sharp relief the urgent work to be done in finding a useful mechanism by which the world can tackle problems that no one country can tackle alone. Amid destruction of the rules must come renewal, and I'm trying to think, as many of us are, about what my role could be in that – in my little world, in my little country, as a citizen of the world committed to doing my best to leave it in the best shape I can to the children of my relatives and friends.

I've got lots of thoughts – too many – jumbling around my head, competing with each other for attention. Maybe some people in the audience need what I do – a process, a means by which I can converse with other people of good faith who care about our land, our people, our country and our world. A process via which to settle on a few basic values; and to be honest about the constraints individuals are under in their individual circumstances. A process to give people fuller rein to work across old political divides to find, encourage and support leaders who will help us all nurture our hope and put the energy that gives us to good purpose.

No one has "the truth" any more. We all know it, in our hearts, though so many of us pretend not to, for fear of what that means, and the consequences that might follow for our careers if we dropped our pretence. And partly because of these left–right barriers we can't seem to get together and talk things through any more. And agree, politely, to disagree on some matters, and have the courage to agree, with relief, on others, and put our heads together to push those common ideals along.

When an old order falls there is the chance to rebuild a better one. This is a time of vulnerability and fear. Thinkers can exacerbate those feelings or facilitate honest conversation to help rebuild community spirit and regenerate a shared value system.

The people in this country and this world need to trust, and need to hope. The left–right debate doesn't engender either.

Could we start again, please?'

In response Salusinszky delivered the standard and by now traditional right-wing critique of traditional left-wing commentators on the war.

My heart sank as I listened. No common ground allowed there. None.

A tiny space opened up briefly when Anne Henderson, wife of the Institute Director, Gerard Henderson, challenged Imre to reconcile Howard's war of 'Iraqi liberation' with

Howard's policy of locking up Iraqi boat people, the overwhelming proportion of whom even Philip Ruddock had conceded were genuine refugees from Saddam.

The left did their cause no good by referring to detention centres as gulags, Imre replied.

No engagement. No honesty. This influential 'intellectual' and editorial writer simply ducked the question, like . . . a Liberal Party minister.

It summed up public debate in Australia for me. Although I'm off the booze, I walked straight into the nearest pub, ordered a beer and read my speech, crying.

In the months that followed, I became paralysed by self-doubt, unable to read or write about the fallout of 'peace' in Iraq. Webdiarist Hugh Driver, a Sydney lawyer, struck a dismal chord:

'I'm just wondering whether scouring the net, posting rants, sending emails, etc isn't just an intellectual exercise that, at the end of the day, counts for very little outside the very, very small circles of consequence that we operate in. Is it just another form of entertainment for modern media junkies?'

I was burnt out. Depressed. I took time off and planned my retirement. Heh, kiddo, get a life!

4

Jack Robertson is one of those 'left-wing commentators on the war' identified by Imre Salusinszky: one of the 'mob' who opposed the Iraq invasion. An 'appeaser' (*Herald Sun* commentator Andrew Bolt) who made up the 'Coalition of the Whining' (the *Australian*). A 'fifth columnist' (*Daily Telegraph* commentator Piers Akerman) and an anti-American 'freeloader' (visiting American neo-conservative academic Daniel Pipes). But labels of any kind are dangerously limiting, as Jack's account of the hard thinking he did during the Iraq war shows. And perhaps in his reflections on history, family and war there lies one answer to my despairing plea 'Could we start again, please?'

Jack has written a 'Meeja Watch' column for Webdiary since 2000, when his critiques of journalism sparked a ferocious online discussion on my profession's future.

I asked him why he remains a lefty when he's been on the losing side of so many political debates for so long.

'My uncle, my grandfather and my brother,' he said. 'Democratic Anzacs all.'

M.K.

Ordinary Australian Appeasers

By Jack Robertson

*I wonder if Howard would give me a
state funeral if he knew what I really stood for*

**Alec Campbell, union man, Vietnam War protester
and the last Anzac, quoted in *Workers Online*, May 2002**

On 15 May 1952, fifty-one years before his third youngest nephew took to the Sydney streets in his first ever anti-war march, Pilot Officer Donald Neil Robertson was shot down and killed by a communist gun crew near the North Korean village of Masan-Ni.

Colin G. King was tail-end Charlie in the final mission flown by Don Robertson and describes it in his memoir *Luck Is No Accident*:

'As we dived on our target, the nasty little black puffs were there menacing our descent path. Quite early in the dive . . . Robertson's aircraft, which was ahead and below me, suddenly rolled to the right simultaneously discharging its rockets. In anguish I watched the Meteor plummeting earthwards, waiting and hoping to see an ejection seat. The aircraft continued its lazy rolling motion, terminating in a great ball of orange flame on the edge of a village . . . Another fine young man was gone.'

The RAAF motto is *Per Ardua Ad Astra* – Through Adversity to the Stars – but in Korea adversity prevailed, and Robertson's climb was ended before he reached the stars.

Surviving classmates from the Point Cook RAAF College achieved the highest ranks and success in business and public service, but Don was posted 'missing, believed killed', and posthumously awarded the US Air Medal for his 'aggressiveness and skill whilst serving in Korea'.

A cockpit photo taken shortly before his death captures a boy grown weary beyond his years and, according to my grandfather Len Robertson, his older son's letters revealed him as 'shocked to his foundations at what he saw and heard in Korea'. What my young uncle meant to convey, of course, was that he was shocked at what he *did* in Korea.

We need to tell the darker side of our Anzac stories, too.

No Australian shared more responsibility for my uncle's killing than Robert Menzies, Australia's first and greatest Liberal prime minister.

Not only was it Menzies who had sent Don to Korea, it was also Menzies who had given him the unlikely chance to become a fighter pilot in the first place.

The post Second World War technical boom had demanded RAAF officers of operational, academic and leadership excellence, and to provide them Menzies conceived of a new cadet school as an exclusive meritocracy.

Len Robertson was a Melbourne factory storeman who'd left school at 14, but if Don's working-class background seemed unpromising it was rendered irrelevant by a national birthright suddenly unshackled from the weight of class destiny – and by an unashamedly elitist father who urged his son to aim high.

Joining the RAAF College beside the sons of toffs and larrikins alike, Don unleashed his aspirations and excelled. The great conservative meritocrat was there to present his graduation rewards: the Queen's Medal, the Sword of Honour as top graduate, the mathematics prize, a commission.

I doubt my grandfather, a Curtin and Chifley voter, felt prouder than he did the day a Liberal prime minister commended him on the Australian he had raised – largely alone, since Don's mother had died when he was a boy.

Within six months that boy was gone, too.

We might have expected some class-war bitterness from Len since Menzies was his generation and yet, unlike him – and his dead son – had never killed for Australia himself. While Private Len Robertson crossed Sinai sands with the Imperial Camel Corps and the 5th Light Horse, student Bob Menzies was earning admittance to the Melbourne bar.

As Bob eased from law to politics, Len fought the Great Depression on Soldier Settlement land.

Had Len rejected all that Menzies represented from the day his son was killed, we'd forgive him. Gazing back from John Howard's 'conservative' Australia, where a war widow sometimes seems like an obstacle to be negotiated with minimum political embarrassment, we might assume that Menzies had taken care to avoid the bereaved Labor man.

But Len was never a class warrior, Menzies wasn't one to shirk his moral duty, and the Liberal Party wasn't always like it is today. After a pause to allow for private grieving, the ordinary Australian Bob instead drove to an ordinary Melbourne suburb to visit the ordinary Australian Len: best Sunday clothes, best china, best room. I suppose the Prime Minister wanted to express Australia's gratitude personally. I suppose he felt a democratic obligation.

There was no publicity on Menzies' part, no attempt at political advantage. Conservative Australian leaders once called such civic grace *noblesse oblige*, I am told, without any irony or embarrassment.

I've been a fierce critic of John Howard for a while now, so when Margo Kingston invited me to write a chapter for a book arguing that he is a conservative impostor disguised in ill-fitting Menzies hand-me-downs I immediately pitched that family yarn as irresistible proof. Don Robertson's youngest nephew – my little brother – fought in Afghanistan alongside Andrew Russell, the SAS sergeant killed there in 2002, and to me the contrast between Menzies' moral courage in facing my brother's grieving grandfather privately and Howard's failure even to invite his dead colleague's widow to the War Memorial wreath laying, where

President Bush specifically praised her husband, seemed almost too symmetrically damning of the smaller Liberal leader to be true.

Which is precisely what it was.

'It's a good yarn,' agreed my dad, when I began checking details about my Menzies story. 'It would be *nice* if it was true, too. But the full story is less clear – and more illuminating.'

For the first time in ages Dad and I started talking properly: about family history, about politics then and now, about the point I'd planned to make with my version of his brother's death. That's how we discovered that we occupy more common ground than we'd realised, even though he's long been a (qualified) admirer of John Howard's story of Australia, while I'm a frustrated idealist, Republican, 'war on terror' sceptic and enduring fan of Paul Keating. We've certainly had our fierce arguments over recent years, but sorting out the truth about his brother's death helped us both recognise again that there are also two sides to *contemporary* political stories.

As Dad said, the fuller story turned out to be more salutary than I'd thought, if somewhat awkwardly so for me. More balanced, more revealing of what Australia has since lost, perhaps even more flattering of Menzies.

And certainly more inclusive, when it comes to the meaning of Anzac.

> The Anzac legend is a story of great valour under fire, unity
> of purpose, and a willingness to fight against the odds that
> has helped to define what it means to be Australian.
>
> **John Howard, on the death of Alec Campbell, 16 May 2002**

The legend as lived by Donald Neil Robertson certainly does contain those stirring chapters our current prime minister claimed on behalf of the last Anzac, Alec Campbell.

Don's valour under fire is told in anecdotes such as Col King's; that US Air Medal for 'aggressiveness and skill' makes it ANZUS-official. His diary records his squadron's camaraderie and fighting unity in Korea, while the UN flag even lent his war a political unity of purpose (though I doubt that's the kind Howard had in mind). And we know that the Meteor Don flew was inferior to the enemy MiG 15: it was out-run, out-climbed, out-gunned. His sorties were usually low-level rocket attacks, where the ground-fire odds were against him, too – fatally so. 'Valour', 'unity', 'a willingness to fight against the odds': even using only John Howard's narrow version of the Anzac legend as our guide, my uncle's story, to use the words of an earlier prime minister, Paul Keating, might contain 'faith enough for all of us'.

But Keating saw much more in our Anzac story than this, and when eulogising the Unknown Australian Soldier at the Australian War Memorial on 11 November 1993 did not intend this poetic closing flourish of his to mean 'faith *defined* for all of us', or '*my* faith is enough for all of us'. That eulogy was an invitation to every Australian to reflect on the meaning of Anzac in their own way, not a prime ministerial lesson in how they should do so. Above all, it was a reminder of who really owns the Anzac story:

'It is a legend not of sweeping military victories so much as triumphs against the odds, of courage and ingenuity in adversity. It is a legend of free and independent spirits whose discipline derived less from military formalities and customs than from the bonds of mateship and the demands of necessity. It is a democratic tradition, the tradition in which Australians have gone to war ever since.'

There was much common ground between Keating and his successor here ('adversity', 'mateship', 'courage') but where was the 'democratic tradition' in John Howard's refusal to listen to sceptics – the 'mob' – on Iraq? Where was the backbench of 'free and independent spirits' in that once-broad church of Robert Menzies' Liberal Party? During the parliamentary debate on Iraq Howard even physically turned his back on Opposition Leader Simon Crean. Turned his back on his own Parliament, his own people, his own democracy. The Unknown Australian Soldier surely would have cried hot tears in his tomb.

I played a privileged official role in that 1993 ceremony, and I saw up close, as Keating approached the podium to speak, our national eulogist's nervousness.

If ever there was an ordinary Australian fit to unite a

people it was that anonymous soldier resting prone on the marble before him; but that single representative of the story of Anzac lay equally open to partisan appropriation at that moment, too.

Keating got it just right: that speech melted stone. As with any living story, the power was all in the listener and the place, and Keating, in his tender, nervous humility, yielded to both. In turn 20 million fellow Australians could find space and faith enough to honour their own private versions of Anzac along with him.

For me every word was for my uncle, his lonelier tomb in faraway North Korea just as beautifully blessed.

This is why John Howard's prescriptive, sanitised version of the Anzac legend, and the way he thinks it defines us as Australians, will never be enough for me. Just as Howard's state funeral eulogy for Alec Campbell in 2002 might have resonated more had it saluted the last Anzac's *anti*-war activism in later life, rather than Howard's recent wars ('Afghanistan, East Timor, Bougainville and elsewhere'), so too Don Robertson's legacy is diminished if we allow it no more than his courage, mateship and struggle through adversity in his attempt to reach the stars.

To tell of Australians dying bravely without telling of Australians killing savagely is an insult to the true magnitude of their Anzac selflessness. Most soldiers who have killed for their country see it as the cruellest sacrifice of all, yet only rarely do we citizens acknowledge it, and modern politicians *never* do. They lacked the moral guts even to keep an honest count of the largely one-sided, automated killing-from-afar they recently ordered my younger brother to do in the Iraq war.

As for what our politicians ordered him to do in peacetime, John Howard's Anzac story has no place for that at all. Not publicly, at least.

I acknowledge your concerns about [allegations of ADF human rights abuse during Operation Relex] and wish to assure you that the government has acted decisively but compassionately to protect Australia's territorial integrity.

Department of Prime Minister and Cabinet reply to Jack Robertson, 18 February 2003

Before he fought in Afghanistan and Iraq – and received two minor wounds looking for John Howard's weapons of mass destruction in the latter – my little brother helped Howard transfer the *Tampa* and associated refugees to Nauru on HMAS *Manoora*. On arrival a handful of recalcitrants refused to leave the ship, and it fell partially to my brother to try to end the stand-off. Straight negotiation got him nowhere; eventually he presented a more unorthodox idea to his superiors, who agreed it was worth a try. I don't know who authorised his plan. I don't know what might have happened if things had gone wrong. Things didn't. His idea partially helped break the impasse, no one was harmed, and Australian soil remained unsullied by unprocessed *Tampa* toes.

My brother won't say how he tried to get those last refugees off the *Manoora*. This worries me because I can recognise taciturnity that is inspired by something more than 'operational security' when I see it. He was more forthcoming when I asked if it could be regarded as human rights abuse, especially by an Amnesty International supporter like me.

'You might call it HR abuse,' he conceded.

He agreed that if they'd known exactly what he'd done to help John Howard develop his election-winning *Tampa* story Australians might have voted in fewer numbers to keep hearing it.

I've read many accusations from refugees against our ADF arising from border protection episodes. Claims about beatings, cattle prods and psychological coercion during Operation Relex have been denied by the government, but they won't go away. The Prime Minister may be right to defend my brother and his RAN colleagues as 'decisive but compassionate', but the danger in his official account of border protection is that, like his eulogy for Alec Campbell, it's not the full Anzac story.

And like my version of my brother's Anzac present, my version of my uncle's Anzac past must also include the darker sides of the story. I have no choice. Don himself, before he died, told that darker side. His father the Labor voter heard it, and retold it publicly on his dead son's behalf even in his grief.

And the Liberal prime minister who sent Don Robertson off to kill and die heard it in turn. And he, at least, had the courage to acknowledge this 'free and independent spirit', this anti-war Anzac among his own nation's democratic 'mob'.

It's May 1952. An unauthorised Australian delegation is preparing to visit Red Peking for a Korean War peace conference. Dr John Burton, who will lead it, is a former secretary to the ALP leader, H.V. Evatt, and a party member himself. With Australians fighting communists, the accusations of appeasement and treachery fly once news of the delegation gets out, much of it from Menzies' government. Just as 'Islamofascism' will be in 2003, 'communism' is a damaging political wedge; soon it will split the ALP catastrophically. Doc Evatt, a principled universalist, is resisting internal pressure to purge his team of all Red tints, real or imagined, but pragmatic colleagues see looming electoral disaster.

When the peace trip hits the papers Evatt's deputy, Arthur Calwell, publicly calls for John Burton to be expelled.

Len Robertson, ex-AIF, has been moderate ALP throughout his voting life: like Curtin, Chifley and now Evatt, a man of principle but never ideology. He has been an admirer of the current Labor leader since his UN role in the creation of Israel in 1948. Len's philosophical touchstone is the one attributed to Voltaire: 'I may disagree with what you say, but I shall defend to the death your right to say it.' On 21 May 1952, only days after he learns that Don is 'missing, believed killed' (doubtless shot down by *Chinese* weapons), he lifts the Melbourne *Argus* and reads: 'Burton says: "I won't resign."' The seeker of peace with the communists is defying ALP Deputy Leader Calwell's latest call for him to leave the party.

The letter my grandfather immediately writes in response – perhaps it is stained with fierce, proud, democratic tears – appears in the *Argus*, following an introduction:

'Pilot Officer D.N. Robertson, 22, of Ivanhoe, the son of the writer of the following letter, graduated from Point Cook in December, winning the Sword of Honour and the Queen's Gold Medal as the outstanding cadet, and the mathematics prize. On Saturday he was reported missing, believed killed, in Korea.

A Father's Letter

Sir – I have this morning read the papers for the first time since the tragic news I received on Friday that my brilliant son had been killed in Korea. I feel, Sir, the loss of my son gives me the right to express an honest opinion of things as they really are.

Who is this Calwell? And who is he speaking for? Has any honest man the right to condemn anybody who tries to conciliate? . . .

No sane man wants to interfere with a person's beliefs and activities, so long as they fail to interfere with the common sense of a large body of the community. My dead son, a sensitive lad with great moral courage, and his soul firmly placed in his Creator's keeping, was shocked to his foundations at what he saw and heard in Korea – so much so that his last letter said it was hard for him to believe that MAN was anything else but 'a lower animal with the biggest brain'.

I am, Sir, a grief-stricken father that has lived for his wife, home and family. I belong to no organisation of any kind, but have admired and supported the late Ben Chifley and John Curtin because they were men with ideals like myself.

Surely this glorious country could be encouraged by your great paper to rouse itself from its selfishness and apathy, and build a society of free, honest people willing to pull together to set an example to all the 'isms' in the world of what we could do in this land.

Surely we would respond IF we had a lead.

L.J. Robertson (Ivanhoe)'

My father and his ageing sister have lately set me straighter on what happened next, and perhaps in the two family stories arising from Len's letter there is lesson enough for all of us, wherever we stand in John Howard's Australia.

Just days after it was published, Dad agrees, my grandfather *did* receive a political visit. Not from the Liberal Prime Minister, though, but from the Communist Party of Australia! With a stupefying lack of sensitivity, they'd deduced that this 'L.J Robertson (Ivanhoe)' might care to speak out from their platform against Menzies, the war and the 'ruling classes'. Len angrily sent them on their way, Dad says, but the fact that it was the self-proclaimed 'progressives' of the day, not the conservatives, who most explicitly tried to hijack my uncle's death is a timely reminder to the fierce critics of John Howard's appropriation of Anzac sacrifice today that appropriation is not restricted to any one side. A reminder to me, too. My own loaded account of Menzies' behaviour in the aftermath of Don's death – with its intention of making the current Liberal leader look smaller in the comparison – shows we can be guilty of the same unforgivable behaviour all too easily.

There is faith enough for all of us.

My aunt also tells of how that letter to the *Argus* caused many of Len's conservative friends to ostracise him as a 'communist appeaser' and 'Anzac traitor'. Dad recalls the AIF veteran's estrangement from his local RSL, as well.

'He was a lonely man, in the end,' he now reflects, and there's surely an equal historical reproach in this for those Australians who threw their white feathers at us 'freeloaders' today in the 'Coalition of the Whining'.

There is faith enough in our Anzac legend for all of us. And, as it turns out, even though I did at first exaggerate my own version of Len's story – obviously picked up in the past from someone in the family – there was a Menzies yarn, after all.

To my father's stunned surprise, when we phoned her together, his elderly sister did remember the story of Menzies dropping by to pay his personal respects to the grieving father who'd stood so publicly on his anti-war principles. Their stepmother had once told her how Menzies – presumably nearby on other business – detoured via Len's home not long after Len's letter appeared. Details of the entirely unannounced visit have the ring of truth: her stepmother described 'racing around the house, shutting drawers, tidying up' and quickly improvising an afternoon tea that was not, 'to her disgruntlement', even consumed.

It's not in the detail, I know, but I can't help seeing a human handshake across the partisan divide. A warm chat about the fine boy Menzies remembered well from his graduation day. An acknowledgement of Len Robertson's principled stand, even if his letter *was* defending the right of some of Menzies' most fervent critics to conciliate. Perhaps it's just my bias again, but I can't quite imagine John Howard – master of spin, stage-management, contrived division – subjecting his political persona to the vagaries of human contact like this. That I can picture his hero Menzies doing so very easily is, I think, illuminating contrast enough.

Whatever the truth of my aunt's memories, Robert Menzies' instinct for forging faith enough for all of us in our definitive national story is firmly on our family's official record anyway. Australia's greatest conservative leader took the time to write a very warm personal letter to my grandfather, the anti-war Anzac. In the end, visit or no visit, not even Menzies' self-proclaimed political heir can disavow this testament to our more inclusive Anzac history.

Yet Howard, and Imre Salusinszky and the other conservative commentators, insist on holding us to a partial interpretation of the Anzac legend that denies its connection with the stories of those more ordinary 'appeasers', the hundreds of thousands of Australians who marched against his war in Iraq.

One of whom has always been proud to call himself – in the family tradition of his Returned Soldier grandfather, his Korean War hero uncle and his fighting brother today – an anti-war Anzac, even though he no longer wears the uniform himself.

Melbourne *Sun*, 11 July 1986:

'Stephen Keeps RAAF Honor for Family

History came a full circle on the muddy parade ground at Point Cook Air Force base yesterday. A Morwell family watched their son, graduating Pilot Officer Stephen ("Jack") Robertson, lead the ranks carrying the Sword of Honour awarded to his dead uncle Don on the same parade ground 35 years ago . . .

Yesterday his nephew [Jack], 20, stood on the same spot as parade commander and carried the sword which has been hanging on his father's lounge wall for years. He was also awarded his own Sword of Honour as the graduate showing the highest leadership qualities.

He said he felt sad, but proud his uncle had given his life for his country. "He led the first parade in the same executive position," he said. "I was definitely proud" . . .

His aunt remembers Don Robertson receiving his sword from Prime Minister Menzies in 1951. "Today is rather lovely and a bit nostalgic," she said. "Don had very high ideals, and I think he would have been proud."'

Postscript: Jack Robertson served in the Australian Defence Force for eleven years, mostly as a helicopter pilot. As he says, he was at the tomb of the Unknown Australian Soldier in 1993 when Keating gave the eulogy. Like former intelligence officer Andrew Wilkie, who resigned in protest over the Howard government's misuse of classified military assessments to justify the Australian role in Bush's Iraq war, Jack served a year as Army aide-de-camp to the former governor-general Bill Hayden, Chief Mourner that day.

M.K.

Part Two

My Australia

5

Waiting for the Great
Leap Forward

*The duty of the journalist is the same as that of the historian –
to seek out the truth, above all things, and to present to his readers
not such things as statecraft would wish them to know but
the truth as near as he can attain it*

London *Times* editor John Thadeus Delane, 1852

On June 20 last year I was sitting on my lounge-room floor, working through the financial implications of retiring to the country to live well, grow vegetables and read history books, when the phone rang. It was my colleague Anne Davies giving me the awful year's latest awful news.

'Margo, we've dropped the ball,' she said. 'The Senate will pass the government's cross-media bill next week.'

Communications Minister Richard Alston had just announced he'd got the support of the four Independent senators needed to pass the bill, Anne advised. My mind went blank.

Chilling news on a winter day.

Howard's legislation would abolish the ban on any media group owning both a TV station and a newspaper in the same city, and it would abolish foreign ownership restrictions on print and television media altogether. The bill had languished in the bottom drawer for over a year, and the journos' union had been assured by the key Senate players that the Senate would *never* pass such a brutal assault on media diversity. Never, ever.

But now it seemed that all it would take to finally seduce the four Independent senators were a few taxpayer-funded baubles – extending ABC news radio in the regions, some extra cash for community radio – and some schmoozing from the Cabinet big boys.

At the other end of the 'democratic' power scale – the elite end?

The bill was Rupert Murdoch's local 'Iraq-war dividend', allowing him to buy a free-to-air television network to complement his Australian print media dominance: a thank-you present for his pro-war advocacy, from the Australian people, by way of John Howard, to the global media mogul who already had everything else. Tony Blair and George Bush were showing similar appreciation overseas. The 'Coalition of the Willing' described it nicely.

For print journalism – and for me – the bill would be catastrophic as it would seal Howard's delivery of the Fairfax stable to Australia's richest, most powerful, most feared and most unscrutinised businessman. As quietly promised before the 1996 election, Howard's bill would at long last allow Kerry Packer to get his hands on the Melbourne *Age*, the Sydney *Sun-Herald*, the *Australian Financial Review* and the *Sydney Morning Herald*. What little scrutiny of Packer's corporate doings there now was – especially from a few crazy-brave Fairfax business reporters – would survive ten minutes. So would Webdiary.

Australia's brackish media pond was already underpopulated by ownership groups, and boasted the narrowest ownership in the Western world. Even if their own latest pro-Rupert rule changes went through, both the US and Britain would still have *more* diversity than we had now. If ours went through, Australia's Big Media club would effectively shrink from three to two – and here those two were business partners.

What do you do? Get depressed, get angry or get out? Turn your back and wander off to grow organic mung beans in peace and harmony? Or lift your chin to look the bastards in the eye one more time?

I told Anne I'd call her back.

I went into my study and gazed at the Jenny Coopes cartoon on my wall: a Murdoch classic I'd picked up at a campaign fundraiser in the early 1990s when Fairfax journos were auctioning the shirts off their backs to stop Packer buying up their professional souls. There Rupert is: at his desk sneering, his newly acquired London *Times* clutched in one hand like a comic book while he crows into the phone in the other: 'It wasn't a takeover . . . It was a PUSHOVER.'

I'd paid a fortune for that cartoon: it reminded me of the origins of my activism on media ownership; of the tactics Rupert Murdoch had once used to grab Brisbane's *Courier-Mail* (the newspaper that had given me my first shot at a career in journalism), side-stepping media laws with disingenuous promises quickly broken. Heavying statutory bodies and pollies. Treating the people – his readers – with contempt. Murdoch's stunted vision of what journalism was 'for' had been clear to me from day one: profit and power.

The cartoon next to the Coopes was even closer to home, a Geoff Pryor ripper – Kerry Packer as lascivious stand-up comedian, fat cigar in hand, late-night tie undone, one microphone raised to those Packer lips, another silenced with his free hand: 'Didja hear the one about the cross-media rules . . .' Howard told Cabinet at the time that Fairfax was 'too liberal'.

In a moment of over-my-dead-body defiance in 1997, during the first battle to stop Howard giving Packer Fairfax, I'd stuck a sticker on the border: 'TRUST ME. I'M A REPORTER.'

To the many great journalists I knew it may well have been the Packers and Murdochs of our world who were destroying our vocation from within, but as far as the Australian public were concerned it was increasingly hard to spot the difference between journalist and proprietor. Or even to bother trying.

One of our early Webdiary debates was on the state and future of my profession. A survey I ran throughout it revealed that readers regarded journalists even less favourably than politicians. It was a Hobson's choice question: who do you trust more? After a long, ferociously engaged debate that wouldn't stop no matter how often I cried 'Enough!', the cold, hard numbers told the story: pollies 51 per cent, journos 49 per cent. The majority of my readers now considered democracy's free press scrutinisers to be less trustworthy than those democratic representatives we were supposed to be scrutinising on their behalf.

OK, Margo, I'll take the bait. Most politicians are a bunch of arrogant, egotistical, power-hungry control freaks who think that their opinions are far more important than anybody else's. They earn their living by distorting the truth. The SAME is true of most journalists. So why is it that journalists are held in even lower regard by the general public than politicians? At least the politicians are usually prepared to SHOW their colours. We all know what side they are on, and what their motivations are . . . We expect [unbalanced and biased opinions] from them. We set a lower social standard for them, and they can expect some returning fire.

Journalists are the spies and snipers in our midst, shooting at the unarmed and easy targets. Unlike politicians, they are unelected and protected from serious criticism. They falsely pretend to be 'impartial' and 'independent', or patronisingly portray themselves to be the same as ordinary people. Some of them even attempt to maintain an ethical pretence, as they generously bestow their wisdom and moral guidance

[on] the peasants. The arrogance of journalists is endless. Journalists are intellectual prostitutes. Their reluctance to criticise the right-wing economic rationalism and globalisation favoured by their media mogul masters is rewarded by an almost unrestricted right to publicise left-wing social agendas. Journalists have the delegated power to pull politicians' strings and make them dance, and they think that this provides de facto membership to the elite. Their own strings – which lead to Packer & Murdoch – are not discussed. If you close your eyes, you can pretend that they 'don't really exist'.

Journalists are beginning to wake up to their true position in the social hierarchy, but they still can't understand the depth and extent of this opinion . . . Have a nice day.

Webdiarist Greg Weilo, 9 November 2000

A little stunned by it all, I'd written a piece called 'Catharsis Complete: What Next?':

'Right. Is there a solution? Ideas PLEASE! As you know, I've been questioning where journalism is, and its future, since experiencing the disconnect [between journalism and the people] on Pauline's Hanson's election trail. Journalists rely on the public to tell them what's happening, and to read/listen to/watch their work. So the journalists and the public have a symbiotic relationship . . . if no one trusts us enough to spill the beans – or if some are confident we'll buy any old bullshit line – then we can't get anywhere near the truth. And if consumers don't believe what we write, or find it boring or irrelevant, we're out of a job. Perhaps we need to restore the "partnership", to use a current buzz-word. I'd like a contract between journos and readers . . .'

I stared at my two cartoons, trying to remember why I had chucked in my legal career to become a journalist in the first place.

Kerry Packer and Rupert Murdoch were laughing at me from my study wall.

I blinked. The moment passed.

I was gunna go down fighting.

6

Closing the Door on
Your Right to Know

*Freedom of the press is not a property right of owners. It is
a right of the people. It is part of their right to free expression,
inseparable from their right to inform themselves*

Kent Royal Commission into media ownership in Canada

Defending Australia's cross-media ownership rules is
not about defending 'me', or even my profession,
really.

Yes, it's an issue I hold dear. Yes, there's self-interest
involved. Journalists like to find out exactly what's going on,
then tell the world exactly what that is. Anything that makes
either half of this job harder gets our backs up. We are
naturally and necessarily information-ambitious: curious
(nosy), precise (pedantic), persistent (arrogant) and, above
all else, *fanatically* protective of our freedom of expression
(blabbermouths).

These are our critical working tools. On every real
news story we investigate, the tools will invariably cheese
somebody off. We try our best to make sure that that 'somebody' is the person who deserves to be pissed off. We don't

always hit the right targets, but we do, at our best, try hard to do so.

And our overall strike rate has everything to do with how much elbow-room our editors, our executives and especially our proprietors allow us.

Sick of us hitting only the easy targets? The dodgy car mechanics, the welfare frauds, the C-list celebrities and the philandering sports stars? Reckon we were too hard on Cheryl Kernot or Peter Hollingworth and too soft on the HIH or the One.Tel gangs?

Then the ongoing cross-media ownership battle is YOUR issue, too.

For Example

1   No Murdoch paper reported Rupert's break-up with his previous wife or his romance with his current one, Wendi Deng. They didn't report the break-up of James Packer and Kate Fischer either (a Lachlan Murdoch 'mate's favour' perhaps?). When Murdoch's *Daily Telegraph* got a story about a relative of James's bride-to-be, Jodhi, getting married at the same time – in much poorer circumstances – Lachlan spiked it: apparently he didn't want to embarrass his mate.

2   Rupert Murdoch and family holidayed at Sydney's Palm Beach in January 2004. A hard-yards freelancer snapped some pictures. Gotcha! The Fairfax *Sun-Herald* ran them. Murdoch's papers, however, didn't even report that the

world's most powerful media billionaire was in Australia. If Kerry Packer had owned the *Sun-Herald*, you – we – might never have known he was here, much less seen him.

But fair enough, eh? I mean, no one likes to pry into other people's private affairs (right, Rupert and Kerry?), and we'd do the same for a mate in unhappy times, too. Try 3 and 4.

3   When One.Tel collapsed investors James Packer and Lachlan Murdoch were right in the thick of it. Yet Packer's Nine Network coverage practically eliminated James from the story, while Murdoch's papers ran a hard 'Lachlan-is-blameless' line (seemingly well briefed by leaks from the boss). Only the Fairfax papers reported the opposing story, as told by One.Tel founders Jodee Rich and Brad Keeling: that these two young moguls-in-waiting were up to their elbows in the rich kids' mischief.

4   In September 2001 John Howard met Murdoch in the US. Neither would say what was discussed. In January 2002 Communications Minister Richard Alston did the same – just before announcing the new media legislation. These meetings were reported only in the Fairfax press. It goes without saying that they would not have been reported had Kerry Packer owned Fairfax by 1997, as planned by him and Howard.

The following big-picture example shows why media ownership diversity is crucial to the functioning of any democracy, and why sound cross-media legislation is as important to you as citizens as it is to me and my journo colleagues. Most of us want to work for you and with you in defending that democracy, not against you, as we often do these days. But *we* need *your* democratic support to do it.

Here's why.

Everybody knows that Rupert Murdoch backed the Iraq war to the hilt. So what? He's entitled to push his views like anyone else, right? Sure. I suppose he's even entitled to use his 'journalism' assets to do so, if he really insists. But, boy, does he insist. On 23 October 2003 Charlie Reina, a former employee, blew the whistle on just how shamelessly Murdoch's number-one American propaganda outlet, Fox News Channel – the 'Fair and Balanced' network – corrodes the democratic pact between government and governed:

'The roots of Fox News Channel's day-to-day on-air bias are actual and direct. They come in the form of an "Executive Memo" distributed electronically each morning, addressing what stories will be covered and, often, suggesting how they should be covered. To the newsroom personnel responsible for the channel's daytime programming "The Memo" is the bible. If, on any given day, you notice that the Fox anchors seem to be trying to drive a particular point home, you can bet "The Memo" is behind it.

The Memo was born with the Bush administration early in 2001, and, intentionally or not, has ensured that the administration's point of view consistently comes across on FNC. This year, of course, the war in Iraq became a constant subject of The Memo [with] subtle hints as to the tone of the anchor's copy. For instance, from the March 20 Memo: "There is something utterly incomprehensible about Kofi Annan's remarks in which he allows that his thoughts are 'with the Iraqi people'. One could ask where these thoughts were during the 23 years Saddam Hussein was brutalising those same Iraqis. Food for thought.'"

About as subtle as a bunker-buster.

Fox's response? 'Like any former disgruntled employee, Charlie Reina has an axe to grind. People are proud to work here. They are proud of the product we produce and understand our daily and future goals.'

This is journalism as seen by Rupert Murdoch: a 'product' of war, just like oil. 'The greatest thing to come out of this [war] for the world economy, if you could put it that way, would be $20 a barrel for oil,' he'd mused beforehand. 'That's bigger than any tax cut in any country.'

But don't just take the word of a disgruntled American Rupert-basher. Read John Howard's hand-picked head of the PM's department from 1996 to 2002, hard-man Max Moore-Wilton. He knows lots about power from the inside, and here's what he said in late 2003 about Murdoch's current media firepower and his willingness to use it:

'In terms of what the Fox network has done during the whole security debate issue, the way in which the *Australian* has refocussed itself in the last 12 months, the impact is enormous . . . I think [Murdoch's] power goes well beyond covert. He doesn't need a prime minister in that sense. He can actually have decisions made overseas that the Australian government may not necessarily support. The biggest change has been the way Rupert has harnessed his [pay] TV networks on issues in the last twelve months. He has harnessed them very, very brutally.'

Australia needs a Rupert Murdoch free-to-air TV network like a jet-setting mogul needs a bicycle.

But again, so what? Fox News Channel is Murdoch's property. He foots the bills, and even if we – and 'sore losers' such as Charlie Reina – despise how blatantly he decrees what editorial line his journalists must toe, surely he's entitled to do so? America is a free country. Nobody is forced to watch Fox, right?

The key lies in assessing the impact of such self-interested editorial interference on the wider workings of a democracy.

What happens when that democracy is not offered an equally accessible, reasonably diverse and opposing array of news angles and editorial opinions to check and balance the Murdoch line? When over time and across a broad range of issues citizens are not offered the maximum opportunity for informed reflection on a variety of subjects? When our habitual instinct for engagement with opposing views is discouraged? This is the crux of the cross-ownership debates.

Let's assess.

In October 2003 a University of Maryland poll on attitudes to international policy revealed the danger with frightening clarity. It found that two-thirds of Americans had embraced at least one of the following false beliefs: (a) that Iraq was involved in the September 11 terrorist attacks or was a proven supporter of al-Qaeda; (b) that weapons of mass destruction had been found in Iraq; and (c) that international opinion supported the war in Iraq.

How come? Most Americans I've met have been pretty frank and open and, individually at least, most seemed equipped with reasonable bullshit detectors. So where does the problem lie for that free-speaking, free-thinking democratic people? With information delivery perhaps?

Truly understanding what influences our views, and how, is almost impossible, but Fox News viewers did top those gullibility tables – fully 80 per cent believed at least one of the above pro-war-lobby fairytales.

It got to the point where even President Bush – as responsible as Murdoch (and US Vice-President Dick Cheney) for spruiking the lie that Saddam Hussein had participated in the September 11 attacks – felt moved to hose that particular furphy down, well after Fox News had helped his administration ramp up support for his invasion, naturally.

It's to prevent precisely this kind of crazy, anti-democratic misinformation partnership that cross-media ownership laws are in place in Australia.

But such nonsense couldn't happen here.

Why not?

We can kid ourselves if we like, but Australians are no more (or less) sceptical than Americans, and we already have the narrowest media-ownership profile in the Western world. Certainly far narrower than in America, and we're far more dominated by individual proprietors. To help mislead those American survey respondents so wildly, Rupert had only a bunch of city newspapers and a single subscriber network at his editorialising disposal. Here he controls 70 per cent of our newspapers, including our only national daily, and with Kerry Packer now jointly owns Foxtel, Australia's only viable pay TV network. Packer in turn owns Australia's commercial TV powerhouse, the Nine Network.

Still happy for John Howard to ease that free-to-air remote gently from your hands while you're dozing – and we all have been dozing, I reckon – and pass it Rupert's way?

Or perhaps you haven't even heard the latest joke about the cross-media ownership laws? I wonder why.

But let's jump backwards first, not forwards, and watch what can happen even when competition laws are in place. I want to pitch you the basic cross-media ownership mantra: *never believe the moguls*.

When I began my career on Brisbane's *Courier-Mail* in the late 1980s there were three big newspaper owners: Murdoch, Fairfax and the Herald & Weekly Times. Murdoch wanted H&WT – which included my paper – to expand his empire, but there was a snag: if he got it, he wouldn't be able to keep all his existing newspapers. Owning both dailies in Brisbane and Adelaide, as he would have, was against competition law.

A law? A mere democratic obstacle. Rupert Murdoch eats them for breakfast.

First he convinced the Trade Practices Commission that he would solve the problem by selling his existing papers in both those cities to Northern Star, an independent media group. The TPC took the deal at face value, which was a pity since if they'd actually read the contract they would have spotted a rat. Northern Star was to be the beneficiary of astounding commercial generosity – Murdoch would print, house, distribute, loss-indemnify and even buy back these two papers via a 'put option' clause if, after five years, Northern Star wasn't happy with the profits.

How Murdoch then planned to get around the original TPC snag if that happened remained unclear, but it was, predictably for many of us journos, a moot point: within months of the sale Northern Star on-sold its new papers, with Murdoch's commercial generosity still attached, to individual executives on each of them. The two instant 'mini-moguls', Roger Holden (Adelaide's *News*) and Frank Moore (Brisbane's *Sun*), were Murdoch loyalists – they were executives at the papers before and after the Northern Star 'purchase'. Both denied being his front men, even though neither had actively sought or bid for 'their' new papers, and neither had actively had to chase the necessary finance.

Dunno about the Adelaide crowd, but every journo in

Brisbane knew the whole thing was a bloody sham. Having got H&WT, and with the TPC finally getting too curious, Murdoch – I mean those two independent owners, Holden and Moore – closed his old papers down. The man thinks media diversity, like democratic accountability, is a drag.

Net result: two great cities became one-paper towns. 'Natural' editorial checks and balances? Gone. A local, mainstream alternative line? Lost.

Adelaide suffered most. Its H&WT broadsheet, the *Adelaide Advertiser*, quickly became the trashiest tabloid in Australia, starving a vibrant city of news and views.

As for me, I was professionally and personally incensed, and for years after I joined Fairfax I pursued the TPC with Freedom of Information requests. The truth of Murdoch's dealings never did come out – there were too many document blackouts – but the Commission did finally concede that it had failed to examine relevant sale documents before approving Murdoch's 'divestment' to the Northern Star.

Assistant Commissioner Hank Spiers said, 'If there had been suspicion of a [Murdoch] link, we wouldn't have gone the way we did', and, on closer inspection of the arrangements, new-broom Commissioner Bob Baxt admitted, 'In legal terms there are ways in which [Murdoch] would be described as the legal owner.' Small-l liberal and former Coalition communications minister Ian McPhee was also less gullible and timid than the TPC, helping force an inquiry into its failure to properly scrutinise Murdoch. This debacle would *never* have happened under the leadership of

Allan Fels, head of the TPC's replacement body, the Australian Competition and Consumer Commission.

Study the history of Murdoch's global rise all over the world, and across the decades you'll find forlorn public servants and politicians littering his wake, telling the same sad story.

Never believe the moguls, please. Never, ever believe them.

It was Labor Treasurer Paul Keating who opened the door to Murdoch's print media domination in Australia and, with the Broadcasting Services Act 1992, put in place what remains the Australian people's only defence: the rule that no media group can own or control both print and television outlets in the same city – Keating's 'princes of print' and 'queens of the screen' legislation.

It's this rule that has ensured Fairfax's survival – just – as an independent third media power. It's a rule that has often been under threat, but never more so than from John Howard now. It's hard to tell which is his greatest motivation for dropping that rule – doing what the moguls want in the expectation of generally favourable political coverage, or neutering the Fairfax journalism culture at last.

As for Kerry Packer and Rupert Murdoch, they've always hated us. And Packer has long wanted us, too.

What these power-players have hated – like many others in their time – is our independent scrutiny. It's inconvenient.

It's awkward. It can challenge and even (if rarely) crimp their power. We've told stories these blokes didn't want told. We've exposed secret meetings and cosy deals they didn't want revealed. Like the ones between each other: between prime ministers and moguls. We've poked our sticky beaks into their affairs – their company tax affairs, say. We've shot off our blabbermouths about it, too. We've occasionally hit the right targets with our journalistic tools.

Whatever its faults, Fairfax is an Australian media company where journalism still works. I've only got away with my activism on media ownership issues because I'm employed there. The same applies to my Webdiary journalism.

Fairfax journos cling tenaciously to the remnants of a true journalistic culture, one backed by a charter of editorial independence and journalist solidarity when journalistic principles are at stake. One where we strive to separate news judgement from the self-interest of owners, boards and advertisers. A culture in which the board picks the editor and the editor decides what is news and is accountable to the staff for that judgement. A democratic workplace culture of the old-fashioned Australian type – which no modern-day power-player either understands or likes. When Keating was treasurer he once strode into the SMH Canberra bureau and brayed at the journalists, 'Your trouble is that no one controls you!'

As for Murdoch and Packer, the notion that a media asset as large and complex as Fairfax could get along just fine under the control of 'no one' drives them nuts. It just doesn't fit into their Citizen Kane view of my vocation: journalism as 'product'; journalism as mogul *power*.

By 1996 Packer had fallen out with Keating's government, which by then was favouring Murdoch over him with its largesse. His media assets duly backed Howard for prime minister. As was the Aussie way of things before Murdoch and Packer stopped competing even with each other, would-be PMs had to decide early on which of the mogul backsides to pucker up to, and then deliver after the election. After the 1996 election Howard duly announced that he would change the law so that Packer could finally have Fairfax.

Murdoch was furious. If Packer could have TV *and* newspapers, Murdoch wanted both, too!

In Opposition the Liberals had – like Packer originally – made big noises supporting a lifting of foreign ownership restrictions as a way of increasing media competition. Now suddenly Howard, the 'global free market' man, was declaring that that would happen 'over my dead body'. Packer was to have it all: the abolition of cross-media rules so he could bid for Fairfax, but a continuation of foreign-ownership restrictions so he'd have no competition in a takeover.

The Australian newspapers of Rupert Murdoch, American citizen, began to snarl.

Howard's new communications hatchet man, Richard Alston, had advocated more media competition for years, but as soon as he took office it was suddenly 'almost a romantic notion to wish for brand-new players'. But don't worry, punters, he soothed, the ABC would always be there to ensure 'that commercial media does not run dead on stories which could harm the interests of proprietors'. His public broadcaster schmoozing was undercut by his leaked submission to Cabinet on how the government could best 'influence future ABC functions and activities more directly' – its main result being the appointment of Jonathan Shier as managing director.

At Fairfax none of us journos were fooled, and throughout 1996–97 we made sure the shit hit the fan. Howard responded by airily suggesting that when Packer bought Fairfax he might have to sell the *Australian Financial Review* – just say – to ensure some semblance of independent scrutiny. And what about letting Murdoch buy – just say – 25 per cent of a TV network? Howard's idea of 'media balance' became painfully clear: he was now trying to keep *both* moguls happy. Fairfax was being carved up before our eyes and we weren't even for sale!

Fairfax Chairman Sir Laurence Street made his displeasure known, as did Rupert Murdoch (anything less than 50 per cent equalled nothing to him). Murdoch's newspapers started mauling Howard, while his tabloid attack dogs such as opinion writer Piers Akerman went after Packer.

Fairfax journos had to dig in at ground level, where the people were. We leaflet-bombed train stations, made speeches, held dinners, circulated petitions, lobbied hard.

Packer was ultimately denied, partly because our democracy worked. In 1997 Howard had yet to tame his backbench – National and Liberal politicians stood up to be counted and said, No way.

Meanwhile Murdoch dropped in on Howard at Kirribilli House on 8 August to say bugger off to 25 per cent foreign ownership of TV networks.

Howard backed down. Of course he backed down – to Rupert, that is. Flip-flop.

You reckon our elected leaders have power? If so it's less than Murdoch and Packer have. Much less.

So why do prime ministers keep giving them more? Because they're looking for powerful allies to help them keep what power they *have* got, or the pretence of it.

Stupid aren't they?

Powerful allies made yet more powerful by political favours *always* retain the ultimate power: the power to change sides at will. The more you give them, the less power you have to say no next time. And they always jump ship sooner or later – once they've used you up.

Never believe the media moguls.

The most illuminating stories about how brutally Australia's mogul power is wielded only ever come out long after the fact. The one I'm about to tell you has never been made public. It will show you how shamelessly the media moguls use their media assets to further their non-journalistic interests, what we reporters are up against, and why I am such a defender of media diversity.

It's not a sympathy pitch. The story will show you why we sometimes don't – that is, *can't* – work on your behalf as many of us would like to. Especially the good Murdoch and Packer journalists. There's plenty of them, and in many ways theirs are the toughest gigs of all.

Remember: there are very few media employers in Australia, and journalists have to feed their kids. So as you read this story keep in mind that a working journo or mid-range media executive in this country only needs to cross a Packer or a Murdoch *once*, on a matter of professional principle, to permanently reduce their employment options by 30, 40, 50 per cent. Or much more, depending on their field, forum and location.

During the stoush over Packer getting Fairfax in 1997, John 'J.A.' Alexander was the editor-in-chief of the *Sydney Morning Herald* for the second time. He was by then a Packer man – effectively a Trojan Horse. He and several journalists close to him believed it was now time Packer owned Fairfax, contrary to the Fairfax board's opposition to John Howard's post-election payback plan.

What this meant was that, unlike during previous media ownership debates, our Sydney flagship would not run opinion pieces opposing the sale.

I managed to sneak an anti-sale piece in when J.A. was away – courtesy of Opinion Page editor Chris McGillion. My piece detailed Richard Alston's record: how his post-election flip-flop contradicted *everything* he'd argued in Opposition. I also tried to nail the outright lies he was telling to get his way.

It was a scary piece to write and a scary piece for Chris to run. He was able to do so because we had a strong editor, John Lyons, who was prepared to debate J.A. on the merits of his news judgement. And John Lyons in turn was bolstered by the democratic Fairfax culture. He knew that J.A. knew that if he did send any editor-in-chief grief back down the line the Fairfax team would try to bloody well publish *that* story, too.

The Fairfax journo culture: lock in together, downwards and upwards, when the moguls come prowling. Of course, when the senior lynchpin is *himself* a Packer man, it gets hairy.

Here we go.

In early March 1997 the cross-media debate is hotting up, and our Canberra communications reporter Anne Davies learns that a Murdoch paper is chasing a ripper: J.A. has just spent a weekend as a guest on the Packer yacht in Fiji. Here is a real test of the strength of our culture.

I'm chief of staff at the *Herald*'s Canberra bureau. Anne confirms the story late on 5 March 1997. I phone the chief sub-editor in Sydney responsible for placing stories and brief him on the yarn. I tell him I've also informed the Fairfax House Committee journos who act as first port of call in the event of a problem with staff or editorial policy. J.A. gets wind of this and rings Anne to demand she not file the story. Anne calls his bluff, replying she'll file the story and that it's up to him to spike it if he so chooses.

J.A. does not so choose.

Why? He knows there'll be big trouble in the news-room if he blatantly censors a story to protect his backside. He knows that such censorship would leak at a very delicate time when Packer is pretending he's not an editorially interferin' kinda newspaper mogul.

Round One to the good guys.

The Packers are beginning to feel the heat, particularly from Murdoch's 'Akermonious' tactical campaign. (And it *is* largely turf-staking tactics; 1997 marks the year the two Big Boys' competing interests will begin to meld into a strategic accommodation.)

A Kerry Packer debate with three Fairfax journos on his Nine Network during his 1991 bid for Fairfax, in partnership with foreign media mogul Conrad Black, hadn't gone down well with the public because he looked and sounded like a bully. So on Friday, 9 May, his son James appears on *A Current Affair*, interviewed by Ray Martin. It's a lollypopper – giggly Ray asks James if he'll marry Kate Fischer, and so on. James says he wants Fairfax for Christmas. He makes promises about how he'd run it. *Never trust those* . . .

Wind back a few hours. In Canberra we get advance notice of James's TV debut as salesman for Packer's take-over bid. I brief the afternoon news conference, and John Lyons slates the pending interview as the page-one lead, with Anne Davies to write the news story, and our Canberra bureau chief, Geoff Kitney, to write a comment piece on James's performance.

By page-one conference time – 6 p.m. – we've seen the interview, courtesy of a Nine Network preview. It had enough juice to merit the lead.

J.A. is running the page-one conference in the Sydney office.

'What's the lead?' he barks down the phone.

'James Packer wants Fairfax for Christmas,' I reply, but he cuts off my briefing of the key news points.

'That's not a lead,' J.A. decrees. 'It's not even a news story!'

I argue the point, but no one backs me up in Sydney. J.A. says Anne's off the news story – and there won't be one. Another Canberra reporter – Tony Wright – will do a 'colour' story on James's TV performance. There'll be no analysis or comment.

Tony hasn't even *seen* the preview, and takes a deep breath. Anne Davies is devastated.

'So what's the page-one lead now?' J.A. demands of me.

Canberra can't supply one. The only other story we have that might make the grade at a pinch is a proposed environment yarn by Canberra reporter James Woodford, which Sydney has told him not to write until Sunday. I call James back to work and he is madly writing right on deadline when J.A. calls.

'The green story isn't worth a page-one lead,' he yells at James. 'What the hell do you think you're doing?'

For the first time ever I take on J.A.

'What the *fuck* do you think you're doing harassing a reporter who's covering for *your* decision?'

I hang up. I'm shaking. Scared.

John Lyons rings. 'Listen. Kitney should write his comment piece and then I'll slip it in after J.A. goes home.'

He's a brave man, John Lyons. Thanks to him, the *Sydney Morning Herald* isn't completely embarrassed on Saturday.

Round Two – just – to the good guys.

God knows what J.A. makes of Geoff Kitney's critical opinion piece on the interview materialising alongside his Saturday morning croissant, but next thing he's onto James Packer, who's in Melbourne staying at Dad's Crown Casino, and arranges for our Sydney finance editor Glen Burge and colour writer Sally Loane to fly down to interview him for Monday's paper. The Canberra bureau is not told, and neither reporter phones Geoff or Anne for a briefing on the key factual and political questions. The first any of us in Canberra know of the blindside move is when we unfold Monday's SMH.

Gotcha! There, splashed all over page one, is a huge picture of a relaxed and comfortable James Packer – and a *news* story on why he wants Fairfax! Even more devastating: inside is a full-page feature expanding on James's case to run us. No sale of the *Financial Review*, he says loftily. He wants that, too. And no agreement to sign off on our charter of editorial independence.

Jesus. Effing. Et cetera.

It's the most humiliating moment in all my years at Fairfax. Here we are running an advertisement for a *competitor*. One who wants to take us over, no less. And naturally the tough questions – on Packer's foreign ownership flip-flops, for example – are not asked.

The producer of *A Current Affair*, Dave Hurley, is predictably (and rightly) scathing: just two days earlier Geoff Kitney's opinion piece has had a mighty go at *them* for going soft on their owner's son. Now the *Sydney Morning Herald*'s gone even softer!

A few months later the Fairfax board sacked J.A. He moved straight over to Packer to run his magazine empire, and now also runs the Nine Network. He's the man who would run Fairfax if Kerry Packer ever got his way and became our owner. And this four-part disharmony of editorial interference – the Packer mogul, the Packer mogul-in-waiting, the Packer 'journalist' and the Packer 'executive' – had given us a very clear glimpse of what that would mean.

Not that we needed it. But maybe you did.

The Fairfax culture fought back in 1997 as best we could. But it was getting weaker under the strain, and would die very, very quickly, and forever, once Packer moved in permanently.

But let's look at it from your point of view, as a citizen of Australia living in Sydney or Melbourne, say. Status quo? Three major commercial groups gathering news and providing analysis for you:

1 Murdoch: the daily tabloids the *Daily Telegraph* (Sydney) and the *Herald Sun* (Melbourne) and the daily national broadsheet the *Australian*.
2 Packer: Nine Network (both cities) and the weekly national magazine the *Bulletin*.
3 Fairfax: the daily broadsheets the *Sydney Morning Herald* and the Melbourne *Age* and the daily national *Australian Financial Review*.

The rest of the major privately owned media – radio and networks Ten and Seven – largely follow the daily press release news and follow-up scoops from these three.

John Howard's preferred scenario is an Australian media landscape so dominated by the two most powerful men in the country that only the ABC could, if it dared, subject either man's corporate empire to independent scrutiny. The Murdoch and Packer journos don't investigate each other's proprietorial doings because if they did their work would not be published and they would lose their jobs. There would be no media players left to defend Aunty. Murdoch's *Australian* savages the ABC as a matter of editorial policy these days, even calling for the abolishment of Radio National, while Packer simply sues it and ties it up in legal knots. These guys hate uncontrollable public media outlets as much as they hate an independent Fairfax.

Result? The Packer–Murdoch Empire would largely decide what news would and wouldn't be broken, and what opinions would get a fair mainstream run, on radio and television and in their newspapers. And their 'news' benchmark would be pretty simple: their own commercial bottom lines.

Paranoid? OK, forget about the immense potential for self-interested skewing of political news and opinion for a moment. Forget that business section. Skip foreign news, war reports, domestic round-ups, election coverage, education lift-outs, arts, health, industry, investment and environment features.

Read the most important pages – sport.

Who broke the Shane Warne–Mark Waugh Indian bribes story? The *Sydney Morning Herald*. Reckon a Packer-owned Fairfax would have? Check out the Packer coverage of Shane's drugs scandal. Warnie's no ordinary 'likeable dill' these days, he's a Nine Network likeable dill – his knockabout public image is a serious Packer investment now, to be seriously protected. Did you see that Ray Martin friendly special with Warne on *A Current Affair* in 2003? Kerry wasn't simply being a loving father-figure to Shane with all that free reputation therapy and rehab. The Nine Network 'owns' cricket and Warne is a star attraction. Journalism is not wanted.

Who broke the Canterbury Bulldogs' salary cap breach in 2002? The *Sydney Morning Herald* forced the Rugby League bosses to act on their own rules and boot the Bulldogs out of the competition for a year. Which network televises the Rugby League? Reckon Kerry Packer would have allowed 'his' Fairfax print journos to nobble the lucrative business end of his Rugby League broadcast season?

But who needs to be hypothetical? Remember the corporate struggle between Packer and Murdoch for broadcast ownership of the national Rugby League competition? After the ARL v. Super League drama, their eventual truce saw the beloved but financially straitened South Sydney Rabbitohs dropped from the merged competition. The Big Two had picked the wrong battler citizens to disfranchise, though, and an extraordinary grassroots movement sprang up to contest the expulsion.

Rupert Murdoch's papers refused to report it – causing one of his sports writers, Ian Heads, to resign in protest, due to 'my deep professional disappointment as a journalist'. (Remember what I said about the longer term career price for Australian journalists who take a principled stand?)

But then Fairfax ran a cheeky advertising campaign pointing out that those footy fans who did want to follow the South Sydney fight-back would do well to buy the *Herald*, and Murdoch's rags suddenly discovered the story. Fairfax had been on it from the start, and not even Rupert and Kerry combined could suppress that kind of public momentum and anger. Or afford to ignore it either.

In a roused democracy not buying the 'product' works, not the actions of an honourable sports journalist who resigns on principle.

Like Ian Heads, every Australian journo has at some time found themselves pushed by their editors, executives and owners until they've stood teetering on their own personal line in the sand.

Some cross it. And cross back. And back again. Some shift it constantly. Some walk away for good – from jobs, from owners, from Australia, from the profession. Some stand firm, and a rare few even push back, including some journalists inside the Packer and Murdoch empires. As individual reporters we Fairfax ones are no better or worse than the Packer and Murdoch hacks. We're just luckier that we're part of a workplace culture that can, when the crunch comes, still – just – put journalism first. Reporters are reporters are reporters – good, bad or indifferent. Because there are so many of us and so few employers each Australian journalist has to cling hard (or not) to whatever professional obligation strikes the right ethical balance for them.

In contrast – because there's only two of them, and they have so much power already – the Australian moguls don't have any bedrock principles at all except getting more money and more power. They want to draw and redraw their covetous lines across our media landscape, anywhere, anyhow and any time they bloody well like. And so they do.

If their mouths are open, never believe them.

If their mouths are shut, never believe them – and be afraid. Be very afraid.

In Round 2003 Rupert Murdoch and Kerry Packer would say nothing in public. John Howard and Richard Alston would do the sales job for them.

7

Unholy Alliances

Those who own or run media organisations are in a position of privilege and influence. They are members of an unelected elite which is not effectively accountable to the Australian people. It is our job as elected legislators to ensure not only that there are reasonable parameters set for the running of successful media businesses but, much more importantly, that these parameters serve the Australian people

Senator Brian Harradine, Tasmanian Independent

On Monday, 23 June 2003, I'm driving to Canberra in response to Anne Davies' phone call, pondering the state of play in the Australian media world.

Howard's cross-media ownership bill, if passed by the Senate this week, will remove the rule that no media interest can own a TV station and a newspaper in the same mainland city. Read: Packer gets Fairfax. Plus the bill abolishes foreign ownership restrictions. Read: Murdoch gets a free-to-air TV station. The Howard plan would also mean Telstra or one of America's transnational media conglomerates could own Nine and Fairfax. It allows a media group to have both a radio and a TV station or a newspaper in the one city, and a newspaper to own TV stations in other cities.

And there are those taxpayer-funded baubles for the four Senate Independents dangling off the tree to help the Big Two get their prezzies at its base. Our money to purchase the moguls' privilege – don't you just love it?

Not that Richard Alston had pitched it to the Australian people that way on Ten's *Meet the Press* the day before: 'The interesting thing this time around, Paul [Bongiorno], is that Murdoch and Packer are already very well entrenched. They are doing very nicely, thank you. It is pretty much the rest of the industry who are out there saying, "We need these changes."'

So that's the super-spin: this latest push has nothing to do with Packer and Murdoch, it's a response to the 'rest of the industry'. Is it? With the exception of Kerry Stokes at Seven, the other biggish players are onside. A sense of inevitability has combined with table-crumb scrabbling to give the bill reasonable support across the industry. Packer and Murdoch have lain doggo this time, and only *The Age* has published an opinion piece arguing the case against the legislation. The Fairfax board and our CEO, Fred Hilmer, now support the legislation. Fred has grandiose TV plans for Fairfax apparently. Some of our journos are with him. The Fairfax culture is not as one this time round, not by any means.

The bill seems to be in the bag.

Paul Keating tries to clear the muck from everyone's soporific eyes. Inspired by an article in the *Sydney Morning Herald* by Eric Beecher of Text Media (a company he later sells to Fairfax), who argues that the media moguls don't and won't influence content, Keating pens a searing *Herald* piece in reply:

'[Beecher's wishful thinking] does not square even with the recent history of News Limited, where the mastheads of that organisation fell slavishly into line with the Group's editorial view on the invasion of Iraq . . .

The Fox News Channel on Foxtel had the same line as the Sydney *Daily Telegraph* and the *Australian*. Ownership does matter . . . Beecher asked "Does anyone really believe either of the enlarged groups would harness its television stations alongside its newspapers as serious political propaganda tools?" The real question is: how could you NOT believe this? . . . An enlarged media company will align its television and its print whenever it suits it. Not every day but when it really counts.'

And on the fate of Fairfax:

'How naive would you need to be to believe that, in the event that the Packer organisation acquired Fairfax, John Alexander wouldn't swoop, falcon-like, from Park Street to Darling Park to do to the *Sydney Morning Herald* that which he has recently done at Channel Nine . . . The crunch point is this. If Senator Alston succeeds in getting the Senate to agree to break the cross-media rule . . . the diversity of our media goes backwards. Pretty simple. [Murdoch and

Packer] get bigger; our range of news and opinion gets smaller.'

Keating goes in hardest of all on the 'rest of the industry', blasting away the 'argument' that what is good for the Big Two will be good for everyone else:

'And poor old Fred Hilmer is helping their case. For all of Fairfax's primacy in news and advertising, Fred thinks it has no future unless it owns a free-to-air television station . . . in advocating changes to the cross-media rule, [he] thinks he is joining Kerry and Rupert in the media proprietors' club. The difference is that each of them is long experienced and accomplished in the game of snatch-and-grab. Devouring a company or two before the main course has arrived. Fred would be still unfolding his napkin as the assets were swept off the table . . . It wouldn't be a game – it would be a shame.'

It's a stunning piece that just might snap some sense back into journalists and readers who care about the future of Australian journalism.

The *Sydney Morning Herald* fails to run it.

The fact that Fairfax editors won't allow such sorely needed editorialising into the paper is why a few of us here fight in the only other available ring.

As both reporters and citizens.

Politically partisan ones? On this issue – absolutely.

Our assessment of the state of play in the Australian Senate in the week starting 23 June: John Howard's Broadcasting Services Amendment (Media Ownership) Bill 2002 is slated for mid-week debate and assent.

Labor will oppose. The Greens will oppose. The Democrats will oppose – we think. The Independents? Len Harris (Pauline Hanson's One Nation): leaning towards 'aye'. Brian Harradine (ex-Labor, ex-DLP): unknown. Meg Lees (ex-Democrat): 'aye'. Shayne Murphy (who resigned from the ALP midway through the Senate term): leaning towards 'aye'. All four voting 'aye' would get it up.

The manoeuvring had been intense the previous Friday. Alston had signalled that the deal was done. The *Australian* had reported before and after his announcement that a deal had been done. It was psychological warfare, designed to hype momentum, split alliances, weaken resolve.

But late on Friday Brian Harradine told reporters that he'd put up an amendment: no owner could have a newspaper and a TV station in the same mainland capital city.

No one knows if he means it, or if he'll vote for the bill anyway if his amendment goes down. But it's shifted the democratic dynamic. Alston's pitch: it's not about the moguls – they're nicely entrenched as they are, thank you very much. Harradine's po-faced reply: OK, so there's no need to give them those big prezzies then, is there?

As the week progresses, the anti-bill lobby decides its strategy: to call Alston's bluff.

Political positions: Labor, the Greens and the Democrats

will support the Harradine amendment, ensuring it gets up despite the government opposing it, while opposing the bill as a whole at the end of the day – leaving it to the four Senate Independents to pass the amended bill. This offers the government a clear choice.

OK, Richard – there's your PM's new cross-media ownership rules, as we, the people, reckon they should be. All your lot has to do is say 'aye'. So – are you with us or against us? Does John Howard legislate for all of us – or only two of us?

Our strategy would fail if the Independents dealt away Harradine's amendment leverage individually. And, indeed, if Harradine wasn't himself simply double-bluffing Alston for a better deal for Tasmania. We could only guess at what subtle inducements had already been offered, although two were pretty clear to me: Lees would get South Australian Liberal preferences when she stood for her new party, the Australian Progressive Alliance, at the next election, and Murphy the same if he stood as an Independent in Tasmania. Harradine was likely to retire at the election, but he *always* extracted a good deal for his home state in power plays where his vote was crucial. Harris? One Nation's Queensland support base had been winnowed away by Howard's shift to the hard social right, and no doubt Harris could use all the vote-winning electoral favours going.

The Independents had been meeting regularly – they recognised that their power lay in acting as one – but the risk for us was that they'd decide whether or not to support the Harradine amendment by majority view rather than on a one-out, all-out basis. We needed to be sure of at least two, including Brian Harradine, who could pull his amendment at any time.

When I arrived at Parliament House it was déjà vu down to the familiar faces of the media company lobbyists at Aussies, the pollies' café. They were smiling.

Bad sign.

On Tuesday, 24 June, I was sitting outside Len Harris's office with Chris Warren, secretary of the journos' union, nutting out how best to sell the case against Howard's bill when something hit me.

'Bloody hell, Chris. The last time I saw Len was in Longreach during the 1998 election campaign – and we had a ding-dong blue over Wik. I'm the worst person to talk to him – he must hate Fairfax.'

I'd done my bit the day before when I'd dropped in on Bob Katter, the National-turned-Independent MP for the inland North Queensland seat of Kennedy. Until the 1997 cross-media fight we'd never had much in common, Bob and I – except that, like Len, we were both North Queenslanders. After that shared battle, though, he'd spoken to me 'on the record' to decry Howard's refusal to overturn the Northern Territory's mandatory jail term laws for children caught stealing for the first time. An early lesson about real democracy: single-issue lobbying across philo-sophical divides can open up common ground elsewhere.

Bob and the other three 'intruder' MHRs – rural Inde-pendents Tony Windsor and Peter Andren, and the Greens' Michael Organ – had all voted against the cross-media bill, and like the Senate Independents had a close working rela-tionship. Bob said he'd deliver Harris a four-signature letter urging him to oppose Senate passage, and cold-called Len's office to give a staffer an earful: 'Listen, I've heard Len is supporting this media thing. He's got to be joking. Vote the lot down. No deals!' Thanks, Bob!

The big-boned goldminer from Mareeba appeared and stuck out a huge hand. Mine disappeared into it.

'Hi, Len. It's been a while. Aboriginal policy day at the Stockman's Hall of Fame?'

'You've got a good memory,' he said, beaming. 'Let's sit down.'

I slipped into the broad Queensland accent I revert to back home and went for it. 'Len, why are you doing this? Stopping Packer and Murdoch owning more and getting even more powerful is part of what you've been elected to do. You can campaign on stopping them taking over all the media – you'd be a hero to your voters.'

'But, Margo, One Nation has no money and very little organisation. How could I get that message across in the media?'

He had me there. Australia's media was a closed shop on this one. With One Nation struggling anyway, if Len opposed this bill he'd be less than invisible in any future election campaigns. Then there were John Howard's fixers.

'So what pressure are they putting on?' I asked.

Len said the government had already plonked the threat of a double dissolution election on his table. If the bill – with all its regional sweeteners added for senators just like Len – went down in the Senate, they'd strip it clean and slam the original back in its place. If Howard won the subsequent election, the Independents would lose everything they'd gained. Len took this nonsense seriously. As well as being proud of getting some community radio money up, and a few minor safeguards, he'd also been heavily lobbied by smaller media groups, who'd said they'd go broke unless they could grow through a change in the law.

'But you know what this would mean, Len?' I asked, preparing to lay down the horror scenario.

He beat me to it, pulling out handwritten notes supplied by another lobbyist trying to claw back lost ground: either the Kerry Stokes man or someone I only learnt of later, CCZ Equities stockbroker Roger Colman. Colman came to Canberra to advise Len and Shayne Murphy despite his day job advising clients which media company's share prices would rise if the legislation passed. Colman later said, 'I was arguing in my capacity as a private citizen. I did not want to be swamped by Kerry Packer.'

Hear that, John Howard? Colman was arguing the

anti-bill case – one contrary to his own financial interests – in his capacity as a citizen.

What a motley crew we last-minute lobbyists were, and we weren't even coordinated!

I gave Len photocopied pages of *Off the Rails*, my book on Pauline Hanson's 1998 campaign, in which I'd reported that my 1997 anti-Packer remarks on ABC TV had triggered congratulatory letters from One Nation supporters and a Hanson press release opposing a Packer takeover on free speech grounds: 'It was truly unnerving that the National Party and One Nation – whose constituencies would never see the small "l" liberal Sydney and Melbourne-based Fairfax papers – joined the Democrats in their total opposition to Packer owning Fairfax, and their support for a diversely owned free press', I'd written.

The book also recorded the first time I'd met Hanson – in a press gallery corridor encounter in 1998. 'So how are you going with your work?' she'd asked. 'I hope you're still safe from Packer.'

But Len needed more than Hanson's retrospective seal of approval. He needed reassurance that he wouldn't be shooting himself in the foot.

'Look, Len. Alston and co are creating a false sense of crisis here,' I said. 'They're trying to convince you that you have to decide now. But you don't. They can only take this to a double dissolution election if the Senate refuses to pass it the second time around, after a wait of three months. You don't lose anything by delaying your final decision till then.'

He took the point, and I pressed my case.

'Len, us journos ran a big campaign in 1997. We had a fundraising dinner, got lots of important support, gave out leaflets at railway stations, had car stickers and badges, the lot. If you hold out now, we'll make sure the public gets the facts on this before it comes to the Senate again, and there'll be public support behind you.'

Partisan? On this issue? Hell, yeah. You reckon that Murdoch and Packer *aren't?*

Like Pauline Hanson before him, Len Harris had long been shunned in Parliament House – by all of us. No one had wanted to talk to Len, the last lingering symbol of the evil One Nation. Yet, as the years went by and emotions settled, I'd come to regret being part of that 'isolate Hanson' crowd when she first appeared. It was a terrible journalistic mistake, not to mention a human one. I wish I'd listened to her. Engaged with her opinions, as I'd just done with Len. So much heat goes out of everything when people of differing views simply sit down and talk.

Later that day I ran into Len at the staff cafeteria.

'Standing firm, Len?'

My heart jumped when he said, 'You bet. There's still a few of us left who don't decide everything on the . . .' He rubbed his right thumb and forefinger together and grinned.

I raced back to my office, found a pile of 1997 'TWO

TOO FEW' car stickers, burst into Len's office and thrust them into his hands.

'I'll do my best, too,' I promised.

Another democratic lesson: never judge an Australian representative's story by his political cover.

Unless that story is the Coalition gospel according to John Howard. One thing was very clear: no one in his 'broad church' would give us the time of day.

Back in 1997 the Nationals were stridently opposed to Howard's Packer present. Queensland MP Paul Neville, for one, had slammed his foot down: 'The more extensive the diversity of media ownership is, the healthier it is for a well-informed community,' he told the media. When Howard backed down, Neville had given his PM a wry public pat on the shoulder: 'It was a decision that reflected common sense and good judgement.'

This time? Neville made some whimpering noises in the party room – and ticked the planned bill.

Larry Anthony was another Nat who'd gutsed it out in 1997, being 'very concerned that these particular proposals might lead to greater concentration of media ownership – in particular in our capital cities.'

2003? Ah, it's *Minister* Anthony now. Tick.

Insiders later told me that in exchange for their silence the National Party had got a good deal for their constituency: my guess was more money for regional telecommunications.

You could hardly blame them, since they now had so little power in the Coalition.

And why should the Nationals stand up to Howard when the Liberal backbenchers, especially those whose capital city constituents would be most hurt by the bill, didn't have the guts to either? It was scary to see how completely Howard had paralysed his parliamentary team's independence of mind.

The starkest – and saddest – personification of this was Dr Brendan Nelson. In 1997 the aspirational, earring-wearing Lib had told Howard that he'd cross the floor to save Fairfax if necessary. Brendan had also attended our Fairfax journos' fundraiser in Canberra, where he'd said that his resolve to stop the Howard–Packer plan had 'strengthened after the response I've had from my electorate . . . The average Australian feels uncomfortable with the concentration of media ownership.'

Back then he was still steering by both his local voters' expressed wishes *and* his own ethical compass, and advertised his stand with a passionate piece in his local paper, the *North Shore Times*, entitled 'A Question of Moral Courage': 'A proprietor with a considerable domestic political agenda controlling a television station and a newspaper in both Sydney and Melbourne, not to mention all the outlets for credible business commentary, is not a legacy we should wish to leave our children . . .'

Classic liberal stuff.

Come 2003 Nelson was nicely entrenched in Cabinet, where grassroots views and legacies to our children didn't count. Not a peep from the Honourable Brendan now. The price of success – and the stink.

Nelson had plenty of Liberal company. Moreton MP and former journalist Gary Hardgrave in 1997: 'If you have fewer and fewer potential employers, journalists might self-censor themselves, might decide not to run certain issues because, let's face it, it might brown off the boss.' Hardgrave had also mocked Packer's lobbying duo, Labor fixer Graham Richardson and Liberal fixer Michael Kroger: 'We thought Richo would finish up running the *Sydney Morning Herald*, with Kroger running *The Age*!'

2003? Tick.

By 2003 Howard had long since abolished the proudest of all Liberal Party parliamentary traditions: the conscience vote. Sure, if you were a backbencher no one could stop you exercising it. It's just that you'd lose your preselection if you did.

Liberalism in the Liberal Party had collapsed long before this issue came to the boil again in 2003, but the contrast between 1997 and a rerun of the same fight only six years later, with the added spectre of an even more dominant Murdoch, made Howard's destruction of Robert Menzies' inclusive legacy agonisingly clear to anyone in Parliament House who cared to be honest about it.

At least the Nationals had required a payoff to sell their souls.

Len Harris now seemed solid. But Anne Davies called with bad news – blindside news.

Suddenly it was the Democrats who were freaking at the thought of a double dissolution. It was a rock-bottom time for the party, and in a DD ballot they'd have to put all their seats on the public chopping block, not merely the usual half. Worse, the determination of their latest defector, Meg Lees, to deal with Howard – nicely boosting both profile and access – had them worried about future irrelevance. And the old split between centre right and centre left had flared again. Anne had heard that Andrew Murray or Aden Ridgeway might seek a fix with Howard. Former Dems communications spokeswoman Vicki Bourne, who'd lost her seat to the Greens' Kerry Nettle in 2001, was rallying the waverers; Anne would pitch in. I ran a recent Webdiary piece detailing the likely bill fallout down to their offices.

Aden wasn't around, but Andrew's offsider assured me that he, at least, was holding the line.

Back in the Independents' corner we'd given up on Lees, who hadn't returned our calls. To me, Meg's position was unfathomable: in trumpeting one of 'her' hard-won baubles – extending ABC News Radio to the bush – she'd lost all 'core impact' perspective.

Labor senators Sue Mackay and Stephen Conroy were working full time on ex-ALP Senator Shayne Murphy.

That left Brian Harradine.

Like Len Harris, he was my job.

The question: would he insist on his amendment? He could easily get a great trade-off for his Tasmanian voters if he gave it away. Would he consider media diversity a matter of bedrock moral principle?

Harradine is not someone whose moral bedrock you can shift, and I had little to go on. I'd left a message at his electoral office the Friday before, asking to speak to him on the matter, and in reply got an email from his senior staffer: 'The Senator has received your query, and asked me to forward you his proposed amendment.'

Brian Harradine always plays his cards close to his chest. He's invariably polite and civil, but he lets his staff do the talking with potential deal-makers and lobbyists. He doesn't cultivate journalists, and he doesn't know the meaning of spin or one-line grabs. Often no one has a clue how he'll vote until he actually does, and when that's the case – if his vote is critical – something extraordinary happens in our Parliament: our senators start working their backsides off. Debate is of the highest quality, and genuinely engaged, because for all anybody knows his vote is still there to be won.

An emailed copy of his amendment: it wasn't much to set our hearts on, but I had a feeling it was Brian's way of letting me know that he was solid.

In 1998 Brian Harradine had single-handedly headed off a race election.

You don't know that, probably. But it's why, in my opinion, Brian Harradine is a statesman. He's 68, Tasmanian, socially conservative and staunchly Catholic. I'm 44, a Queenslander, and a socially progressive feminist. If there's one single Australian politician I'd choose to have representing me on a vote of genuine bipartisan importance to Australia's future, it might just be him.

It seems eons ago now, but Australia was at flashpoint over Howard's Wik Bill in 1998. The High Court had asked miners and pastoralists without freehold to share the land with Aboriginal people who could prove a traditional connection. Howard wanted to nobble such judicial activism as far as possible. Harradine's was the key Senate vote. He was stuck between a ruthless government and an equally determined coalition of Labor and Democrats. His sympathies were with the Aboriginal people, but he feared terrible consequences unless they conceded ground. He gave lots away – too much for many – but held firm on four sticking points, all of them bottom lines for Howard. When the Senate passed the Wik Bill in a form unacceptable to Howard just before Christmas in 1997, Howard threatened a double dissolution, and when the Senate stood firm just before Easter in 1998 he was ready for a race election.

Like Brian, I was horrified. In my view it would have torn rural and regional communities to bits. It was unthinkable, including for the rural reps, some of whom – for all the 'redneck' jibes of inner-city progressives – are among Australia's busiest black–white bridge builders. But the

Nationals were trapped by their core constituency, the pastoralists.

And there are no limits on what Howard will do to wield and retain power. None.

But in June 1998 Howard realised he'd painted himself into a nasty corner. Hanson's One Nation won 23 per cent of the vote in the Queensland state election. Part of her platform? Abolish native title altogether. (This is what Len Harris and I had blued about in Longreach – Len drafted that policy.) Those numbers scared the pants off Howard and the Nationals. If Howard did what he'd been threatening to do – offer Australians an explicit vote on land rights – One Nation might decimate the National and Liberal vote in some seats, and turn away Liberal voters in his safest seats in Melbourne and Sydney.

John Howard suddenly needed an escape route. Desperately. Harradine sensed the high stakes shift immediately and offered talks. And everyone except me wrote that he was the one who had blinked.

They were dead wrong.

The Wik people had fronted Parliament House in traditional regalia during the Senate Wik debate to dance for their land. I'd watched them ask Brian to join in. And I'd watched this elderly, very proper, very devout Catholic gentleman take off his shoes and socks, accept a spear and dance their land-honouring dance alongside them. I've never been so moved in all my years covering politics. I knew Brian wouldn't back down.

When John Howard really wants something from you he invites you to tea. Howard invited Brian to tea. A few little words were changed in Brian's sticking-point amendments before Howard emerged to announce himself victorious. The country bought it. Race election threat over.

Brian invited me to tea.

Nothing much, he explained quietly, when I asked what he'd really given up to break the impasse. Nothing important to the Indigenous people anyway.

Just his right to claim victory over Howard in public. That was basically all it took to get John Howard to back down. Even on the crucial 'right to negotiate' (the native title claimants' right to negotiate with miners and pastoralists on land use) – the bottom line that Howard had said he'd never, ever budge on. Harradine's amendments retained the right to negotiate by giving the Senate a veto power over any state laws attempting to water it down.

All Brian gave away on Wik was his right to claim victory. Better that an Independent senator look like a loser than that the country be torn apart by one stubborn little chap who didn't want a race election any more but would have pulled one on us anyway rather than appear to back down.

Brian Harradine is a great Australian. One day someone will tell his story in the detail it deserves.

Tuesday evening, 9 p.m. I sat in the press box in the Senate chamber and watched the cross-media debate. Our democracy on show. Then again through Wednesday morning, noting with disgust that Alston rejected any amendment giving any consolation to the public – even a benign Democrats one requiring commercial TV stations to correct and/or apologise for errors of fact, which would have brought them into line with the SBS and the ABC requirements. No, no, no, said Alston. No more accountability. Lots more power.

Who *are* you working for, Richard? Who do you represent? We'd find out pretty soon.

A second-day highlight: Greens Senator Bob Brown produced Keating's spiked *Sydney Morning Herald* piece and read the whole thing into Hansard.

I cringed when Brown got to Keating's last paragraph:

'Australia is a continuing story of takeovers and amalgamations. In this country, the number of institutions shrink rather than expand. This should not be allowed to happen with the major media companies and their respective organs. If Fairfax were not independently owned this article would not be published by the other major media outlets.'

Harradine grinned. Alston spat chips. I was glum, proud and angry. It had taken a politician to get a vigorously dissenting Fairfax opinion piece into the mainstream public realm during a debate crucial to the future of vigorously dissenting Fairfax opinion pieces by way of a vigorously dissenting Fairfax leak – a backwards one, journo-to-polly.

Speaker after speaker rose to commend democratic

principles dear to my heart, but I was trying to read the faces of the Independents, especially those of Brian Harradine and Shayne Murphy. The ex-Labor senator was being subjected to intense government pressure, and rumours abounded that he was on the verge of dealing on the Harradine amendment. If that happened at any point in the debate, with Meg Lees gone Len might waver. And then Brian's amendment leverage – if he *was* going to persist with it – would crumble. The ripple effect: the flighty Dems might want to grab what *they* could get . . .

Brian was still giving nothing away. Democracy, I thought, is bloody exhausting.

At 5.12 p.m. on Wednesday, 25 June 2003, Brian Harradine stood to speak: 'I move these amendments to protect against media proprietors having undue influence in the metropolitan media markets. My amendments are quite straightforward. They would ensure that a media proprietor could not own both a television licence and a newspaper in the same mainland capital city.'

Alston's scam was sprung when Shayne Murphy rose to announce that he would support Harradine.

As Murphy spoke, Alston walked to the back of the chamber, put his foot on the banister and stretched his leg for a long time. Then he walked down the aisle towards his seat, jaw set, stopped, put his hands behind his back and stared into the distance. For a long time. Finally he strode to his seat and, still standing, turned to his advisers in the advisers' box.

'We'll get the Dems in a few months,' he murmured.

He would send his precious bill – you know, the one that had *nothing* to do with Packer and Murdoch, but was all about helping the 'rest of the industry' grow and expand – back to the House of Representatives immediately, setting up another John Howard double dissolution trigger.

Round . . . whatever . . . to the good guys.

What was Alston in democratic politics for, I wondered. What sort of difference did he want to make, and for whom? I'd tried to figure it out as, enraged, he blew the cross-media legislation super-spin away like a parliamentary greenhorn.

'This is a *watershed* amendment! This amendment goes to the absolute *heart* of the cross-media reforms!' he yelled across the chamber.

Bluff called, Richard.

In his frustration Alston pointed the bone:

'It is the JOURNALISTS whom you ought to be worried about, not the media proprietors. It is the JOURNALISTS who are the players in debates like this. There are JOURNAL-ISTS running around and into politicians' offices pushing their lines. I know JOURNALISTS who can BARELY SLEEP at night, pushing a line on this issue. THEY are the players. It is not the proprietors who are ringing up and arguing the case; it is the JOURNALISTS who are pushing the case . . .'

I was suddenly very tired.

Brian Harradine was scathing:

'The decision was overwhelming tonight – I think it was 36 to 29 – and that is a message that the people of Australia are giving the government in this matter. The people do not want further concentration of power in the major players in the media. Why doesn't the Government pass the amended bill? Possibly because it is a bit more concerned about the effect it would have on the big media owners than they care to admit. Perhaps the real aim of this bill was to allow the big owners to get even bigger. I urge the Government not to reject this amended bill just because it does not allow for media moguls to create a cross-media company which could dominate a particular city's media or which could be a dominant national force . . .'

He looked Richard Alston square in the eye and hit him, and the 'liberal' impostors around him, with some fatherly liberal democratic advice:

'I remind Senator Alston that 16 years ago I made a speech about the then broadcasting legislation. The Minister will remember that, because he came in as a senator the year before, from memory. On that occasion I referred to a statement made by Mr Davidson in 1956, when he was the Postmaster-General [in the Menzies government], in which he talked about television licences. He said: "Television stations are in a position to exercise a constant and cumulative effect on public taste and standards of conduct, and, because of the influence they can bring to bear on the community, the business interests of licensees must at all times be subordinated to the overriding principle that the possession of a licence is, indeed, as the Royal Commission said, a public trust for the benefit of all members of our society." That has been my view over a period of time, and Mr Davidson's comments about the public trust issue have been seared into my mind ever since.'

I shook with relief afterwards. I took a few deep breaths, got a beer from the office fridge, drank it quickly and walked to Brian's office. When I saw him I burst into tears and started raving.

'Oh, Brian . . . I was hoping you'd see this as a core principle . . . I'm so grateful. Thank you for doing this . . . it's so important . . . you're so rare . . . you really care about the public interest . . . what will we do without you . . . ?'

He put his arm on my shoulder. 'Margo, I feel like you're a daughter to me.'

I kissed his cheek.

Postscript: James Packer joined the Liberal Party in late 2003. He voted for his mate Malcolm Turnbull, a sometime business partner of Kerry Packer, for preselection for the blue-ribbon Sydney seat of Wentworth. Turnbull won.

Part Three

Whose Australia?

8

Brian Harradine had once walked straight out the front door of Parliament House, kicked off his shoes and danced like a delighted kid with the visiting Wik people, jointly to honour the sacred soil where our national Parliament stands. And I'd cried.

Canberra insiders who spend every day up close to its innermost workings – pollies, journos, public servants, lobbyists, policy wonks – routinely forget what our democracy really is: the Australian people. Rarely, if ever, do we contemplate the symbolic power of its physical presence through the eyes of the citizens who constitute its heart, soul and mind. Inevitable, really: familiarity breeds indifference, if not contempt.

All the same, on the odd occasion that I rushed through the Public Foyer when I was still part of the Canberra press gallery, I'd see citizens doing exactly that: standing or wandering about their national House, being quietly awed. Schoolkids, oldies, uni students, out-of-towners, Canberrans. And visitors from other countries around the world – some democratic, some not – checking out what the Australian version of the world's 'least worst' system of governance looks like, and in what sort of House it lives.

If they'd been unlucky enough to try to do so on 23 October last year they would have seen a national capital and a national House in lock-down mode – lock-down and lockout. John Howard was taking no chances. The notional excuse was the now familiar 'national security' line but, as events would show, it had more to do with politics than any war on terror.

Before I take you behind the barricades to relate what Howard's 'G'day, Mr President' sounded like through press gallery ears, a Webdiarist friend will describe what she saw and heard from outside those excluding lines, and another will report her experience as an 'invited guest' to hear George Bush's speech. My 'outsider' friend is one of the many anonymous Australians who would have liked to have given George W. Bush a rather more democratic reception to our national House than the one he got from our PM on our behalf – a reception more consistent with the vision of those who shaped Australia's democracy.

M.K.

Outside the People's House

By a Citizen of Australia

> *Myths are so intimately bound to the culture, time, and place that unless the symbols, the metaphors, are kept alive by constant recreation through the arts, the life just slips away from them*

Joseph Campbell, American thinker

It'd been years since I'd ridden my pushbike, but on the October morning when George Bush came to Canberra there were so many radio warnings of road closures that I decided to cycle up to the protest rally at Parliament House.

I needn't have bothered – cycling, that is.

I'd expected to see a crowd thousands strong, but I found just a sprinkling of people behind police barricades on the lawns leading up to Capital Hill. How different from the solid mass of humanity in Sydney's Hyde Park back in February at the No War! march – which was actually more of a slow shuffle than a march at the outset. The size of the crowd there had meant it took three steamy hours before my little group could make its way out of the park and up past David Jones, cheered by the sight of shoppers waving from the pedestrian overpass.

The atmosphere in Canberra was much less warm, in more ways than one. The brazen confidence of the Sydney crowd was gone. There was less eye contact and fewer smiles. The Sydney–Canberra cultural divide was part of the difference, but I also remember thinking, Times have changed – and so fast!

Despite my little 'No Blood for Oil' badge, I hardly counted myself as an anti-war activist. A certain world-weary pragmatism – which Margo calls 'a failure of hope', and of which I am not proud – had made me believe from the outset that Australia would go to war in lockstep with its ANZUS big brother. It had all seemed so inevitable, even as I added my voice to the rhythmic chants in Sydney. Yet by the time of the Canberra rally what had started as pragmatism had hardened into bitter resignation – so much so that I was silent. Not once did I raise my voice in protest. Not against Bush. Not even against war.

Then why make such an effort to get to this rally? Dusting off my bike, pumping up the tyres.

I had a bee in my bonnet, that's why. About the way that we, the people, were being excluded from our Parliament. The people's place. Our House. *Ours*.

In one way there was nothing new in that exclusion. The public gallery is full of officials at each state opening of Parliament, so the rest of us can't get in. But to be barricaded away from even the outermost edges of Parliament – away from the marvellous Aboriginal mosaic on the forecourt, with all its ancient symbolism of a gathering place – irked me, and worried me, too. (And that was long before I found out that Bush's Canberra visit was not even an official state one.)

I feared that in the turbulence of the moment the damage to a central symbol of our democracy would go unheeded. That is what my protest was about.

Why such strong feelings about something so abstract?

I'm a migrant from Europe, a place where most public buildings are encrusted as deeply with symbolism as with ancient grime, and Australia's national Parliament had really impressed me at first glimpse, a decade ago: the clarity of design intent, the simplicity and self-confidence. I loved it.

I especially loved the way the architect, Romaldo Giurgola, had honoured the original vision of Canberra's designer, Walter Burley Griffin; loved how he hadn't shirked from meeting Griffin's challenge: let's make the national House a living embodiment of the Australian democratic process.

Years earlier in the Parliament House shop I'd found a school students' guide, *Interpreting the Art and Design of Parliament House*, a joint 1989 publication from the Royal Australian Institute of Architects and the Parliamentary Education Office. This modest little booklet was full of inspiring stuff:

'It was Griffin's intention that the city's physical form and land use pattern would express Australian democracy and the national identity. Griffin set out to clarify and define, interpret and proclaim the essence of the democratic experience. His plan for the federal capital would be charged with self-evident truth, its landscape would have meaning for every citizen. By moving about the city, engaging in everyday life, the powers and responsibilities of government institutions, together with the rights and responsibilities of each individual, would become manifest.'

The student guide describes how Griffin's design makes the landscape pre-eminent by aligning the parliamentary triangle with local landmarks and by keeping the buildings low. The only structure to rise to dominance would be a 'Capitol' building at the central point, on Capital Hill; Parliament House was intended for Camp Hill nearby. The Capitol building would eternally symbolise 'that in a democracy, the people stand above their elected representatives'.

The people standing above their elected representatives. What a brilliant contrast to the lofty pomp of the Palace of Westminster, in my native land, with its high iron railings and its towering presence dwarfing visitors as they crane their necks to see Big Ben. I relished the idea of the people being above their elected representatives. How egalitarian, I thought.

How Australian. How wonderful.

Yes, I knew that Griffin's idealism had been compromised along the way. His central Capitol, envisaged as a 'gathering place and forum' for all Australians, was never built. When parliamentarians decided in the 1970s to build a new Parliament House for the 1988 bicentennial to replace the 'temporary' Old Parliament House, they chose to locate it on Capital Hill, not Camp Hill.

As it turned out, Giurgola's steel flag-mast firmly echoes the outline of Griffin's pyramidal Capitol building and, explains the student guide, 'provides the visual climax required on Capital Hill'. Giurgola did his best to honour the original intent by designing broad, sweeping lawns so that people could use to walk right across the top of their elected representatives. Every time I'd catch a glimpse of those lawns when driving about Canberra I'd think of Griffin's vision of our democracy: the people above their parliamentarians. Because Canberra is derided and resented by so many Australians I treasured that positive feeling about my hometown. And I confess that when visitors from overseas and interstate came I felt a little swell of pride in pointing out the symbolism.

So fair enough that those 1970s politicians nudged themselves up Capital Hill, away from Griffin's original site, because we, the people, still owned the high ground. A reasonable trade-off.

Then in mid-2003 a terrible thing happened to Parliament House. We got booted off that high ground. Our right of way was blocked on those lawns, barred by ugly barricades, huge white Lego blocks placed across the most visible representation of Australian democracy. Sure, we could still get up to the roof – but only after subjecting ourselves to airport-style security checks at the public entrance and then crowding into a lift. That's a long way from simply strolling up to the building – our House – and then, free and proud, up our lawns onto our roof.

And our national House caretakers? Aside from some

indignation from our Opposition senators, those barricades went up with none of the public outcry that Griffin might surely have expected.

Kicked off our own roof. That was bad enough. But on the day of the Bush visit our exclusion went one step further: we were cordoned off to a sideline location, down by the Old Parliament House. Even if our imperial visitor had had eyes to see and ears to hear, he could not possibly have learnt the views of Australia's people, stuck way down there.

Our sample of democracy tried, though. I stood there on that October morning listening to the speeches. Bob Brown, Carmen Lawrence, Andrew Wilkie and many others, each stirring ripples of applause from the 'mob'.

I can't recall much of what they said, but I do remember the discomfort I felt; I'd kept my bike helmet and sunglasses on as I walked – I felt somehow safer dressed that way.

How odd.

I put it down to being a bit unhinged after the sleepless night we Canberrans had endured so that this President, who'd arrived the previous evening, could sleep soundly in his bed. Who would have thought that we'd have FA-18 fighter jets roaring across the skies in the bush capital?

Still, whatever the explanation or excuse for my helmet and sunglasses, I can sadly say that on that Canberra morning it was a case of 'see and be unseen' for me, not 'loud and proud' as at the peace march in Sydney. How odd.

Disappointing, too.

A bit slumpy shouldered, I set off for home before the imperial cavalcade even arrived.

As I watched the Bush speech to our national House on TV, I leafed through my little Parliament booklet for solace, pausing to read quotes like this one from Prime Minister Billy Hughes almost a century ago:

'We in Australia have fought, are fighting and shall continue to fight to the end – for those free institutions which, to free men, are dearer than life itself. We fight not for material wealth, not for aggrandisement of Empire, but for the right of every nation, small as well as large, to live its own life in its own way. We fight for those free institutions upon which democratic government rests. In Australia what the people say goes; whatever they choose to make, that they can make.'

What the people choose to make they can make, eh? That wasn't how it felt, Billy, outside the people's House in October 2003.

I went back to Parliament House some weeks later, after one of Margo's 'save our democracy' Webdiary raves, and found a second book in the shop – this one glossier and more grown-up than the first. Published in 1988, it was called *Parliament House Canberra: A Building for the Nation*, and had a foreword by Manning Clark in which the historian said: 'Parliament is a place where men and women of vision tell the people what Australia might be. We have been told that without vision the people perish. The Members of Parliament are the custodians and interpreters of that vision.'

I read on, and on almost every page found similarly inspired words and imagery that seemed from another era. The past is another country . . . Only fifteen years after its publication and already there was a whiff of innocence, of an era long since passed, about the book:

'It is democracy itself, rather than politics, that is embodied in the building . . . The only explicitly political references built into the structure are the Australian coat of arms over the public and Executive entrances and in the Houses of Parliament; and what allows one to think about the effacement of the political, as in some measure crucial to the whole idea of the building, is the fact that three of these are more or less transparent and the fourth, a bas-relief, so delicately figured as to be almost invisible.'

The book notes, too, that this place, 'which is essentially the house of the Australian People', has little to say about that people, with its diverse origins and traditions, 'for people will come to the building, and may be allowed to speak for themselves'.

Not any more. Ruefully I continued and found this:

'The central concept of the Constitution – that the Parliament is the People – is symbolised in the Foyer. This is the primary public space within the building – the "People's place" (in the same way as the chambers might be considered to "belong" to the parliamentarians). As the public's room, the Foyer is the most luxuriously appointed space in Parliament House. Rich polished marbles and timber marquetry offer a sumptuous contrast to the much simpler materials of the chambers. Individuals can cluster in small groups against the columns, unlike the monumental open space of the Forecourt, where people assemble as a crowd.'

No, we don't. Not now. The passage reminded me of a couple of paragraphs by Giurgola from the young Australian citizens' booklet:

'Architects can only make signs which are reflecting [the] human condition. As people give meaning to those signs they become symbols and thus unforgettable. Australians often consider themselves as alien to symbols and yet, for a society formulating its own identity, it is precisely the language of symbols which is the most efficient and natural form of communication, as is expressed in the arts, in movies and in icons.

On the day of the Opening by the Queen, a large throng assembled in the Forecourt, and a demonstration for land rights by Aboriginal people took place. It was a civilized demonstration culminating with a little girl offering a red, yellow and black bouquet to the Queen, who graciously accepted the gift. It was the first time that the Forecourt was seen crowded, the Honour Guard being careful not to step on Michael Nelson Tjakamarra's mosaic. It was a moment in which the elements of the building forming the place acquired a full significance for everyone.'

That was it.

When I read that description my abstract motivation for pedalling up to Parliament House on that Canberra morning crystallised. How could it be that our period of direct, unfettered access to our own House had been and gone, in the blink of an historical eye? Just fifteen years, 1988–2003.

The little student guide contained a list of study questions for our young Australians. One asked the kids about the extent to which our new Parliament House was truly the people's House. A fine question, I thought, and how fortunate it was that our younger citizens at least were still asking themselves such things. I even rang the Parliamentary Education Office to find out what sort of responses students using the study guide were giving to – and getting from – their civics teachers these days.

'It's out of print,' I was told. 'Check the website.'

On the parliamentary site I found lots of cyber stuff for Aussie schoolchildren. I just couldn't find any of the exquisite historical context, or the depth of grown-up democratic analysis, or any of those inspiring quotes, that the original kids' guidebook had offered us all.

And no sign, sadly, of that excellent question about whether the House is truly the people's.

9

Natasha Cica writes:

'I was only able to see George Bush address the Australian Parliament because I am enough of an "insider" there to wangle an invitation from Duncan Kerr MP, for whom I worked in 2001. I went because I was curious – not so much about what Bush would say, but more about how he would be received by "insiders": pollies, press, parliamentary staff and other wanglers of invites and the occasional publicly funded sausage.

I wrote this piece because I was stunned at the transformation inside Parliament House that day. I've worked in that building on and off in a range of jobs since 1995, and I've never seen us, the people, so marginalised in its proceedings and treated with so little respect as Australians. Even when the logging industry held the entire building to physical and political ransom in the dying days of Keating, the occasionally drunk and often abusive demonstrators were handled pretty much with soft kid gloves.

I sent this piece to Webdiary because I had a feeling most of the other "insiders" from that day wouldn't tell the story as I saw it, and that other editors wouldn't touch it. That was pretty much confirmed when I saw the media's analysis of the interjections made by senators Bob Brown and Kerry Nettle. I was stunned by the poison spat by most commentators in their direction (one gutsy exception was

Matthew Franklin writing in the *Courier-Mail*), when all they were really doing was saying things many Australians inside and outside that building agreed with – including lots of pollies who chose to be quietly supine on the day, and lots of journos, too.'

Dr Natasha Cica is a Fellow at the Centre for Applied Philosophy and Public Ethics and a Lecturer at the University of Canberra. She has worked as a research specialist in the Department of the Parliamentary Library, as an adviser to Labor MP Duncan Kerr and Liberal MP Petro Georgiou and at a public policy think tank in London. She comments widely on media and justice issues.

M.K.

Inside the People's House

By Natasha Cica

> *You can judge politicians by how they treat refugees;*
> *they do to them what they would do to everyone else*
> *if they could get away with it*

Attributed to Ken Livingstone, Mayor of London

Thursday, 23 October 2003, Canberra
03.00 a.m.
Woken from sleep. Again. Helicopters, fighter jets.

05.00
More helicopters.

07.30
Rise, shower, breakfast. Radio says Canberra hospital ward cleared in anticipation of presidential emergency. Infectious diseases. Wonder: is this a joke?

08.00
Leave house. Drive towards Parliament House.

08.25
Stuck in traffic jam somewhere near Parliament House. Swarm of policemen in baseball caps.

08.45

Closer, but still stuck. Very large policeman with gun and baseball cap outside car window, inserting round mirrors in drains on approach to Parliament House. Wonder.

08.50

Closer, but must park outside ring-road. Start walking.

09.00

Stopped by security official on ring-road. Show invitation. Am allowed past.

09.03

Stopped by security official. Show invitation. Am questioned further. Mention first official and am allowed past, on proviso am checked by third security official in pink shirt.

09.05

Security official in pink shirt demands invitation and name of inviter. Both provided. Proceed.

09.07

Another security official reluctant to let me proceed. Despite invitation. Mention first, second, third official. He relents.

09.08

Walk past Stars and Stripes to ministerial entrance. Present invitation. Encounter gaggle of Coalition wives in large, elaborate hats. Vowels like Prue and Trude from *Kath & Kim*. Think: bit too early for Melbourne Cup? Is this a joke?

09.10
Attempt entry. Everything beeps going through security. Shoes, watch, earrings. Fillings, presumably. Wonder: do hats beep? Cleared to enter. Walk round building. Many Prues and Trudes, many loopy rope barricades. Many men with curly wires coming out of ears. Wonder: is this *The Matrix*?

10.15
Meet Member of Parliament for coffee. She's been to anti-Bush demonstration and asked for pass by security official to proceed into Parliament House. (What pass for an MP? Since when? She was obliged to jump barricade.)

10.45
Am escorted to chamber entrance by Member of Parliament. Wonder: will we need to jump barricade? Meet another member of parliament handing out dove badges. Peace, yeah, am all for it. Take one.

10.47
Walk towards stairs. At bottom of stairs, security official demands invitation. Duly presented. Walk up stairs. At top of stairs, security official demands invitation. Duly presented. Walk towards security screening area. Join long

queue. More Prues and Trudes, many hats. Near end of queue, take mobile phone from bag to turn off. Security official says must cloak phone. Leave queue to cloak phone. Resume long queue. More Prues, more Trudes. Nearing end of queue, security official inspects invitation and notes no Texta mark on back. Sorry? Leave queue for Texta mark – green. Resume long queue. Stand behind random ambassador. Very friendly – says some diplomats not so happy about security, complaining lots, but he has no problem, the world has changed forever, he likes Australia. Asks what dove is for.

11.03

Everything beeps going through security. Hear rumours that Melanie McDonald née Howard exempt from security check after complaint.

11.05

Am directed up more stairs. Find myself in area behind soundproof glass, not public gallery – that's full. Chairs here all full, too: many security passes from US Embassy. Note closure of entire public gallery of Australian Parliament to Australian public. Wonder.

11.06

Security/courtesy official politely asks if visitors from US Embassy would mind accompanying her. To fill empty seats at back of press gallery, in open area of parliamentary chamber, so invited guests to public gallery may sit there after all. None shows interest. None moves.

11.07
Security/courtesy official repeats request. Tell her as invited guest am happy to sit in one of those empty seats if they don't want one. Not possible. Wonder why, aloud. Offer only extends to people who won't make a disturbance. Wonder, aloud, why as an invited guest of Member of Parliament I'm suspected of potential disturbance. No hat? Remember dove.

11.08
Walk off, turn corner into another closed area. See spare seat near glass near American journalist. Sit.

11.09
Security/courtesy official says please vacate seat for one away from window. Tell her would rather not, thanks, need to see what's happening to take notes for article. Remain in seat.

11.10
Parliamentarians enter chamber. Listen as American journo is coached by baby-faced spook from US Embassy on who is what in chamber. 'That's the Foreign Minister. D-O-W-N-E-R. Yes, really.'

11.11

Announcement of President. All parliamentarians in chamber stand. All in public gallery below me stand, including school-children in green and gold tracksuits. Security/courtesy official runs up, exhorts us all to stand as matter of courtesy. In the distance eighteen members of press gallery stand. There are empty seats behind them.

11.15

Howard speech. We are a terrorist target 'not because of what we have done, but because of who we are'.

11. 25

Crean speech. Joining 'most warmly' in the Prime Minister's welcome. 'Above all, Australia looks to itself [as an] independent people.' Wonder. 'Honesty is the foundation stone of that great Australian value – mateship.' Baby-faced spook smirks and snorts. Involuntary memories of *Tampa*. Excision, anyone? Look at Americans around me in what passes today for public gallery. Wonder.

11.30

Bush speech. 'Man of steel – that's Texan for fair dinkum.' Rudd laughs. Latham looks gloomy. Brown interrupts. The Speaker responds: 'The sergeant will remove Senator Brown from the House.' Bush winks. Howard reddens. Man in long black coat with tassel tries to remove Brown from the House. Brown sits, sergeant retreats. Episode assiduously avoided by Australian parliamentary television. Episode caught on American TV and beamed to world. I love free speech. Bush continues. We celebrate 'the spread of freedom'. Wonder: is this Vegemite? Remember Victory Gin. Kerry Nettle interrupts. The Speaker responds: 'The sergeant will remove Senator Nettle from the House.' Feel bit sorry for sergeant, approaching, tassel waving. Bush responds: 'I love free speech.' Coalition applauds, many Labor also. Wonder.

11.55
Bush ends with God. Entire Coalition stands and ovates. Assorted Labor, Greens, Democrats remain seated. Entire Labor frontbench stands and claps, limply. Latham looks gloomier. Bush moves towards Labor frontbench. Shakes all hands. Howard beckons, Beazley rolls on down, tank-like, beaming. Abbott sits like bouncer in rear of chamber near door throughout. Wonder. Bush moves towards door, Abbott marshals Coalition human shields to block Greens' petition about unlawful US detention of Australians David Hicks and Mamdouh Habib. Speaker 'names' Greens. Motion passed to suspend them from House. Coalition applauds.

12.00 noon
Leaving chamber, escaping excited Prue/Trude scrum, more hats. Walk directly into Mrs Habib, looking sad. Wonder.

12.05 p.m.

Attend Amnesty International meeting as guest of Member of Parliament. Strangely, Ruddock absent. Wonder if has now handed in his Amnesty badge. Addressed by Melbourne lawyer who works in US on 'war on terror' cases, including Hicks and Habib. Counts 3500 detainees, including Guantanamo Bay. Discusses unlawfulness of arrests and detention, conditions of detention, military tribunals. Recalls rule of law, separation of powers. Describes torture – systematic, deliberate, ongoing. Unlawful, immoral.

Wonder aloud why this is not news in Australia.

10

A Day in the Life of Our House Under Siege

Political systems have much more frequently been overthrown by their own corruption and decay than by external forces

Robert Menzies, 'The Sickness of Democracy', from
***The Forgotten People* radio broadcasts, 1942**

The anti-democratic hustle

On 8 October 2003 John Howard's government lied to the Australian people to obtain their Parliament's consent to hold a special joint sitting for President George W. Bush. Manager of business Tony Abbott told the people's House:

'The government has decided to deal with the visit of President Bush in precisely the same way that the Keating Government dealt with the visit of President Bush Senior on 2 January 1992. As well as the formal Parliamentary proceedings, there will obviously be an opportunity for all members of this Parliament to mix with President Bush, and very possibly to meet him.'

Senior ministers would hold talks with the President, Abbott said, adding, 'Of course, there will be similar opportunities for the Leader of the Opposition and senior shadow ministers. This Parliament spends a lot of time dealing with what might be described as politics as usual, but it is important to put politics as usual aside for this day.'

The 1992 speech by Bush Senior was the first time any foreign head of state had addressed our Parliament. There is nothing in the Constitution to allow it and no precise rules in place. But his visit had gone well. Australians had generally supported our participation in the UN-endorsed coalition to drive Iraq from Kuwait, and the man who'd masterminded it arrived as a largely uncontroversial figure. 'Politics as usual' was put aside by making Bush Senior's stay a state visit. He was welcomed at Kingsford Smith Airport on his arrival in Australia by the Governor-General, Bill Hayden, with Prime Minister Keating in attendance; there was a state dinner hosted by the Governor-General at Government House, a non-partisan parliamentary dinner hosted by Keating, and meetings with government, Opposition and even farm lobby leaders. The President mixed equally with all our representatives after his speech to show his respect for the honour we, their electors, had extended to him; and he treated our media congenially and with even-handedness throughout.

AUSTRALIAN PRIME MINISTER: Thank you for coming. And just before I invite the President to say a few words, just to outline, first of all, the structure of the press conference so we can operate smoothly . . . I hope we'll be able to take a roughly even amount from both the Australian and visiting press . . .

AMERICAN PRESIDENT: My [opening] remarks, Mr Prime Minister, will be very brief. And I simply want to, once again, thank you, thank all of our official hosts, and thank the people of Australia for the warmth of the reception on this visit . . . And I'll be glad to take my share of the questions.

At that joint press conference Australian journalists asked Bush Senior about half of the twenty-two questions he fielded. Presumably when Abbott told Parliament that this next Bush visit would proceed in 'precisely the same way' both our press gallery and elected representatives felt reassured.

The anti-democratic sting

Contrary to Abbott's pledge, the government already knew that, unlike the visit by his dad, the visit by Bush Junior would NOT be a state visit, but a partisan 'working' one, as a guest NOT of the governor-general, our head of state, but of John Howard.

The President would NOT 'very possibly . . . meet' our parliamentarians, or even 'obviously . . . mix' with them.

He would NOT 'of course' meet senior shadow ministers.

He would NOT hold a press conference.

The government knew all this *weeks* before Abbott misled Parliament to obtain our consent.

Documents I obtained from the Prime Minister's Department under a Freedom of Information request show that at a planning meeting with John Howard's department on 17 September 2003 a member of Bush's Advance Team said that the 'visit was to be short – just the basic wreathlaying in the Hall of Memory – *no official state visit*, no ceremonial greeting, gun salute etc'. A draft itinerary dated the same day – and which remained largely unchanged – provided for no meetings with Labor shadow ministers and no mixing with or meetings between parliamentarians and Bush.

The visit was always going to be the George 'n' John Show, with Bush shadowed by Howard at all times so that he appeared in practically every image captured of the President. There'd be no public opportunity for any Australian to voice their opposition to his foreign or trade policies directly or question his plans for our ANZUS future. Rather than seek to unite all Australians behind our most important ally via demonstrable expressions of our true shared values – engaged debate, freedom of speech and of the press and democratic inclusion – Howard would prevent almost everyone who disagreed with him from speaking with Bush at all.

I reckon that if our parliamentarians had known that it was going to be 'politics as usual' – only much worse than usual – there'd have been uproar in both our Houses. The Senate had already censured Howard twice over Iraq, and many non-government MPs may have refused to attend Bush's speech at all.

Doubtless that's exactly what John Howard reckoned, too.

The anti-democratic announcement

Australians got their first hint of what was to come via a leaked White House press briefing in early October, which named our Prime Minister as 'John Major' and gave American reporters minute-to-minute details of Bush's Canberra itinerary.

Asked by Neil Mitchell on Melbourne's 3AW on 3 October whether he intended to recall Parliament for 23 October – not a bad idea since Bush had already told his media gang he'd be arriving to deliver a speech there at 9.55 a.m. sharp – Howard said, 'Well, I'm looking at the present time at some of the details – final details – of his program and when I'm in a position to announce exactly what's going to happen, I will do so.'

Mitchell later pressed the matter.

MITCHELL: Okay, I've just got a message through. Apparently in the United States journalists have been told that the President will be addressing the Australian Parliament on the 23rd of October – is there something the White House knows that you don't?

HOWARD: Well, that may be the case, but I'm not in a position to say anything at the moment.

MITCHELL: That's what's being said in the United States.

HOWARD: Well, a lot of things are said in the United States that I don't have control over.

MITCHELL: Okay. Is it wrong?

HOWARD: When I'm in a position to formally say something, I will.

On 5 October Howard announced that Bush would speak to our Parliament.

On 8 October Abbott asked it for our permission. Labor moved an unsuccessful amendment requiring a full working day. The Greens' Mike Organ unsuccessfully circulated an amendment requiring Bush to 'invite questions from the floor for a period of no more than 60 minutes' following his speech. Tony Abbott closed the debate with 'What the government is doing is precisely what the Keating government did on 2 January 1992.'

The anti-democratic plants

Howard's con began to become clear in the planning decisions made by Parliament's supposed trustees: the Speaker of the House of Representatives, Neil Andrew MP; and the Senate President, Senator Paul Calvert.

Despite the ever-tightening straitjacket of the party-discipline duopoly, our Parliament remains structurally separate from the government of the day and manages itself independently of it, protecting the ideal of our Westminster system of democracy: that Parliament in its entirety represents the sovereignty of the people *over* the governing executive.

This means that the Speaker of the House of Reps and the Senate president, elected by the members of their respective Houses – not the prime minister and his cabinet – run the Parliament. These two nominally non-partisan trustees are responsible to all our elected representatives for its smooth functioning, including an even-handed defence of parliamentary privileges. Every senator and MP has equal rights to use the Parliamentary Library; to book rooms for meetings and forums; to seek and receive answers from ministers and departments to constituents' questions; to host guests of their choice; and so on.

Parliament decides the rules for its own deliberations, including disciplinary measures for rule breakers. *Parliament* decides the rules for media reporting of its activities. *Parliament* decides the rules for its security. And non-party staffers who serve our elected representatives are employed by the *Parliament*, meaning they owe their duty to *Parliament*.

That, in turn, means the Australian voters who elect the members of Parliament. Not John Howard and his – or any other's – political majority. Liberals Andrew and Calvert are minding *our* sovereign parliamentary trust – and cracking our working whip – 'for all of us'.

For Bush Junior's visit, however, none of this would apply. Our two trustees would instead lock us out of our own House, shut down its workday routine, humiliate its occupants and hand both security and control over media access to its American guests. The effective result would be the temporary occupation of our sovereign Parliament by a foreign sovereign power.

Here are some of the unprecedented planning measures these two Liberal Party plants took in the service of the George 'n' John Show.

1 Expelling the people from Parliament House
For the first time ever, members of the public were to be banned from entering Parliament House.

2 Suppressing protest outside Parliament House: visual
a   For the first time ever, protesters were to be banned from gathering on the lawns outside the public entrance, and instead ordered to assemble down the hill, at Old Parliament House. (Banishment to the stamping grounds of Menzies, Holt, Gorton and Fraser for all those small-l liberal dissenters, John?)

b   For the first time ever, a screen would be erected at the public entrance – large pot plants. (Parliament security chief Terry Crane later told Senate Estimates, 'It was designed to create a visual barrier for the President's arrival.' ALP Senator John Faulkner asked, 'So no member of the public could see the arrival?' Crane replied, 'They probably would not have been able to see it clearly from the "authorised assembly area" [anyway], but that was the purpose of the pot plants.')

3 Suppressing protest outside Parliament House: aural

For the first time ever, the use of a public address system at protests would be banned, while organisers wielding loud-hailers were directed to 'turn their backs to Parliament House'.

4 Banishing Parliament House staff

For the first time ever, Andrew and Calvert would instruct all staff except those considered 'essential' for the parliamentary sitting itself to take the day off. Australian taxpayers were to pay $2 million to bring our politicians back to Canberra to do no democratic work beyond listening to a speech. (Not everyone folded to Howard's commands: library chief John Templeton decided that his staff, though not directly involved, were still essential: 'We had in the building on the Thursday all senators and members. My judgment was that a lot . . . would take the opportunity to use the library services, because there were no formal proceedings going on beyond the end of President Bush's address . . . A fair bit of work was done . . .')

5 Allowing political staffers to use the Public Foyer of Parliament House as a party convention room

For the first time ever, party-political staffers would occupy the Public Foyer. A Coalition rent-a-crowd would greet Bush with an American-style razzamatazz welcome, complete with cheers and flag waving. (Remember: 'The central concept of the Constitution – that the Parliament is the People – is symbolised in the Foyer. This is the primary public space within the building – the "People's place".' Not during the George 'n' John Show it wasn't.)

6 Ceding responsibility for Parliament House security to a foreign power

For the first time ever, our Parliament House trustees handed authority for security to a foreign power. For the first time ever, Parliament's security board was shunted aside, not even convening to consider intelligence reports and make its own security recommendations.

Instead the American Advance Team arrived in September and summarily announced its requirements. One precedent-shattering example will suffice: for the first time ever, our trustees allowed visiting close-protection officers to bring their personal firearms into our House. And 'we' – that is, Andrew and Calvert – didn't merely say yes to each such security demand, 'we' also relinquished overall security control.

7 Ceding control of Parliament House media access to a foreign power

For the first time ever, our trustees relinquished control over media access to the Prime Minister and his department, who handed it straight to the Americans.

To pull this off Howard used one of his favourite anti-democratic tricks: outsourcing, an administrative mechanism that delivers the precise 'service' required yet has an inbuilt firewall in case the heat starts to rise – as in this instance it eventually would. Media liaison was outsourced to Daniel Bolger, a low-level private contractor without authority or leverage when it came to 'negotiating' equitable access to the President for Australian *and* American journalists. But Bolger's report to the government after the visit exposed the reality. 'All media arrangements were cleared by and distributed by the Prime Minister's office', he wrote. Those with the duty to oversee media arrangements in our Parliament – Andrew and Calvert – were not even listed in Bolger's report as 'key stakeholders' with whom he liaised.

Result? For the first time ever, Australia's parliamentary media would have less access to a visitor on their own daily news beat than would the American President's press corps.

The anti-democratic welcome

At 9.50 p.m. on 22 October 2003 John and Janette Howard climbed the stairs of Air Force One at Canberra Airport and disappeared inside, where presumably our Prime Minister shook George W. Bush's hand in a private 'working' welcome to Australia. A short time later both men and their wives emerged, all four waving to a non-existent crowd, before descending to the tarmac. Next morning golfers were kicked off the Royal Canberra Golf Club greens adjacent to Yarralumla's Government House, while Bush (without Howard) called on our head of state in a nineteen-minute visit at which presumably Governor-General Mike Jeffery welcomed Bush to Australia on behalf of 'all of us'. It was his *only* encounter with the President.

Anti-Democratsville, Canberra, Texas

So how did our ANZUS partner respond on the day to our total acquiescence to its demands during planning and preparation? In just the way any superpower would upon discovering that a junior ally doesn't have the guts, self-respect or constitutional seriousness to treat its own Parliament with proprietorial care, of course: they trashed all the agreed arrangements.

They rolled right over the top of us and rubbed our noses in the dirt.

1 No flashy photography in the House, please

Neil Andrew had at least said no to one demand, repeatedly refusing – including in writing – an American request to allow TV cameras into the House of Representatives for Bush's speech. He could not have done otherwise: our rules are that only the Parliament's cameras are allowed in, and these operate under strict guidelines, including no filming of any politician 'without the call'. It's a rule the press gallery has long protested, but our Parliament has decided it wants to preserve its dignity, and it's very strictly policed. Any Australian journo who sneaked a camera in would get their media group expelled from Parliament House, quick smart.

But the American media had decided they wanted to film George's speech and so film George's speech the American media did.

How on earth did this happen?

Not only were all politicians, journalists and guests

security-screened before entering the building, but the Americans had further demanded we be screened again before entering the House of Representatives' chamber itself. Under US orders our security officers set their machines to maximum and subjected anyone in the conga line who 'bleeped' to close individual scrutiny.

How close? The *West Australian*'s Karen Middleton, a fifteen-year gallery veteran well known to security, progressively jettisoned all metallic accoutrements before finally suggesting in an embarrassed whisper that the bleeping problem could only be the bleeping wire in her bra.

Paul Kelly, Australia's senior political journalist, got stuck outside the Reps' chamber on a different snag: his press pass – which had been deemed 'valid ID' in the agreed security plan – was now summarily dismissed as 'inadequate' by *American* security officers. As Press Gallery President Malcolm Farr later pointed out in a Parliamentary Privileges Committee submission, 'This . . . led to the farcical situation where . . . Kelly was allowed into the White House to talk to Mr Bush, but not allowed into the Australian Press Gallery to cover his speech.'

And yet.

And yet, just down the corridor, Australian security officers were waving in American journalists with nothing but a smile. No searches, no scanners, *nothing*. If the extreme measures elsewhere were for real, then this was a serious security breach.

Need proof? Well, 'our' security officials allowed CNN

to openly walk a TV camera into 'our' House of Representatives, contrary to all those explicit refusals by their supposed boss, Neil Andrew.

When Senate Estimates hearings later sought the truth behind the American exceptionalism, Labor Senator John Faulkner pointed out that this rogue camera 'could have been a bazooka, for all I know'. Parliament security chief Terry Crane replied that the inner-sanctum breach didn't matter because everyone had been screened when they entered the building.

FAULKNER: But there was security screening up there, wasn't there?

CRANE: Not for the pool that arrived.

FAULKNER: Was there for the Australian media?

CRANE: Yes, Senator.

FAULKNER: Take for example Paul Kelly, the Editor-at-Large of the *Australian* newspaper, quite a prominent Australian journalist. He got harangued for about half an hour and fluked, effectively, getting into the press gallery in the chamber. And yet these other characters were just whisked in without any second security check at all. How do you justify that?

MICHAEL BOLTON (PARLIAMENT'S JOINT HOUSE DEPARTMENT HEAD): You make a risk assessment at the time and the risk assessment was —

FAULKNER:	The risk assessment was that Mr Kelly was a risk?
BOLTON:	No.
FAULKNER:	These characters carrying movie cameras were not a risk, is that it?
BOLTON:	They [the Americans] were happy for them to be there, and to get in quickly, and therefore that was done.
FAULKNER:	You told me that you were in charge. Are you saying that whoever is in charge of the President's security within Parliament House overrides your authority?
BOLTON:	No, the risk was in relation to the American President, and they were happy for them to be there and cover the thing.
FAULKNER:	Let us just get it right, Mr Bolton: you do not know whether they were happy or not, do you?
BOLTON:	They were under the control of the media liaison officer [Bolger] who brought them into the building, and who controlled their access. He asked us to do various things and we accommodated that. [*Bolger says he knew of the Speaker's written refusal to allow cameras in.*]
FAULKNER:	And is this media liaison officer a security expert?
BOLTON:	Probably not.

Australians as second-class citizens in their own Parliament? You bet.

2 We know where you live, buster

John Howard was happy to 'accommodate' the Americans outside Parliament House, too. Through an FoI request, I discovered that less than forty-eight hours before Bush arrived, the Americans suddenly demanded 'the home addresses for all the key people the President will be encountering during his visit'. No reason was given, and Australian officials madly sent emails to ministers and Defence Force chiefs. Only one registered bemusement: 'Perhaps POTUS [Bush] is thinking of "red alerting" them all, or they are now on his Christmas card list.'

A 'red alert' is military slang for an unannounced, uninvited and highly inconvenient party at someone's home. The email joker was too generous; the party usually ends up also being fun.

3 Move along, nothing to see here

Howard also stripped the Australian Federal Police of command outside Parliament House, as Network Ten's Greg Turnbull discovered while setting up near the War Memorial to film Bush's arrival – at the agreed location, with all his agreed passes in order. An Australian cop made the team move, on orders from the US Secret Service. Turnbull sought out the AFP officer in charge: 'I said, "This is our country, we're at our memorial, we're working for Australian audiences and we've got all the proper accreditation",' Turnbull recalls. 'He said there was nothing he could do, and we had to shift.'

4 Security postscript

All that overt security was just for show. After Bush had left town, the *Canberra Times* revealed that the Americans had demanded so much security on the Bush routes that the AFP had been forced to dress up *civilians* as policemen to make it look like they were on the job. Nearly *one in nine* of the local 'police' contingent was actually an unsworn-in public servant. Many of them were dressed in AFP overalls and vests and deployed around such sensitive locations as the Lodge, the US Embassy and Parliament House. Extra security?

Breaking Australian laws, more like it.

Impersonating a police officer is a criminal offence. Impersonating a democratic prime minister is merely a political one.

The anti-democratic media lockout

For the first time ever, no Australian media members were allowed in the presidential motorcade or in the core pool of journalists following Bush – Yanks only need apply. This meant that if anything newsworthy happened – a logistics hiccup, a spontaneous public walkabout, hell, an *assassination attempt* – no local reporter would witness it. To keep Australians informed, we had to rely on American reports – if *they* considered it newsworthy enough to mention to their American audiences, that is. The press gallery protested when the program was finally released.

Howard's office drop-kicked responsibility to Daniel Bolger. Bolger threw up his hands, causing some desperate journos to call the Americans direct. Response? Get lost, you don't have the required security clearances. How do we apply? Don't bother. Lo, on the morning of the speech Howard said he'd let two token Australian journos in to report the barbecue lunch, after all. His chief spinner, Tony O'Leary, called it a 'favour' to the gallery. Thanks, John.

And yet.

And yet, as with security, having got all the media control they wanted during planning, on 23 October our American visitors broke many of the agreements anyway, summarily excluding authorised local media time after time. Just three examples.

1 Make that lock-in

For Bush's War Memorial wreath-laying ceremony in honour of Australia's war dead (to which Howard forgot to invite Australia's most recent war widow), Australia's designated journalists and photographers arrived early to secure good positions. When the White House party arrived they instructed the Australians to move, so the spoon-fed American contingent could commandeer the premium places. Afterwards they literally locked the Australians inside the Tomb of the Unknown Soldier for twenty minutes – while the George 'n' John Show posed for those same American reporters outside.

2 Or rope-in

The agreed photographers' position in the Public Foyer for the President's entry was to be behind a roped-off barrier, and Australian 'shooters' and TV crews assembled early in the best 'first come, first served' tradition, organising themselves so that everyone would have a clear shot. As the big moment approached, however, Australian security – at the direction of the Americans – ordered them to move the barrier and themselves back. Why? Our shooters, who to their credit refused to budge, soon found out when US photographers arrived and were permitted to take up positions in front of the rope barrier. AAP veteran Alan Porritt, who's photographed presidential visits since LBJ came all the way, was not happy. 'The last time I looked I didn't see a new star added to the US flag or Stars and Stripes replace the Union Jack on ours,' he wrote to his Press Gallery President. 'I object to being told by foreigners what I can do in our Parliament House in our country.'

3 Or plain old-fashioned censorship

Howard left Bush's side only once in Parliament House – when Bush met with Simon Crean. The Network Ten crew stood outside the Cabinet Room to film Bush's arrival to meet the Opposition Leader – as agreed – until a young American woman listlessly chewing gum abruptly waved them away.

'No press,' she announced.

Daniel Bolger did nothing. A Ten cameraman asked Bolger's assistant what the hell was going on.

'The President's saying he doesn't want anyone, so . . .'

No one? Of course not. '[D]espite this change, the US subsequently took a US pool TV camera into the meeting', Bolger reported.

A petty snub for Simon from George, or just generalised contempt for Australians?

Call me suspicious, but I found it odd that just as Bush's actions denied Australians footage of the meeting, so Howard tried to ensure they would not see any other images of Crean with Bush. Under Howard's agreed arrangements, only a photographer from Auspic, the government photographic unit, was allowed to shoot that meeting – with a promise to distribute the photos to the press gallery for publication. But after Auspic gave *Sydney Morning Herald* photographer Andrew Meares the pictures, a panicking shooter rang to say that Howard's office had now forbidden their distribution.

Meares was incensed, but faced with an awful dilemma: distribute the shots and he'd probably cost someone their job. Crean finally got the photos by invoking his rights as an MP. It was the Opposition Leader himself, in the end, who passed them around the gallery.

Welcome to John Howard's idea of putting 'politics as usual' aside for the day. Bush was to be his alone. He wanted NO pictures of the Opposition Leader with 'our' ANZUS ally, and he didn't mind trashing prior agreements to ensure it.

The anti-democrat

Actions speak louder than words in the end, and from the emerging events of 23 October the Australian people might begin to extract a clear understanding of Australia's relationship with the United States, John W. Howard to George W. Bush style. Under Howard ANZUS is not an alliance, it's a political tool, a partisan plaything. It's also a one-sided walkover. For many of us watching from the inside that day, Howard's proclaimed respect for *his* Westminster Parliament – *his* fellow representatives, *his* head of state, *his* office, *his* Liberal Party, *his* voters and *his* country was revealed as just more super-spin.

The anti-anti-democrat

In an apt end to a shaming day, our Parliament House was witness to tough, experienced Australian reporters – still reeling from ejections, bans, lockouts and broken promises – racing around begging the Americans for an ironic favour: to let them film *their film* of the extraordinary events that had transpired in our Parliament House.

The CNN 'rogue camera' footage was flashed around the world within minutes of Senator Bob Brown's interjection during Bush's speech. Also recorded by CNN for all to see was the back view of the Coalition's human shield around the two dissenting Greens, a barricade that physically stopped Senator Nettle giving Bush a letter from the wife of one of two Australian citizens detained at Guantanamo Bay. From Washington to Moscow the interjections were reported as proof of Australia's enduring tradition of 'robust' democracy.

By the skin of our teeth.

In the wake of that dangerous outbreak of democracy Howard reneged on yet another media agreement: that the Auspic man – the only photographer allowed in the press gallery viewing area that day – would provide pictures to the media. From his spot he'd got the only front view of Brown and Nettle rising in their places to interrupt, and of that rugby 'rolling maul', but the PM hadn't meant pictures like *that* of course, and again his office ordered the photographs not be distributed. Luckily *Canberra Times* photographer Graham Tidy managed to get one shot of the closing scrum, recording for posterity those Liberals who used physical force in our national House in those ugly moments.

Fronting the guard, with his arms spread wide like a goalkeeper?

John W. Howard.

We heard what was said on that historic occasion, John, and by whom.

We saw what was *done*, too.

So let's compare and contrast Brown's actions and words with yours.

Here you are in *our* House that morning, explaining to us, the Australian people, just why you and George are such mates:

'Mr Speaker and Mr President of the Senate . . . The things that unite the Australian and American people are shared values: the belief that the individual is more important than the state, that strong families are a nation's greatest asset, that competitive free enterprise is the ultimate foundation of national wealth, and that the worth of a person is determined by their character and hard work, not by their religion or race or colour or creed or social background.'

Looks good on the page, John. Sounds even better on the nightly news. But let's see how those fine sentiments stack up with your actions.

1 'The individual is more important than the state', John

Throughout Bush's speech Howard's backbench performed with all the spontaneity of a Stalin audience. 'Hear, hear' they cried in unison and laughed as if vocally choreographed at Bush's attempt at a joke (or was it?) that in Texas 'man of steel' means 'fair dinkum'. When Brown stood to make his solo voice heard over Howard's State Choir, the state shouted the individual down.

Howard's Speaker then tried to use the office (and muscle) of the state to eject Brown; next a state goon squad tried physically to block Brown and Nettle from approaching Bush as he left. Finally Tony Abbott used the state's majority to pass a motion having Brown and Nettle suspended for twenty-four hours, without the state bothering to order a vote of MPs before doing so, as required by Parliament's rules.

In fact Abbott's move was itself a breach of rules since his own request back on 8 October had been for 'no proceedings' in our House that day except the two welcomes and Bush's speech. And so that's all we authorised.

Look it up in Hansard, Tony. Your government didn't have our permission to put or pass *any* motions that day.

Oh, and by the way, John – not only had the Greens' MP Mike Organ, in his 8 October amendment, sought the state's permission to ask Bush questions from the floor; Brown had also asked, well before being forced to use such unconventional tactics, if he could give a speech. The state said no. Brown chose to speak anyway. It was the only opportunity he could do so, thanks to your ban on Bush mixing with our elected representatives.

The individual is more important than the state, John?

2 'Strong families are a nation's greatest asset', John

So what was Brown's beef with the President, then? Saving the whales? Bringing down the ruling classes? No.

Brown's interjection was: 'Respect Australia. Return the Australians to this nation for justice. If you respect the world's laws, the world will respect you.'

He was appealing, on behalf of the families of David Hicks and Mamdouh Habib, two Australian citizens held in Guantanamo Bay without charge, trial or outside contact, for a fair go.

He was asking Bush to treat two members of our national family in the same way he'd treated the *American* citizen John Walker in the same plight. Walker's family had asked Bush to ensure that his American Bill of Rights protection against the misuse of state power was honoured. Bush's state had done so, granting Walker due judicial process under US law. Bob Brown wanted the same standards applied to our citizens.

This was no anti-American opportunist's grandstanding stunt. It was a courageous gesture of moral principle and human compassion, expressing the profound concerns of not just his own partisan supporters, but also those of millions of Australians of all political stripes, including many true Liberals.

John Valder – former head of the Sydney Stock Exchange, former head of the federal Liberal Party and a former key supporter of John Howard – told me later that he went public with his opposition to the Iraq war only after getting nowhere with polite private letters to Howard and the American Embassy seeking due process for David Hicks. Brown, too, had spent months futilely pursuing the government through formal channels before resorting to a direct approach.

'Strong families', whether individual or national, always look after their own. The wife and son of one of those detained citizens were Brown's guests in Parliament that day, but when Kerry Nettle tried to hand their letter of appeal to Bush she was physically prevented from doing so by the Prime Minister's strong political family – his back-benchers.

As John Valder lamented to me later, Howard has raised them to be obedient: 'The sad thing about the Liberal back-bench is that they don't have the guts to stand up. They're hand wringing. If no one on the backbench will stand up and risk [their] preselection, it shows the power Howard has over people.'

Strong families – a nation's greatest asset, John?

3 'Competitive free enterprise is the ultimate foundation of national wealth', John

Kerry Nettle's interjection called on Australia not to sign a free trade agreement with the US. As I write this we've signed up, yet argument rages over whether what we got is a 'free trade' deal at all. It's certainly not for our sugar farmers, even though Deputy PM John Anderson once described any FTA that excluded them as downright un-Australian.

Howard's election-year response to his own failure to reap a sweet bumper crop from all his past ANZUS fertilising of Bush? Great loving spoonfuls of public cash has been heaped onto the existing $150 million sugar industry subsidies. There goes that nice line about 'competitive free enterprise', John.

As for George, his White House – and our ANZUS ally's Congressmen – folded to the ultra-protectionist US farm lobby with barely a fight. Maybe Nettle had a point of order after all.

4 'The worth of a person is determined by their character
and hard work, not by their religion or race or colour
or creed or social background', John

Howard's tactical response to Brown's assertion of our Parliament's proper function was to trash the 'worth' not merely of Brown as an individual representative, but of Greens politics entirely.

The week after the speeches to Parliament by Bush and Chinese President Hu, Brown tabled a Senate motion urging Parliament's Procedures Committee to consider major changes to the way in which such events were conducted in future. The government's response was a coordinated assault of withering viciousness. On 28 October Brown was denounced as 'a political terrorist', while the Greens Party was a 'new and sinister element' in our democracy, one akin to Adolph Hitler's Nazi Party. The 'terrorist' line came from Northern Territory Senator Nigel Scullion, who'd been in the middle of the scrum on 23 October, as was the acting Senate president presiding over his slanders, Ross Lightfoot. Brown's political crime had been to speak out of turn; Lightfoot, who had coyly admitted that senators Brown and Nettle could have 'walked into my elbows', also allegedly hissed to Kerry Nettle that she should 'die'.

These were the senators who now claimed *Brown* was the anti-democratic danger.

The blanket denunciation of the Greens as 'Nazis' came from Queenslander George Brandis, a Liberal moderate I normally respect. He'd stood up to Howard on his anti-terrorism and ASIO laws, yet that didn't stop him playing hatchet-man-in-chief to help his Prime Minister wreak revenge on Brown and co for spoiling his big moment:

'The commonalities between contemporary Green politics and old-fashioned fascism and Nazism are chilling. First of all, the embrace of a set of political values which will not brook the expression of legitimate difference. The second feature of contemporary Green politics which bears chilling and striking comparison [to fascism and Nazism] . . . is not merely their contempt for democratic institutions, but a very cynical willingness to use those democratic parliamentary institutions to achieve anti-democratic ends . . .'

Think about Bob Brown, the gentle Tasmanian doctor who once went to jail to save some unique wilderness, a beautiful Australian corner of our planet that today we're glad we still have.

Now think about what Adolph Hitler did to our world.

All this was said in our House.

But who, throughout the Bush visit and afterwards, was really refusing to 'brook the expression of legitimate difference'? Who really was showing 'contempt for democratic institutions'? Who really displayed a 'cynical willingness to use [them] to achieve anti-democratic ends'? And which Australian party leader really – if Howard's bovver boys insist upon throwing cheap insults about – does that Nazi description better fit?

Of his ugly jibes, George Brandis later told me, 'You can come back at me and say the Liberal Party is what I'm saying the Greens are, if you like. It's my job to argue my party's position.'

No thanks, George – it's too nasty a shot. But maybe it's time some of your Liberal Party colleagues had a good look in the democratic mirror, and especially at their behaviour leading up to and on 23 October. Perhaps you should all re-read Benito Mussolini's definition of fascism, too, just to ensure that you really know what it is before you make such accusations in our Parliament again: 'Fascism should rightly be called Corporatism, as it is a merger of State and corporate power.'

Il Duce should know, since he invented fascism as a modern political force. Which Australian party do you really think he'd be more comfortable with?

Democratic actions speak louder than democratic words

In the course of defending his interjection and his reputation during that ugly Nazi debate, Senator Bob Brown said of a representative's democratic duty to his electors, 'it is not what we feel or think [in the House], it is what we DO that matters'.

So what about George Bush's actions on 23 October?

'I love free speech,' the planet's most powerful democratic leader had said when Nettle interrupted.

Brown had smiled, spread his arms, and replied, 'We do, too.'

The Coalition guffawed and applauded as if Bush possessed the sharpest wit of all time, but they'd have done no less had he said, I love free pretzels.

The President didn't explain why he wasn't holding a free press conference after his 'free speech', which Bolger's report said he'd refused point-blank to do.

And John Howard?

His actions on that day were one long exercise in disrespect for a Westminster parliament. From his loaded 'welcome' speech – Howard could have saved time by combining those four 'shared values' into one: 'Vote neo-liberal' – to his stewardship of the mêlée at the end, he treated our House with contempt.

Don't just take my word for it. Way back on 18 November 1996 the parliamentarians had debated the most appropriate way to respond to the upcoming speech of Bill Clinton in the House. Many felt that a standing ovation would be in order, and even the Speaker was happy to accept whatever 'spontaneous' gesture ensued. Not so the Member for Bennelong, one John Howard MP, who sternly reminded the House, 'It is unparliamentary to clap.'

But not if the applause is for a Republican President, eh, John? Or – as the people's House would very soon discover to its lasting shame – a communist dictator. Then it's compulsory and orchestrated.

But history will record that John Howard MP did do at least one thing in our House on 23 October 2003 that was 'individual' and 'spontaneous', not just the next staged act in his George 'n' John Show. When Brown stood up in our sovereign Parliament, as its democratic champion and hero, John Howard's face blushed as red as the flags that would greet China's President Hu when he showed up the next day.

Postscript: democratic navel-gazing

One minute past midnight, the beginning of a new day.

The press gallery was empty save for me. As a member not tied to early deadlines and news stories, I'd been able to stand back and take in the shocked stories of reporters, photographers and cameramen on the run. I'd also blown my top at fellow gallery members, incensed at some of the things our committee had conceded. Government-only photographers at official functions? Howard had to be kidding. Agreeing to exclude independent shooters was the first step on a very slippery slope. Where were the complaints? And where was the media exposure of this stuff? We had to draw a line here – it was getting serious.

Only Mark Riley had bothered to report the public's lockout from Parliament, Bush's refusal to give a press conference and the planned exclusion of the Australian media from Howard's barbecue. Even then our editors had buried his stories on page six, with the same old chestnut: 'We don't want to be seen to be navel-gazing.' Navel-gazing! This stuff was fundamental and the Australian people had a bloody right to know about it.

What the hell was the Press Gallery Committee

doing allowing Daniel Bolger – a paid contractor of the government – to retain his press gallery pass as a working journalist? ('We're about to remove it,' one committee member advised.) What the hell was the Press Gallery President, Malcolm Farr, doing swanning around as a 'guest' at the Lodge barbecue while his working colleagues weren't even allowed to report it? ('What ARE you on about, Margo? I'd have gone too!' was the standard journo response.) But we were the ones who wrote the columns and filed the news stories – why the hell weren't we bellowing to the people of Australia about all this? People were watching the Bush visit intently – or trying to.

People *wanted* to know what had really happened inside our House.

Maybe it took someone now outside the gallery hothouse, yet intimately familiar with its workings, to stand back and see the bigger picture. I wanted to explain why this wasn't navel-gazing. What had just transpired wasn't the usual game media and politicians play, it was a sustained assault on fundamental freedoms, and even something as apparently frivolous as a barbecue invitation was no mere consolation perk for the Press Gallery President, but an invitation for us all to surrender completely. I thought that by accepting his free lunch Farr had just signalled to Howard that we considered the loss of our free press adequately compensated.

'Malcolm should have boycotted the barbecue in protest!' I railed – to the rolling of many eyes.

I took a deep breath and wrote a long, detailed Webdiary piece recording the day from the inside, especially the media aspects. 'Parliament Greets Bush: A Day in the Life of Our Faltering Democracy' attracted my biggest readership since the Iraq war. This wasn't navel-gazing. This was NEWS.

Some colleagues were as angry as I was. The *Australian*'s political columnist Matt Price dissected the media travesty in a searing cover story for the paper's Media supplement the following week. 'Bushwhacked', the headlined roared. 'They came in force, took over our Parliament, captured our media and held them to ransom for 21 vital hours. How did we let it happen?'

Most pollies got their first inkling of what had been done in their name through Matt's piece. As I write, multiple parliamentary inquiries are underway, including an investigation into the media's shabby treatment to which Malcolm Farr contributed a damning submission on the press gallery's behalf.

And *that* wasn't navel-gazing either. Like everyone else who works at Parliament House, we journalists have got some serious professional thinking to do.

Of great phrases and vital truths

No true democrat would have permitted it to happen.

If George W. Bush could not visit our Parliament without shutting the place down, treating its occupants like near-criminals, and privileging his own entourage's petty needs over our constitutional rules, protocols and traditions, then he shouldn't have come at all. And if John W. Howard wanted a personal, 'working visit' with no obligation to observe bipartisan niceties 'in precisely the same way' as Australia had done when Bush Senior dropped by, he had no right to convene our Parliament so Bush Junior could speak there.

In the 1997 Sir Robert Menzies Memorial Lecture in London, Howard had said of his self-proclaimed political mentor:

'Menzies had a deep respect for the political freedoms and personal liberties, the parliamentary democracy, the rule of law, and a free press that were Britain's great gift to Australia. It is no exaggeration to say that these principles constitute the foundations on which Australia's strengths as a nation are built.'

Yet had Menzies been there to witness the way Howard treated that 'great gift' on 23 October last year he might have stormed around our national House in a regal rage, ramming a copy of his famous 1942 wartime broadcast 'The Task of Democracy' into every Liberal Party face he encountered:

'What then, must democracy do if it is to be a real force in the new world? It must recapture the vision of the good of man as the purpose of government. And it must restore the authority and prestige of Parliament as the supreme organic expression of self-government. The truth is that ever since the wise men gathered about the village tree in the Anglo Saxon village of early England, the notion of free self-government has run like a thread throughout our history. The struggle for freedom led an English Parliament to make war on its king and execute him at the seat of government, confined kingship itself to the Parliamentary domain, established the cabinet system and responsibility, set in place the twin foundations of the sovereignty of Parliament and the rule of law on which our whole civil edifice is built.

The sovereignty of Parliament – that is a great phrase and a vital truth. If only we could all understand it to the full, what a change we would make! Sovereignty is the quality of kingship, and democracy brings it to the poor man's door.'

Robert Menzies was a great Australian democrat. John Howard is a democratic fraud.

11

The Forgotten People

In our time, we must decide our own belief.
Either freedom is the privilege of an elite few, or it is the
right and capacity of all humanity

George Bush, address to the Australian Parliament, 23 October 2003

There are fascist tendencies in all countries – a sort of latent
tyranny . . . Suppression of attack, which is based upon suppression
of really free thought, is the instinctive weapon of the vested
interest . . . great groups which feel their power are at once subject
to tremendous temptations to use that power so as to limit the
freedom of others

Robert Menzies, 'Freedom of Speech and Expression', from
***The Forgotten People* radio broadcasts, 1942**

15 June 1989

Prime Minister Hawke commends to the House of Representatives a government motion expressing outrage at the Tiananmen Square massacre of 4–5 June: 'The unanimous passage of this motion will mean that not merely the Government but the Parliament and the People of Australia will have put on the record for all time the totally unacceptable nature of the barbarity which has been practised and the tragedy which has eventuated in China.'

The motion is carried unanimously.

5 September 1995

In the company of Michael Lightowler, Australia's ambassador to China, and Carmen Lawrence, Minister for Women, I tour a site near Beijing hosting women from around the world, gathered for the United Nations World Conference on Women. We see Chinese police and women representing China's puppet regime in Tibet assault two Tibetan-born Australian women peacefully protesting against China's brutal occupation of their land of birth, as is their right under the host nation agreement between the UN and China. Mr Lightowler grabs our citizens and puts them in his car.

Led by a Chinese security officer, a large group of the harassers surrounds the car and hurls abuse. The security officer bumps Lightowler and tells the Australians to get out of the car.

Lightowler yells, 'I'm the Australian Ambassador. These two people are Australian citizens and I have consular responsibilities to protect them.'

An angry Minister for Foreign Affairs, Senator Gareth Evans, directs Lightowler to 'personally make strong representations about the unacceptable treatment of the Australian women'.

19 August 2003

John Howard announces that Chinese President Hu Jintao has accepted his invitation to visit Australia. Without prior consultation with Parliament, he decides that Hu will address it – in defiance of what a unanimous all-party Senate inquiry later finds was a 'widespread assumption' that only US presidents would be so honoured, to reciprocate for Australian prime ministers invited to address the US Congress.

8 October 2003

Howard writes to the House of Representatives and the Senate seeking their consent. Despite disquiet among the Liberals, other parties and Independents, the two major parties quash their concern for fear that rebuffing Howard would harm Australia's trade relationship with China. The House of Representatives consents.

9 October 2003

The Senate consents, over the objections of Brian Harradine, the Greens and the Democrats, who all urge that Hu should instead address a function in Parliament's Great Hall.

Senator Harradine says:

'Whatever else might be said about President Bush, at least he is the democratically elected head of the United States. China is a one party state, and the people of China continue to be oppressed by a one party state. This is a sad day if we accept a proposal that we fete President Hu in the democratically elected chamber of this parliament to address its members, all of whom have been democratically elected and stand against gross violations of human rights. Let us take a stand on this.'

Senator Bob Brown says:

'[Howard's invitation] is all to do with money, the big dollar. It is a decision that is abhorrent to those of us who value human rights, human dignity, democracy, and liberty – the very things that Prime Minister Howard said he stood for in going to war in Iraq. These ideals would be sacrificed for this "ceremonial day". [President Hu] was the supreme leader in 1989 in the crackdown on Tibetans in Lhasa. He was there; he directed it. Forty people were killed and hundreds were imprisoned. The right of religious expression and political rights were totally taken away under sufferance of death and torture of the seven million people of Tibet. Since then he had a major role in the crackdown in Tiananmen Square, for which an earlier Prime Minister of this country shed tears. This man is now being invited to take the podium in the House of Representatives, with the elected representatives of this parliament muzzled. If Prime Minister Howard were in China and moved to represent the Liberal Party, President Hu would put him in jail. If Opposition Leader Simon Crean were in China and moved to set up either an independent trade union or the Labor Party, he would go to jail.'

Soon after Parliament's consent is obtained, Chinese Ambassador Tao visits Speaker Neil Andrew and Senate

President Paul Calvert to stress his 'hope' that 'there would be no demonstrations [and] that the President would not be embarrassed by any people demonstrating and causing disruption'. He mentions Bob Brown by name. Andrew and Calvert then order that protesters must gather down the hill and out of sight.

There'll be no need for pot plants this time. President Hu will slip into Parliament House through a side door.

(Revealed in Senate Estimates by Calvert on 3 November 2003.)

21 October 2003
The Chinese Embassy sends the following email to Fairfax newspapers:

'President Hu Jintao of China will soon come to visit Australia. This visit will be a major event in China–Australia relations with profound significance. Now both the Chinese and Australian sides are working to ensure the smoothness and success of the visit. However, we have learnt that some anti-China forces in Australia, such as organizations for independence of Tibet or Falungong, are planning to disrupt the visit by issuing open letter or putting up political advertisements in local papers at the time of the President's visit. To make sure that the visit will be free from such disruption, we hope that your paper will not publish their open letter, carry their political advertisements or any of their propaganda.

It is our wish that with the success of the visit by President Hu, the friendly relations and cooperation between the two countries will grow further.

Yours sincerely,

Feng Tie

Press Counsellor, Chinese Embassy in Canberra'

Fairfax newspapers reply:

'I'm afraid that our policy on accepting or refusing advertisements does not provide for such requests. It is, naturally, our wish that relations between Australia and China should continue to improve. However, we do not believe that goal would be served by censoring advertisements or other legitimate expressions of opinion.

Kind regards,

Michael Gill

Australian Financial Review editor-in-chief'

The Chinese Ambassador now tells Andrew he fears people might falsely use the invitations of official guests of parliamentarians to sit in the public gallery of the chamber. Andrew gives permission for Chinese Embassy staff to join Parliament's security officers to vet guests, with photographic ID required if the Chinese so demand.

(Admitted by Andrew in a statement to the House of Representatives on 3 November 2003.)

23 October 2003

Andrew defies the rules of the joint meeting agreed to by the Parliament for 23 October, which decrees an immediate adjournment after President Bush's speech to Parliament, and at Tony Abbott's request suspends Greens senators Bob Brown and Kerry Nettle for twenty-four hours so they cannot attend the Hu speech in the chamber. The expulsion also breaches the chamber's rules, which require that a vote be taken on expulsion if two or more people call out no to an expulsion order. (Several voices are clearly heard saying no.)

A Senate committee will later find that Andrew also had no power to order a senator to leave because he has no authority over senators. The Clerk of the Senate, Harry Evans, will also advise that Brown and Nettle could have sought an urgent injunction in the High Court to annul the expulsion order as unconstitutional, creating an international incident.

Yet Andrew issues an unprecedented directive to Parliament House staff to use 'preventative force' if necessary to stop senators Brown and Nettle from entering the House of Representatives to hear Hu's speech at the joint sitting on 24 October. Calvert countersigns the order without seeking the advice of his Senate clerk, Evans, or anyone else on its legality. Appalled, Evans instructs Senate staff that 'no Senate officer is to lay hands on a Senator or physically interfere with a Senator in any way'. He will later explain to Senate Estimates: 'The basis of it, firstly, was that it would be highly undesirable to have Senate officers assaulting a

Senator; secondly, that the authority for keeping Senators out of a meeting of the Senate was extremely dubious, to say the least.'

Andrew also makes the unprecedented decision that official guests of the Greens – Australian citizens of Tibetan descent Dhondup Phun Tsok and Mrs Tsering Deki Tshokoto, and Chin Jin, an Australian of Chinese descent and Chair of the Federation for a Democratic China – will be banned from sitting in the open public gallery. Calvert consents.

Neither Andrew nor Calvert advises the Greens' parliamentarians that their guests will be diverted from the public gallery.

24 October 2003

Speaker Andrew and Senate President Calvert wait at the side entrance of Parliament House to greet President Hu. A white car pulls up but instead of Hu, Chinese Foreign Minister Li Zhaoxing alights to express 'some concerns'. Andrew, Calvert and the Foreign Minister adjourn to Andrew's office, where Li says Hu is worried about 'two Green Senators in the chamber and three guests – "dissidents" he called them – in the gallery, who were likely to interrupt the President's speech'. Li names Chin Jin.

Andrew assures Li that the Greens' senators will not get in, and that Chin Jin will not be in the public gallery. 'The Speaker repeatedly gave them assurances, as best he could, that that was not going to happen. They seemed satisfied with that.'

(Revealed by Calvert to Senate Estimates on 3 November 2003.)

When the Australian Tibetans arrive at Parliament House Chinese agents point them out to Australian security, who call Andrew. The security officers take them to the enclosed, soundproofed gallery. They cannot follow Hu's speech because Andrew does not provide translation devices.

Chin Jin is in the office of his host, Greens MP Michael Organ, when Organ is told the fate of the two Tibetan guests. Two officials from the Department of Foreign Affairs escort Chin Jin to the security check area, then into the soundproofed area. Two Chinese officials closely watch the three guests while talking on mobile phones.

Three Parliament House security officers block senators Brown and Nettle from entering the House of Representatives. Senator Brian Harradine boycotts Hu's speech. John Howard makes no mention of human rights or democracy in his welcome to Hu, but stresses the trade relationship.

Several Liberals refuse to applaud Hu's speech, including NSW Senator Bill Heffernan, who also pointedly fails to use his translation device during the speech.

After Hu's speech, NSW Liberal Senator Marise Payne muses over coffee, 'I have to say something about Tibet.'

At the joint Hu–Howard press conference, Howard states, 'I can say very confidently that it is a strong relationship built on mutual respect for each other's traditions.'

That evening Speaker Neil Andrew refuses to tell the Australian people what he's done, declining to comment when the media calls. The next day the *Sydney Morning Herald* and the *Australian* break the story of the Chinese Foreign Minister's intervention.

27 October 2003
Chin Jin writes to Webdiary:

'I am one of the Greens guests to Hu's address to the Australian Parliament.

I want to say that the occurrence in Canberra last Friday put the Australian Government and Chinese leader Hu Jintao on test, and both failed. Not long ago, Hu said the CCP [Chinese Communist Party] would not employ their traditional approach in dealing with opposition. Last Friday was a test to his words; Hu failed to keep his political promise and employed the same measures to pressure the Australian Government to ban three Greens guests access to his speech. That meant that what the Chinese leaders say is one thing, and what they do is another thing.

The Howard Government also failed the test. The principle and spirit of democracy could be thrown into garbage when confronting the lure of economical interests.

Senator Brown and his colleagues are great heroes of this democratic country. They stand up and speak up for the values of democracy, for those who are suffocated in

China, including Tibet. [T]his man of courage and principle had set me up a brilliant example to achieve democracy and freedom in China, no matter how many hardships I will encounter.'

18 November 2003
Paul Bourke, Executive Officer of the Australia Tibet Council, sends a submission to a Senate committee investigating the events of October 23 and 24:

'The exclusion of the Tibetans represents an extension onto Australian soil of the denial of rights that Tibetans suffer in their own land. It is hoped that the unfortunate exclusion of the Australian public from our own Parliament at the behest of an undemocratic foreign government is not repeated in the future.'

6 February 2004
Labor leader Mark Latham says a Labor government would ask the House of Representatives to elect an Independent Speaker to restore the honour of Parliament. He says either of the two NSW country Independents, Peter Andren and Tony Windsor, would make 'fine' Speakers.

12

The Girl We (Almost) Left Behind

Australia's first military casualty in the war against terrorism was farewelled yesterday by his widow and the baby he never knew . . . [Kylie Russell] chose to bury [her husband] in a grassy grave surrounded by bushland and kangaroos

Sydney Morning Herald, 2 March 2002

Halfway through his speech to the Australian Parliament on 23 October the President of the United States said, 'In Afghanistan, the first casualty among America's allies was Australian: Special Air Service Sergeant Andrew Russell. This afternoon, I will lay a wreath at the Australian War Memorial, in memory of Sergeant Russell and the long line of Australians who have died in service to this nation.'

On the Opposition benches, Labor MP for the Perth seat of Cowan, Vietnam veteran Graham Edwards, blinked. Kylie Russell lived in his electorate and the Parliament's most respected veterans' advocate had met her after the vehicle in which her husband was travelling drove over a landmine on 16 February 2002. Andrew Russell was Australia's first combat death since Vietnam and Edwards thought he'd have heard if his widow was in Canberra. At the first opportunity he made a call.

Kylie was grocery shopping in Perth with Leisa – born eleven days before her father's death – when Edwards rang. It was the first she'd heard that Bush would lay a wreath, let alone one in honour of her husband. She turned off her mobile to avoid the media.

'What do you do in that situation?' Kylie said later. 'Do you just stand there, or go and finish the grocery shopping before going home and falling apart?'

The *West Australian*'s Robert Taylor was in Canberra to help cover the Bush visit and confirmed that, Bush's praise for Sergeant Russell notwithstanding, Kylie and Leisa had not been invited to the wreath-laying ceremony. After conferring with his Canberra-based colleague Karen Middleton, he rang the Prime Minister's office to find out why.

Because it was the first the PM knew of the dedication, he was told.

Bush laid his wreath. Robert wrote the story for his paper. Kylie Russell went home in shock. No one in the government – no one – bothered to contact her. She would hear nothing from John Howard – the man who sent her husband to war – for another week.

The next day her electoral representative, Graham Edwards, hand-delivered a letter to the Prime Minister's office:

'I write to urge you to contact the widow of Sgt Andrew Russell, and apologise for her not being invited to attend the wreath-laying ceremony in honour of her husband at the War Memorial . . . Those who lost loved ones and those who were victims in Bali have been brought to Canberra on two occasions and quite deservedly treated with a great deal of compassion, sympathy and given much support in the process of healing . . .

Why was Mrs Russell not extended the same comfort and support at this most important time, when both you and the President of the United States made much of the sacrifices of our Defence personnel? Mrs Russell is a constituent of mine, and I know she has been very active in seeking a better deal for war widows, and that she has at times been critical of you, your Government and your Ministers. I believe the people of Australia would be affronted if this is the reason she was not invited to attend the ceremony at the War Memorial or the barbeque at The Lodge.'

It's hard to imagine how Kylie must have felt, yet with her husband's death surely hitting home all over again, and her official snubbing still sinking in, she found the civic grace and resolve to write this letter to the editor of the *West Australian* the next night after the ceremony:

'Despite one's opinion of George W. Bush and his visit to Australia, he is the President of the United States, and as such it is a great honour for me, my daughter and our family for him to honour my husband SGT Andrew Russell in his speech to Parliament and at the National War Memorial. His visit to the War Memorial should be viewed as an honour to all those fallen in the name of freedom. It is a shame that the leader of our own country has not shown this same honour to our veterans and widows. This outspoken widow has far from finished the campaign to improve veteran entitlements, and therefore will continue to be ignored by our own government as a result.'

Kylie had first put her head above the citizens' parapet after her husband's death to let Australians know what a raw deal the government gave the families of soldiers killed on active service. Andrew Russell's was entitled to a miserly $13,000 tax-free annual pension.

Miserly?

Well, the widow of a federal politician gets $50,000 a year. To pick a random comparison, John.

Webdiarist Polly Bush later pointed out that my sister Gay Alcorn had interviewed Kylie, now 30, for *The Age* in early 2003, describing her as 'a petite, pretty woman with a sandy-haired one-year-old baby on her knee, [who] has chosen not to play the silent heroine but to prod into the politics of war':

'One year on, she keeps almost frantically busy. She works part-time as a nurse, studies health education at night, and has forged close friendships with a few women whose husbands died in the police force or fighting fires. "As soon as I stop, it hits home and that's when I fall apart," she says. "I can't afford to fall apart because I've got a daughter who can't have her mother lying on the floor crying when I need to function 24 hours a day for her.

"Everyone knows John Howard only comes to Perth when the SAS [based in Perth] are going away, or when it's an election. He uses those guys extraordinarily to aid his political agenda, and he promises them all when they go away we'll look after your families, and as soon as anything happens he doesn't want to know about it." Mrs Russell says she is not fighting to improve her own position. She and Andrew had life insurance and had almost paid off their home. She is forsaking her privacy to help future war widows because something positive might come out of her husband's death.

"When Drew died I got the phone call from the Prime Minister and the phone call from the chief of the army. I had a visit from the Minister of Defence, the Minister of Veterans Affairs. Everyone wants to know you, everyone promises they will look after you," she says. "Then you start writing a few letters to these people, when you start realising that things aren't all that good and then no one, all of a sudden, wants to be your best friend.'"

Three days after being snubbed by John Howard, a distraught Kylie spoke briefly to her local paper just once, before retreating: 'I don't know if I wasn't invited because I have been a thorn in Mr Howard's side, but if so I hope he can live with himself after denying me and my daughter an opportunity to be part of something we would have remembered forever. No apology will bring that back.'

She gave that interview after Karen Middleton had tenaciously flushed out John Howard. That morning, on ABC TV's *Insiders* program, other guests were visibly startled when Middleton mentioned Thursday's fiasco – which only Karen's paper and the *Canberra Times* had reported – and incredulous at the PM's explanation: that he hadn't been *told* that the President was going to honour Andrew Russell.

So on his visit to thank Australia for our 'war on terror' sacrifices, Bush was supposed to jog the Australian war leader's memory about them? Lest he *forget*?

Come on, John.

So why, really, hadn't Kylie been invited to the wreath laying? Or to hear Bush speak in Parliament in person? Or to have lunch with him at the barbecue? The story was a personal one, yes, but these were valid questions journalists had a duty to pursue. Other Australian soldiers were still in wartime danger, their dependents daily stricken with anxiety. They, especially, had a right to have the question asked: why was the woman who had sacrificed more than any other Australian in the US-led 'war on terror' not John Howard's and George Bush's 'guest of honour' on 23 October 2003?

And why hadn't John Howard contacted Kylie Russell to apologise?

The PM, watching *Insiders*, rang his chief spinner Tony O'Leary to order an urgent phone call. But not to Kylie Russell – to Karen Middleton. O'Leary withdrew the first embarrassing 'explanation', and Karen's Monday by-line duly passed on Howard's next excuse to Western Australians – including, presumably, Kylie Russell.

'It was an "oversight", and the Prime Minister will be writing to her to apologise,' his spokesman told Karen.

Howard's strategy was soon clear: to 'kill' the story. It might have worked, except that Karen felt personally bound to press him for an explanation of the 'oversight'. I also picked up the thread – I felt Howard's treatment of Kylie Russell shamed every Australian. However, Karen advised me not to contact Kylie: every media call was reminding her that the first time her daughter had seen her father was in a coffin. Instead I focused on Howard's accountability – the right target. Two facts eventually became clear.

1   As with the Bush barbecue list, Howard decided who would attend the wreath laying – including which ministers and defence personnel. Howard's attendees included members of the SAS who had served in Afghanistan with Andrew Russell. Veterans' Affairs Minister Danna Vale – who'd personally met Kylie – knew nothing about the ceremony except this: when to be there and where to stand. It was John Howard's 'baby', and the Russells' wasn't invited.

2   No one outside Howard's personal office, including

his department, which administered the practical arrangements, had knowledge of Bush's special tribute until they heard his Parliament speech. (We still don't know if Howard or his staff did.)

So for once Howard couldn't shift the blame to a public servant, on a story that threatened to trash his carefully crafted image as the 'Anzacs' Anzac' PM. To salvage it, Howard treated Kylie Russell not as a human being, but as a pressing political problem to be neutralised.

Howard made no public statement, instead bunkering down behind his spinners in stonewall mode. It's a painfully familiar story to Canberra journos. Here's the script.

On Monday, 27 October, I asked Howard's media minder David Luff how this 'oversight' could possibly have occurred.

'It was an oversight that she wasn't invited.'

Yes, but '*How* could you forget to invite the widow?'

Long silence.

Then: 'That's all I want to say. We're going to write to her, and it's best not to discuss it until she receives the letter.'

'Will you write today?

'Shortly.'

'Today?'

'Shortly.'

'Today?'

'Shortly.'

Sigh.

'When did the government know the wreath was going to be laid for Mrs Russell's husband?'

Long silence.

Then: 'We're writing to Mrs Russell so it's not appropriate —'

'David, that's *not* the question I asked.'

Long, long silence.

I finally broke it by asking if he could put me through to the logistics person in the Department of the Prime Minister and Cabinet who oversaw the Bush trip and might be able to help. David said he'd get back to me. He didn't. Instead, by early evening, he'd been authorised to tell the media that Howard's letter to Kylie had now been sent.

On Wednesday I rang Tony O'Leary to ask when Kylie would receive it.

'We put it in the mail.'

Ordinary post?

'What do you suggest?' he snarled.

Hand-delivered, as Graham Edwards's letter to Howard had been? Or Express Post?

Oh, and did Howard's written apology explain the 'oversight'?

'He sent it to Kylie Russell – why don't you ask her? We're not answering questions about the letter until she gets it.'

I tried one last time: exactly how had that 'oversight' occurred?

'I'll inquire how it occurred.'

Was Howard reviewing procedures to ensure such an oversight would not happen again?

'I don't know.'

He didn't call back.

Kylie Russell received Howard's letter a *week* after Bush laid a wreath in her husband's honour. Graham Edwards received his reply the same day as Kylie. Karen Middleton, who had been speaking to Kylie, sensed that Howard's letter – which she said was in similar terms to Graham's – may have made matters worse, with its bureaucratic tone. But it was the lack of accompanying mementos that really hurt.

John Howard sent her no video of the wreath laying, no photographs, nothing.

Personally, I find it almost impossible to accept Howard's stated excuse at face value. This was a thank-you visit for our 'war on terror' sacrifices, after all, and Australia has made only one 'ultimate' sacrifice in that war so far; also some of Andrew Russell's own Afghanistan comrades were present at the War Memorial that day. To me, it beggars belief that Kylie and her daughter were an 'oversight'.

Still, if we do accept that, Howard's delay in apologising and his grudging language in dealing with Kylie's hurt is a glimpse behind the carefully managed Howard façade.

It is also illuminating for larger reasons to reveal the subtly different ways and contexts in which our Prime Minister *is* prepared to concede that certain past mistakes – for which he is not *personally* responsible, of course – might be worthy of a prime ministerial apology.

Here's the letter John Howard sent to Graham Edwards on 29 October:

'Dear Mr Edwards,

I have received your letter of October 24 about Mrs Russell.

As you may now know, Mrs Russell's failure to be invited to attend the wreath laying ceremony at the Australian War Memorial last Thursday was a most regrettable oversight.

President Bush had indicated in his speech on the same day that he would dedicate the laying of his wreath at the Tomb of the Unknown Soldier to her late husband, Sergeant Russell, and the long line of Australians who had died in service for our country.

I can assure you that neither Mrs Russell's activities nor criticisms of the Government in relation to war widows in any way contributed to her failure to be invited.

I have written to Mrs Russell extending the Government's deep regret that she was not invited to the War Memorial at which her presence and that of her daughter would have been entirely appropriate.

Yours sincerely,

John Howard'

Through Karen, Kylie Russell has given me permission to publish the Prime Minister's letter to her for the first time:

'Dear Mrs Russell,

Through a most regrettable oversight you were not invited to the ceremony at the Australian War Memorial last Thursday at which the President of the United States laid a wreath at the Tomb of the Unknown Soldier.

The President had indicated in his speech earlier that day that he would dedicate that wreath to your late husband Andrew and the long line of Australians who had died in service for our country. In doing so, President Bush also honoured the service of Australia's military to the cause of freedom.

I am very sorry that you were not invited to an occasion at which your presence and that of your daughter Leisa would have been entirely appropriate and, I know, moving for you.

On behalf of the Government I extend to you my apologies for this oversight.

Yours sincerely,

John Howard'

Only Karen Middleton and I were still on the story – Howard's feet-dragging and his minders' stonewalling had seen to that. Edwards had obtained Kylie's permission to ask Howard a question when Parliament resumed the next week, and Karen and I wrote weekend columns on the fading affair, hoping to help get Graham's question listed. Mine recorded online fury. Webdiarist Greg Carroll asked, 'Hasn't Mr Howard heard of the telephone? He's really got a problem with that word "sorry", hasn't he?' John Boase wrote, 'Anyone who could remember to invite [former Wallaby captain] John Eales to a barbecue could SURELY remember to invite Mrs Russell to a wreath laying.'

That Friday John Howard had warned that 900 Australian soldiers still faced danger in Iraq: 'I certainly haven't forgotten them . . . naturally we are concerned about their safety.'

Hang on, John. You personally decided your wreath-laying guest list and 'forgot' to include Kylie Russell; you also 'forgot' to put her on the barbecue guest list you personally compiled – yet you 'remembered' to include those six Australian businessmen whose companies between them had donated more than a million dollars to your Liberal Party.

Does money, not blood sacrifice, earn inclusion in 'your' Australia, John?

Graham Edwards lost both legs in Vietnam and so remained seated on 3 November to ask John Howard his first question in our Parliament since George W. Bush and Hu Jintao had addressed it:

'How does the Prime Minister respond to the statement made by Mrs Russell, in referring to his [oversight], when she said: "I hope he can live with himself after denying me and my daughter an opportunity to be a part of something we would have remembered forever."'? Has this oversight been investigated, and can he advise the Australian people how such an oversight could possibly occur?'

Howard stood to make his very first public comment on the matter:

'I am indeed very upset that the oversight did occur. I want to renew to this House the apology that I have extended in writing to Mrs Russell. I want to take the opportunity of saying that, whatever the circumstances of it, as the head of government, I accept responsibility as inevitably in these things the head of government must. I also take the opportunity of saying to the honourable gentleman that suggestions made in some newspaper articles – and, indeed, contained in a letter that he wrote to me – that the failure to invite her might have been in some way due to the fact that she had been critical of government policy in relation to benefits for the families of deceased Defence personnel have no substance of any kind – no substance at all. I can only say that I am profoundly sorry that it occurred. I apologise to the lady concerned. It was an inexcusable oversight, and I can assure the honourable member that, whatever the lead-up to it was, it was not malicious. It was a mistake and, as the head of government, I accept responsibility.'

But did he? Did he really? Here's the active sentence again: 'I want to take the opportunity of saying that, whatever the circumstances of it, as the head of government, I accept responsibility, as inevitably in these things the head of government must.'

Notice the subtle side-stepping of *personal* blame? Notice that he gave no explanation for how the 'oversight' occurred either, or said whether he'd investigated it?

I watched Howard give that answer, and I watched his backbenchers' heads drop as he gave it.

'How come he gave a much stronger apology to the Parliament than to Kylie Russell *herself*?' I asked a gallery colleague as we left the chamber. ('Very upset . . . inexcusable oversight . . . profoundly sorry . . .')

'Because he was on TV,' he replied.

The next day I wandered down to Aussies café in Parliament House after watching John Faulkner question Prime Minister and Cabinet departmental staffers in Senate Estimates. They had said Howard's office was handling the Kylie matter, and I'd given Faulkner some background on the story and suggested he press the matter. He declined. Labor wasn't keen on playing politics with personal tragedy, he said. He was right: there was nothing more to be said.

Karen Middleton sat with Graham Edwards, both looking glum. Kylie was going bush, Graham said, to get some peace – she was doing it hard. Karen had asked colleagues at ABC TV to put together a video of the wreath laying, and Fairfax photographer Penny Bradfield was gathering some good stills. Karen would ensure that Kylie would have a record of the moment the world's most powerful man honoured her late husband by name.

Andrew's daughter, too.

What the hell happened to Australia on 23 and 24 October 2003?

The Bush and Hu visits were exercises in democratic exclusion, and Kylie Russell was the human face of that exclusion. That *attempted* exclusion – for her strength and dignity and courage throughout give all of us hope that attempts by our leaders to sideline the Australian people from our democratic process will, if the media remains vigilant, always fail.

Karen Middleton reminded me that even the toughest journalist's tool kit can include a tender human touch.

As Kylie Russell went bush, John Howard went to London to attend yet another grandiose Anzac ceremony: opening a new memorial to honour Australia's fallen in the bloody European wars of last century. It was a huge, complex logistical undertaking, but Howard had long planned it with maximum care and diligence.

It was profoundly important to him *personally*, he explained, since both his father and grandfather had made enormous sacrifices during the Great War, although neither had been killed, thankfully.

It went off like clockwork. There were no 'oversights', and no one was left behind.

Part Four

Their Au$tralia

13

I had coffee with George Brandis after his 'Greens are Nazis' speech to Parliament, and said a number of my Jewish friends were very upset by his remarks. He looked startled. He said that after he'd made it he'd rung Colin Rubenstein, head of the privately – and secretly – funded think tank the Australia/Israel & Jewish Affairs Council (AIJAC), who'd endorsed it. On *Lateline* the next night Brandis said Rubenstein had contacted him to say 'he supported it and he was pleased it had been given'.

'Colin Rubenstein doesn't represent mainstream Jewish opinion,' I replied, appalled, 'and many Jewish people vote Greens.' George Brandis's mouth fell open.

I've avoided participating in debates on the Israel–Palestine question for the same reason that most journalists and politicians in Australia and the United States have. History professor Juan Cole of Michigan University put the reason succinctly: 'Most people in public life have frankly been intimidated into just being quiet about it (including every single sitting member of the US Congress, not one of whom ever criticises any action of the Sharon government and survives the next election); this is an incredible degree of political intimidation.'

This intimidation, and the internal pressure on those in the Jewish community who do not support Zionism or the Sharon government in Israel to shut up about it outside the community, means people such as Colin Rubenstein and AIJAC Chairman Mark Leibler dominate the media and politics on the matter, purporting to speak for the Jewish community. There are, however, elected community groups in each state, which join together in the Executive Council of Australian Jewry, established in 1944. The Jewish spokesman for the Council had condemned Brandis's comparison of the Greens with the Nazis.

At the time, debate was raging about the powerful behind-the-scenes lobbying led by the Rubenstein–Leibler crowd to force NSW Premier Bob Carr not to present the Sydney Peace Prize to Palestinian Dr Hanan Ashrawi.

A Jewish friend cried out in conversation with me, 'I feel ashamed to be Jewish!'

'No. Please don't be ashamed, please,' I said. 'One of my heroes is Ron Castan [who before his death ran the Mabo case for Aboriginal land rights in the High Court]. His is the true Jewish way – to struggle for human rights for all. Don't be ashamed – get involved!'

So I gulped three times and asked the only Jewish member of the NSW Parliament, the Greens' Ian Cohen, to write a piece for Webdiary on how he felt about the Brandis attack and the Ashrawi furore. I published it and one by my colleague Antony Loewenstein supporting Ashrawi, to find that a Jewish reader called my editor demanding immediate removal of the whole entry from the website.

However, once attempts to censor two Jewish Australians were out of the way, the door opened to a fantastic

Webdiary dialogue that included Jewish, Muslim and other Australians on both sides of the debate anxious, even relieved, to participate.

The night Kerry O'Brien interviewed Hanan Ashrawi on the *7.30 Report*, I suggested to the *Sydney Morning Herald*'s Canberra intern that she have a look. She was mesmerised.

'I've never heard the Palestinian view before,' she said. 'I never knew there was another side to the story.'

I then commissioned Antony Loewenstein to research the Ashrawi saga for this book.

By the way, I sought Colin Rubenstein's comment on George Brandis's claim that he'd endorsed the Greens and Nazis speech. He repeatedly refused to answer my question during a lengthy email exchange. And I copped this in an article on AIJAC's website:

'Probably the worst accusation came from Margo Kingston, web diarist for the *Sydney Morning Herald*. She claimed on Nov. 14 that Jewish backers of Sharon "seem to have the power, money and clout to dominate public debate and wield enormous political and financial power behind the scenes. The Ashrawi debacle has exposed this secret power." A more clearly stated racist conspiracy theory I have never seen in the mainstream media in Australia.'

M.K.

Taking Back the Power:
Hanan Ashrawi

By Antony Loewenstein

> *This whole debate has been invaluable in opening up the
> ability of people in or around the Jewish community to have a view
> that was only tolerated before*
>
> **Ian Cohen, NSW Greens MP**

The Hanan Ashrawi affair left me fiercely proud of my
Judaism.

My maternal grandparents arrived in Melbourne from
Vienna in 1938, and my paternal grandparents in Perth from
Dresden in 1939. All four had fled Nazi persecution; all four
were regarded in Australia as enemy aliens. My grandparents
lived in the general community, but were not allowed radios
and had to report weekly to the police during the war. It was
a bizarre war for Antipodean Germans. Some males, not
even naturalised, were placed in the Australian Army for the
duration. Others, including a number of family friends, were
transported to Australian internment camps – Tatura in Victoria and Hay in NSW – although conditions were markedly
superior to those of refugees today.

Some things never change, though. Here's the President
of the Victorian Legislative Assembly in 1939 referring to

my grandparents and others – the tiresome Jewish 'reffos' – as 'slinking rat-faced men, under five feet in height, with chest of 20 inches, willing to work for a few shillings pocket money plus keep . . . it is horrible to think such people would marry Australian girls or bring their under-nourished women here'.

Most of my extended family were unable to leave Europe and were killed in the death camps of Poland.

I was brought up in a Jewish home that was progressive but observant; all festivals were celebrated and I regularly attended synagogue. Then one day I brought home a girlfriend who was Polish and non-Jewish – an unacceptable combination. My parents rejected her. They couldn't understand why I didn't feel uncomfortable about Polish 'involvement' in murdering family members. I was nineteen.

I began moving away from observance as I sensed Jewish intolerance, and began questioning the underpinnings of my belief. Then I started fighting my religion's assumptions about Israel and Zionism.

I had been taught from a young age at Sunday school that Zionism was the right of the Jewish people to their own homeland and sovereignty over the land of Israel. Despite centuries of attempted assimilation, early Zionists believed that Jews throughout the world were continually persecuted, making a Jewish homeland essential. The formation of Israel in 1948, partly due to the world's guilt over the Holocaust's devastation, was a victory for Zionism; the British and American power brokers had little interest in Palestinian self-determination. Today the state of democracy in Israel is far removed from the tolerant, socialist utopia that was the dream of Theodore Herzl, the father of Zionism.

> [Hamas spiritual leader] Sheik Yassin is marked for death and he had better dig deep underground, where he won't be able to tell the difference between day and night. We will find him in his tunnels and liquidate him.
>
> **Zeev Boim, Israel's Deputy Defence Minister, on Army Radio, 17 January 2004 (Yassin was assassinated on 22 March 2004)**

For many who suffered in the Holocaust 'Never again' is an overarching mantra. In an Israel stricken with suicide-murderers that sentiment is an urgent imperative and a daily silent plea. But can there ever be a hierarchy of suffering? And what of Palestinian nationalist ambitions?

I am no longer an observant Jew. If I had to label myself I would choose 'culturally Jewish', to try to capture that sensibility that merges a deep knowledge of Judaic history and tradition with a secular embrace of humanism and compassion. Am I therefore still 'truly' Jewish? I would hardly be as interested as I am in Israel, Palestine and twenty-first-century Zionism if I'd been born atheist. And religiously lapsed or not, I have absorbed the values of my parents, who brought me up to believe in testing, questioning and challenging established power.

Seeking out the truth.

If ever Jews needed such intellectual tools it was during the Hanan Ashrawi affair.

The Ashrawi story is both very simple and very complicated. The simple version: Hanan Ashrawi, a Palestinian and human rights activist, campaigner for women's rights and Christian, was chosen as the 2003 recipient of the hitherto uncontroversial Sydney Peace Prize. Manufacturing both 'Jewish' outrage and sickening slanders, a small number of powerful, self-declared Jewish 'community leaders' set out to intimidate, threaten and bully the award committee into changing its mind. Along the way some non-Jewish politicians buckled under the pressure, a few others stood firm and, thanks to a small number of courageous public figures and journalists, the Jewish and non-Jewish community got a rare glimpse of how unseen power is wielded in Australia.

The controversy also exposed to a wider Australian public the mechanics of the global information war over how to get peace in the Middle East, the core issue in the intensifying confrontation between the Islamic world and the West.

It also showed how fundamentalists seek to hijack the debate in an escalating war of ideas between Zionist absolutism, whose template is the Likudian touchstone of a holy land given to the Jews alone by God, and Jewish humanism, with its belief that the land must be fairly shared with the Palestinians, who have equal rights.

Baruch Kimmerling, a professor of sociology at the Hebrew University of Jerusalem, believes 'politicide' is at work, which 'has, as its ultimate goal, the dissolution of the Palestinians' existence as a legitimate social, political and economic entity'. Israel continues to build settlements on Palestinian land in defiance of international law and numerous UN resolutions, and in April 2004 George Bush unilaterally declared the West Bank settlements permanent.

Of the Jewish community worldwide, Kimmerling says 'too often the Jewish "Diaspora patriotism" makes overtime. Most of them have an over-simplified black and white perception of the Jewish–Arab conflict and automatically presume that everything the Israelis are doing is correct and just, and every Arab is evil and a terrorist.'

This perception has also prevailed in Australia, and Kimmerling wrote to New South Wales Premier Bob Carr supporting the choice of Ashrawi: 'There are few international figures in the present,' he argued, 'who deserve a peace prize more than the outstanding Palestinian leader, intellectual and peace activist – Dr Hanan Ashrawi.'

The Israeli–Palestinian agony is the definitive security debate of the day, shaping all others, and it came to Australia with Ashrawi.

For the first time a Palestinian voice was clearly heard by the nation. 'We [Palestinians] had to spend decades proving to people that ours was not a land without a people, to give to a people without a land,' Hanan Ashrawi told a public forum in Sydney after accepting her prize in November 2003.

In the power struggle to prevent her voice being heard and any legitimacy bestowed on Palestinian claims, a number of individuals found themselves caught up in manoeuvring behind the scenes. One of the bravest was Bob Carr, and one of the most unlikely was a young Sydney journalist who emailed the Premier's office hoping for an interview and got the shock of his professional life when Carr's spin doctor, Walt Secord, rang back in mid-November 2003 to ask, 'When suits you, Antony?'

Bob Carr is one of the most hard-headed media manipulators in political Australia. On this issue, however, he put himself equally hard on the line on principle. I found him frank, passionate and peeved at the way certain of his own powerful donors and supporters in the Zionist community had conducted themselves over Ashrawi.

The pressure on Carr to back down began with a Glenn Milne column in the *Australian* on 13 October 2003, liberally drawing on an Australia/Israel & Jewish Affairs Council press release. Milne wrote that Ashrawi's 'fluent, polished English, natty dress sense and passionate statements of the Palestinian position made her a media favourite in the West'. The 5 September AIJAC press release stated that: 'Her fluent, polished English, neat attire and passionate statements of the Palestinian position made her a media favourite in the West.' Milne's column trumpeted the internal agonising within the Labor Party over its virtually unqualified support for Israel, and linked it with the upcoming Ashrawi visit.

Bob Carr recalls: 'I got a call from [Labor powerbroker]

Laurie Brereton on the morning of the Glenn Milne article, saying "I strongly recommend in response to the article that you don't reconsider your position. It's very important that you don't be seen to pull out of this. Colin Rubenstein's hand is all over this."'

Carr said of the Executive Director of AIJAC:

'I do think [Rubenstein's] playing partisan politics. He's said to be close to the PM's office, he's a former candidate for Liberal preselection. At the Australian–American Leadership dialogue [a high-level meeting between both countries' business and political leaders] on August 14–16 2003, which was the first time the Ashrawi thing had been raised with me, he came up to me and said "Ashrawi is a Holocaust denier." I said that would concern me if it's true, and I don't know if it is true [there is no evidence that Ashrawi is a Holocaust denier] . . . Palestinians are a brave people and they've taken a brave risk for peace. And I thought that should be rewarded by a bit of recognition from an Australian politician whose got a record with engagement and support for Israel.'

In a stunning illustration of how politicised the Australian Defence Force has become since *Tampa* and September 11, Colonel Mike Kelly, an Australian Army officer serving in Baghdad, emailed Carr in early October demanding he abandon his support for Ashrawi: 'It would be hard to explain to a soldier here who has just lost both legs in a terrorist attack why an Australian State Premier (supposedly an ally in this war) has been in effect comforting the enemy.' His email naturally found its way onto the front page of the *Australian*.

Carr demanded Kelly butt out of domestic issues and be mindful that 'the Australian mission in Iraq is not to engage in a war with the Arab world or the Palestinians but to remove Saddam Hussein and find and destroy weapons of mass destruction'. And in a private letter to General Peter Cosgrove, Chief of the Defence Force, Carr demanded an explanation:

'If [Kelly] thinks he has a role in a domestic political debate he is wrong-headed. I object to a serving officer intervening [and] this decidedly breaks with tradition. I am not aware of any precedent. Colonel Kelly gave his communication to the media, or gave it to somebody who did. How does this fit with the relevant rules for a serving Army officer?'

Like Carr, the corporate sponsors of the peace prize – the City of Sydney, Gilbert & Tobin, PBL, Rio Tinto and Citigroup – were pressured by elements of the Zionist lobby to withdraw their financial support. Carr said he heard of 'one company which received pressure from New York, or a request from New York head office that they shouldn't be part of this'. (Carr was unwilling to reveal the name of the company or the CEOs with whom he spoke about this matter, though a source has confirmed that Citigroup's New York office was pressured to influence its Australian counterparts.) Representatives from all five sponsors have now said that various degrees of pressure were exerted on them to withdraw, with one senior executive revealing that 'people contacted all corporate sponsors to withdraw support and withdraw publicly'.

For some, inevitably, such pressure was too much. The then Sydney mayor Lucy Turnbull withdrew the City of Sydney's support for the peace prize just weeks after endorsing Ashrawi as the winner. 'I would be failing in my duty if I were not to take these hard decisions in the light of my conscience,' Turnbull said, before retreating into silence. The impression of surrender was overwhelming, although the mainstream media's pursuit of the story behind this development was almost non-existent. Many people saw a direct link to her husband's preselection battle in the federal seat of Wentworth, with its high proportion of Jewish voters. Bob Carr told me, '[Turnbull's withdrawal] made me all the more determined to do it. I presumed her pulling out was due to sensitivity to what was happening in Wentworth. My instincts as a politician tell me that.'

Former Federal Court judge Justice Marcus Einfeld suggested Lucy Turnbull's decision was power politics as usual:

'[Turnbull] is relatively inexperienced in politics, certainly in this type of political confrontation. I've known Lucy since she was a child. The heavies of the Jewish community would have been pretty heavy for Lucy, I would have thought. I wouldn't be surprised if some people tried to pressure Malcolm to pressure Lucy. I don't know if that is a fact, but I wouldn't be surprised.'

Initially the *Sydney Morning Herald*'s Alan Ramsey was the only mainstream journalist who shrugged off Zionist lobby intimidation. With the cold, cynical eyes of the veteran political reporter, he wrote that 'almost always, in politics, money is at the root of the greatest grovelling'. The Director of the Sydney Peace Foundation, Professor Stuart Rees, gave Ramsey the transcript of a stunning conversation between himself and former Foundation chairwoman Kathryn Greiner. 'I won't be subject to bullying and intimidation,' he had told Greiner. 'We are being threatened by members of a powerful group who think they have an entitlement to tell others what to do. This opposition is orchestrated.' Greiner responded with the brutal realities of the pressure being placed by Zionist forces on Sydney University, the Peace Foundation, the corporate sponsors of the prize and Bob Carr: 'They'll destroy what you've worked for. They are determined to show we made a bad choice. I think it's [businessman] Frank Lowy's money . . . The foundation will be destroyed.'

Frank Lowy, the billionaire owner of Westfield shopping centres, called Carr direct to question the Premier's motives. 'He is the only person from the Jewish community who rang me directly,' says Carr:

'[I]t was a courteous and respectful call. It wasn't lobbying, unless you argue that the mere fact that he made a call can be said to represent pressure. He simply said he'd been asked to sign a petition criticising me on this, and he wanted to pay the courtesy. I explained my position.'

Ramsey had blown the story wide open, yet mainstream media outlets barely responded to his initial column. A senior ABC journalist told me he thought Ramsey was shocked by this failure, because 'if he hadn't been, he wouldn't have come back and written that second article'.

Sydney University had refused the use of its Great Hall for the ceremony, and Ramsey's follow-up column revealed the reason: a senior member of the Jewish community had pressured Chancellor Kim Santow, who was anxious about future donations and financial support. A university staffer commented, 'The whole affair stinks like a dead rat under the floorboards.'

Ramsey's piece also challenged the Zionist lobby's reading of Israel–Palestine and took to task AIJAC's national Chairman Mark Leibler for his comments to ABC radio's Linda Mottram about Ashrawi's language. Asked about Ashrawi's insistence that all violence against civilians, 'whether [by] suicide bombers or Apache helicopters', be condemned, he had loftily asserted, 'What [she's] doing is equating those who blow up innocent civilians, women and children, with actions by a country to deal with terrorists. That's not good enough, because the Israeli violence [is] not violence. The Israeli action is there simply to protect the civilian population.'

Rees says that Ramsey's contribution to the debate was crucial: '[Ramsey's columns] exposed the business of the pressure [and] he linked into the international pressures that came from Israel and the Jewish community.' Even so, the ensuing media focus concentrated on various personality conflicts within the Jewish community rather than seriously investigating the depth and intricacy of Zionist influence on political power.

Most of that lobbying came out of Melbourne, home of the Australia/Israel & Jewish Affairs Council, and increasingly jarred with the more conciliatory tone emanating from Sydney. Yet Michael Gawenda – Editor-in-Chief of *The Age*, a Fairfax stablemate of the *Sydney Morning Herald* – didn't think the issue worth exploring.

'It was a very Sydney story,' he told me, 'which received little coverage in *The Age*, perhaps too little coverage.' Gawenda was being disingenuous; *The Age*'s fence-sitting editorial on Ashrawi indicated it would not pick up a story that was beginning to make Melbourne heavies Rubenstein and Leibler look out of touch with the emerging mood. '[*The Age*] said there has been a distortion of her [Ashrawi's] track record,' Gawenda advised me. 'We also said that Jews, like any other group, have a right to lobby and forcefully put their position. We were disturbed how quickly people reached for images of Jewish financial power and secret influence.' Yet such 'images' were exactly what had been exposed in Sydney as all too real.

In early 2004 the *Australian Jewish News* reported that political donations information released by the Australian Electoral Commission showed that the Liberal Party has been the most successful party in attracting support from Jewish donors and their associated companies. Among the donations was that large one from Frank Lowy, one of the invitees to Howard's barbecue for George Bush.

The Australia/Israel & Jewish Affairs Council is privately funded by several Melbourne business leaders, is philosophically right wing and has enjoyed great influence as the self-proclaimed voice of mainstream Judaism in Australia.

Stephen Rothman, President of the (elected) NSW Jewish Board of Deputies, says that AIJAC does represent mainstream Jewish opinion – although the robust discussions in the Jewish community during the Ashrawi affair, reflected in the *Australian Jewish News*, suggest otherwise.

AIJAC also vigorously and successfully claims to 'represent the interests of the Australian Jewish community' to politicians and the public, and its influence stretches across both major political parties. Mark Leibler and Colin Rubenstein have long-time associations with the Liberal Party: Rubenstein has run for Liberal preselection, while Leibler is a partner in the Melbourne law firm Arnold Bloch Leibler, for which John Howard gave a fiftieth anniversary speech in April 2003. Leibler was also one of the few invitees to the Howard barbecue for Bush. (Both Rubenstein and Leibler refused to be interviewed for this chapter. The only other person who refused was Lucy Turnbull.)

Federal Health Minister Tony Abbott, after a speech to the annual general meeting of the Victorian Zionist Council in late October 2003, joked, 'Did I get anything wrong? Colin [Rubenstein], you better correct it so I get the script right.' In the speech itself Abbott asked, 'What is it, then, [for Ashrawi] to proclaim moral equivalence between an Israeli leadership striving to preserve a liberal, pluralist democracy and a Palestinian leadership running a one-party statelet dedicated to destroying its neighbour?'

Mark Leibler could have sued for plagiarism.

John Howard and Alexander Downer were also happy to act as AIJAC proxies over Ashrawi's award. Downer was simultaneously transparent in his distaste for a Palestinian getting the prize at all and his means of undermining any who did: 'I'm surprised that anyone is being chosen from that region, but if you wanted to choose a Palestinian, you'd choose someone like [former Palestinian PM] Abu Mazen.' Howard publicly agreed with Downer's sentiments and tactics.

But Bob Carr sees a clear warning in the affair for the Zionist lobby. He feels they harmed their cause by being too sensitive to public expressions of the Palestinians' case:

'I think they're producing too much hostility among journalists, who are sick of being called to account as a result of complaints [to] their newspapers or TV stations from Colin Rubenstein and others. I think they should be much more relaxed about the fact that, in a pluralist media, there will be criticisms of Israel appearing.

I've got to caution them to be a little more selective about their fights with journalists, and I think whoever fed that [early] interpretation to Glenn Milne – I presume it was Colin Rubenstein – and whoever lobbied Lucy Turnbull – I don't know who that was – did a great disservice to the Israeli cause in Australia, and the Jewish community.'

These are the comments of a lifelong friend of Israel.

The Ashrawi affair had implications for the larger Australian community, not just the Jewish one. It exposed significant shortcomings in our political and media elite, and the way a small number of powerful figures could exert a disproportionate influence, often in underhand ways, on the workings of our democracy.

Amid the pressure on the peace prize committee to retract their decision, something curious began to happen in the Australian debate. By the end of October, after Ramsey's incendiary columns, unfamiliar voices started being heard in the public domain.

Our media is filled almost daily with images and stories of Middle East violence against civilians or military targets in Tel Aviv, Ramallah and Jenin. The Ashrawi affair introduced something new by blowing away some of the taboos around discussion of the conflict. For the first time people began to talk to each other openly and in good faith about complex, sensitive subjects that had their roots in the European horrors of the last century and the means by which the West dealt with its guilt, the creation of Israel.

Jewish groups invisible to the wider community were suddenly being heard. Barbara Bloch of the Sydney-based organisation Jews Against the Occupation says that 'the media started getting interested in the dispute within the community and that was probably one of the first times it's been so publicly explicit. There's been a sense in the past that we keep it all inside, don't air our dirty linen in public.'

Exchange of emails mid-November 2003
The debate shifted the agenda in Australia from demonisation of Israel to forcing Ashrawi to respond to Palestinian terrorism. The vast majority of the Jewish community stood united, as the many emails and calls I received demonstrated.

Gerard Steinberg, an Israeli academic, regular correspondent for AIJAC's *Review* magazine and originator of an online petition against Ashrawi

A) Hanan Ashrawi got the prize. B) The Jewish Peace Camp got an unprecedented exposure in the Australian media. C) For the first time the Australian public and intellectuals were exposed to the complexity of the Israeli Palestinian conflict, while usually they are mainly fed by right-wing propaganda of the self-appointed 'Jewish leaders'.

Baruch Kimmerling, Israeli academic

Ultimately the issue generated great public heat. It started in the letters pages of the *Sydney Morning Herald* and the *Australian*, where powerful people named by Ramsey stated their case. (The papers did not, by and large, investigate the matter in their news pages.) Sydney radio buzzed. Everybody had an opinion and, for once, the 'middle grounders' had their say, too.

Ben Saul, an Oxford tutor in public international law, in a letter to the *Herald* of 24 October, said that much of the opposition to Ashrawi was based on 'ideological blindness, wilful malevolence or provincial political opportunism'. Ashrawi has been 'a rare and precious voice of reason and has encouraged Palestinians to reject violence, despite continuing Israeli territorial expansion and systematic political oppression'.

On the other side, Ian Fraser, in a letter to the *Australian* of 6 November, wrote that pro-Israeli lobbying was legitimate and those who argued against it were displaying inherent bias:

'The tiny percentage of the world population that is Jewish has every right to campaign on issues that are of concern to them, just as the 1.3 billion Muslims do. In Australia, there is a powerful pro-Palestine lobby consisting mainly of Muslims, but also including the far Left. They vilify anyone who has a good word to say about Israel. But the best example of the pro-Palestinian lobby is the 57 Islamic states using their numbers to bash Israel at every opportunity at

the UN. Most critics of the Jewish lobby are activists themselves, only on the other side.'

Strong views, yes. Hysterical and one-eyed, no. Capable
of fertile engagement? Absolutely. Ordinary people were
emerging, and they wanted to talk with each other, not shout
across the chasm that has so often separated Israel and Palestine. The Zionist censors were being left behind.

Billionaire US financier George Soros and *Sydney Morning Herald* literary editor Michael Visontay are just two
among the many who are forging a new way forward. In
November 2003 Hungarian Holocaust survivor Soros
told the Jewish Funders Network in New York, 'There
is a resurgence of anti-Semitism in Europe. The policies
of the Bush Administration and the Sharon Administration contribute to that. If we change that direction, then
anti-Semitism will diminish. I can't see how one could
confront it directly.' Soros is contributing millions of
dollars in 2004 to the Democratic Party and affiliated
organisations to unseat Bush in the November presidential election.

A typical AIJAC response would be reactionary outrage,
an escalation of the same old shouting wars: Jewish 'Never
again' versus Jewish 'self-blame'. A speech given in early
December 2003 by Isi Leibler could stand as an example.
Isi, who lives in Jerusalem, is the multi-millionaire brother

of Mark Leibler and Senior Vice-President of the pro-Zionist World Jewish Congress. Although he no longer has formal ties with AIJAC, Isi maintains close links with members of its board. Speaking in Melbourne, he argued that the greatest threat to Israel came from self-hating Jews:

'If you [Australian Jewry] have worries it should not be about goyim [non-Jews], but about your internal enemies – Australian Jews who publicly criticise those who exposed that bad woman, Hanan Ashrawi. The day that Jews feel they cannot express their views and lobby against enemies of Israel, that is the day when the Jewish community begins to unravel.'

Michael Visontay, deeply unsettled by the Ashrawi affair, instead countered the Soros line in the context of Ashrawi's visit in an equally measured way. The logic of the Zionist lobby critics, he argued, often seemed to be that:

'unattractive behaviour by some Jews can legitimise antipathy to all Jewish people, unwarranted as that may be. What it's really saying is that Jews are not free to engage in the full range of behaviour that is allowed from other groups (although Muslims would feel a kinship here), because if they act in a way other people find unacceptable, then it legitimises an illegitimate view of Jews. In short, Jews have to be good, not bring attention to themselves, turn the other cheek, don't speak out, don't cause trouble.'

I believe the possibility of nuanced expressions like those of Soros and Visontay will prove to be one of the Ashrawi affair's greatest legacies in Australia.

Certainly the spirit of that engagement found a correspondence in the thinking of those caught up in the Ashrawi controversy in the wider, non-Jewish community. For Bob Carr the key to the future of Israel and Palestine lies in moderates on both sides staking out the fertile middle ground together. He is a politician more known for right-wing social and economic policy; on Ashrawi he advanced the debate in a way few political progressives ever could:

'I think the Australian public, rightly or wrongly, is drawn to what might be called an "even-handed" view of the Middle East dispute, and that's something for those who passionately support Israel to think about. [They] have to learn to let things pass. I say that out of respect, respect for the suffering of the Jewish people in the last century.'

The NSW Premier believes the enormous public interest around Ashrawi stemmed from:

'[outrage at the] bullying of a woman, people against the policies of the Sharon government and a sense that people were overplaying their hand, trying to use a privileged position to blot out the other side. A sense of outraged even-handedness. Some of these factors overlap. The Middle East dispute is a conflict with two sides to it, and we should hear both sides. I think there is war weariness.'

Carr has no doubt that something earthshaking occurred. He says that – elections aside – he has never known an issue to so electrify the public mood:

'The minute Lucy Turnbull made that announcement about pulling out, there was an avalanche – I choose my words carefully – of public reaction, and I witnessed it across Sydney. Nobody has raised any issue with me as they raise the Ashrawi affair, in my entire premiership or, going back further, as Leader of the Opposition. Forest controversies, urban planning controversies, tax rises for poker machines, electric privatisation or workers' comp reform. This has been extraordinary.'

And Hanan Ashrawi?

Upon her return to Ramallah in November 2003 she spoke to journalist Jon Elmer of her visit to Australia:

'I have received many awards and have spoken all over the world and this is the first time that such a small minority managed to spew forth so much poison, lies, disinformation, slander, defamation. It was a process of dehumanisation and exclusion. But it backfired. It mobilised people who were either intimidated or who were not active. It also brought out people from the Jewish community who felt that this was way beyond repair.'

Hanan Ashrawi did collect her peace prize. But if there was truly a winner in the affair, it was open debate; and if anything was lost, it was only our fear of talking about the most important issue for world security and the war on terrorism, for all of us.

For me, the affair changed my life.

I was thrown into it when a column I wrote for the US website ZNet defending Ashrawi's prize was quoted by the British *Independent*'s veteran Middle East correspondent Robert Fisk. On 4 November, under the headline 'Since When Did Arab Become a Dirty Word?', Fisk noted that 'a Jewish writer in Sydney has bravely defended [Ashrawi]', and when Margo Kingston's Webdiary republished my ZNet article and linked to Fisk's column, the local response was electric.

Within twenty-four hours I tasted a little bit of the pressure Carr, Rees and Ramsey were experiencing. An Israeli emailed: 'When the next suicide bomber or car bomb goes off, think about the consequences of your words, because words, like lives, can never ever be returned.' I've been labelled a 'self-hating Jew' and 'a pawn in a wider media relations battle'. A caller reminded me that I 'would have been gassed with the rest of us' even with my 'fucking anti-Semitic and pro-Palestinian ideas'.

This sort of bile – rendered more unbearable by the uglier re-emergence of vicious Jew-hatred worldwide – is just the beginning.

Yet the Hanan Ashrawi affair has left me fiercely proud of my Judaism – fiercely proud, and fiercely defensive, and finally determined to go on the offensive. Identity is not a matter of who you are, it's a matter of what you do. For Australian Jews – and Muslims and anyone else – who care about the ongoing tragedy in the Middle East, there's much to do, starting with the reclaiming of Judaism from the Zionist fundamentalists.

I don't want men such as Colin Rubenstein and Mark Leibler telling Australia what it is to be Jewish in the third millennium. They have no right to steal my heritage.

Of course they should be free to try, as Visontay says. But I'm free to lobby against them, too. I'm free to call their bluff. The internet is opening alternative media forums: new Jewish ideas and new, aroused Jewish voices are being heard every day.

Mine is going to be one of them. This controversy has left me with the feeling that I have been silent for too long. As Baruch Kimmerling wrote in 2002, describing the destruction of Israel's social fabric due to the occupation, 'I accuse myself of knowing all this, yet crying little and keeping quiet too often.'

I'm going to visit Israel and Palestine for the first time – despite the outrageous Israeli Defence Force restrictions on 'foreigners' who want to get into the occupied territories. Since visiting Auschwitz in 1998 I've felt increasingly drawn to examining the confusions between Zionism and Judaism, but before the Ashrawi affair I'd always made excuses: fear, paranoia, sheer bloody-mindedness. Now I want to see for myself the kinds of Israeli actions that Israeli peace groups such as Gush Shalom bear witness to daily, in the name of my Judaism:

'This week, the soldiers continued to shoot and kill in the alleys of Nablus. This week, the bulldozers continued to destroy fields and olives groves, to build walls and fences that rob hundreds of thousands of their livelihood. This week, Sharon made more promises that he has no intention of keeping. This week, the Israeli Defence Force announced that soldiers are permitted to shoot at demonstrators, both Palestinians and Israelis.'

But I claim no special rights or knowledge about what's needed in the Middle East simply because of my background, education, friends, family or religion.

The Ashrawi debate has made me question my motivations throughout it and my place within it. Being Jewish explained my initial interest, but as the months have passed, I have come to see that my involvement was driven by much more – by a desire to respect and embrace the totality of the person my parents taught me to be, not simply the traditions and superficial clothing of Judaism.

Question authority. Challenge established power. Seek out the truth.

14

Recognising the importance of the non-government sector
and the positive values arising from it, what are the lessons
for policy? The first thing is the very important maxim for government,
any government, on any issue: 'Do no harm.' These social
networks are neither established by, nor controlled by government.
They are voluntary. That is their strength

Peter Costello, 'Building Social Capital' speech, 16 July 2003

Thirtieth July 2003 heart-starter: the Fin Review's political correspondent Laura Tingle reports that Peter Costello will cancel the tax deductibility of donations to, and the tax concessions of, charities whose core activities include 'attempting to change the law or government policy'.

As I researched the history of this bombshell, I began to suspect that it was no one-off attempt to gag charities and other non-profit non-government organisations (NGOs) that did not keep out of politics or toe the government line. Rather, it looked part of a long-term, coordinated strategy to discourage organised participation in our democracy by citizens.

My suspicions were heightened when I read an August 2002 speech on NGOs by Gary Johns. Johns, a former ALP federal minister, was now a Fellow at the government's favoured neo-liberal think tank, the Institute of Public Affairs. In his speech he stated that politically active

NGOs threatened 'to mediate the effects of the ideology of individualism and self interest' in the cause of 'the greater good'. He argued that the 'communitarianism' promoted by many NGOs, national and international, was, shock horror, 'a vehicle for the idea of citizenship', that dreadful concept the neo-liberals have sought to banish by calling citizens mere 'customers'. Participatory democracy, for Johns, threatened established power because 'democratic life encompasses more than the periodic business of government and elections'.

Neo-liberalism is the dominant ideology in Australia, Britain and the United States. Its premise is, in the words of Margaret Thatcher, that 'there is no such thing as society – there are individual men and women, and there are families'. Its tenets – total freedom of movement for capital, goods and services; lower spending on social services such as health and education; deregulation of everything that could lower profits, including environmental and worker safety laws; reducing the safety net for the poor; privatisation of public assets; and the elimination of the concept of the 'public good' or 'community' and its replacement with 'individual responsibility'. It also derides any call for corporate social responsibility.

To neo-liberalism, organised groups of citizens pushing for the 'common good' are threats to the power and privilege of those who benefit most from neo-liberalism – global capital and the multinational companies, which have governments over a barrel. According to Johns, 'a cardinal tenet of liberalism is to keep democracy in its place, to regard it as an activity of limited application'. The task of the state is 'to depoliticise much of life, to make it less amenable to public dispute'. In other words, to control public opinion by minimising the public contest of ideas.

Could it be that, as well as his attempt to deliver Australia's mainstream media to Murdoch and Packer and his government's relentless attacks on the ABC and cuts to its funding, Howard also had an agenda to expel the informed dissenting voices of NGOs from the public debate?

Journalists routinely rely on information and analysis from NGOs to test the truth of what a government is saying; without that resource governments would get away with blue murder.

NGOs can also be a great help to governments that care about their citizens. Take a 'peak body' called the National Alliance of Young People in Nursing Homes, for which I moderated a forum at the fringe festival of the 2004 ALP national conference. Different groups such as the MS society come together in this peak body to collect the facts and advocate the case for young people who have profound disabilities or have been severely injured in accidents or assaults, and who because of a big gap in the system often have no choice but to live in nursing homes designed for old people. A philanthropic foundation funds the Alliance, which through its contacts with young people, their families and their friends around the nation knows the problems and has ideas to help solve them.

Its entire purpose is to lobby government for change, just like many other peak bodies of disparate grassroots voluntary groups with common needs or issues. Such peak bodies are a source of great expertise and experience for governments that care, and a means by which ordinary people can employ someone with expertise and experience to articulate a strong case to government for change. Costello's plan could mean the end of an organised voice for young people in nursing homes and for many other disadvantaged and marginalised groups. Without the help of tax concessions many would fold.

But what if, say, a government doesn't really want to know what's gone wrong, or who is suffering, or which environments need urgent repair or protection?

Imagine a world where no one articulate and informed spoke for the powerless or for those whose values don't match the dominant ideology of 'money is everything'. Imagine a world where there was no one to check the government's claims, or ferret out its misinformation, or expose flaws in the system that hurt real people; a world where dishonest governments could spin tall tales without fear of exposure. Who would benefit? The people?

The denial of the facts in the pursuit of short-term profit for big business is already happening. In 2004 the Union of Concerned Scientists, a group of sixty prominent scientists including twenty Nobel Laureates, issued a statement asserting that the Bush administration had systematically distorted scientific fact to get its way on the environment, health, biomedical research and nuclear weapons. The *Sydney Morning Herald* reported that 'The documents accuse the Administration of repeatedly censoring and suppressing its own scientists' reports, stacking advisory committees with unqualified political appointees, disbanding government panels that provide unwanted advice, and refusing to seek independent scientific expertise in some cases.'

(Howard's government is following the Bush lead. In 2003 the *Sydney Morning Herald*'s Aban Contractor revealed that in late 2002 the Department of Education, Science and Training censored its own report on the state of higher education, deleting findings that the government's HECS increases in 1997 had lowered the participation of mature-aged students and students from lower socio-economic backgrounds. This left Minister Brendan Nelson free to argue that his government's 2003 decision to raise HECS fees even more would have no such effect.)

I commissioned Paddy Manning, the founding editor of *Ethical Investor* magazine and now a property writer on the *Australian*, to investigate for this book whether activist charities really are under the gun in John Howard's Australia.

M.K.

Keeping Democracy in Its Place

By Paddy Manning

Independent activity, involving, at times, opposition to the State, is not opposed to democracy; it is essential to it. Democracy resides in participation in organisations, in the openness, the publicity, of struggle

John Anderson, Australian philosopher

Behind the term 'non-government organisations' (or NGOs as they are known in the trade) are the charities, churches, clubs, associations and unions that 4 million Australians give time or money to each year.

Professor Mark Lyons of the University of Technology Sydney writes that 'non-profit organisations make an important contribution to society through their demonstration of, and thus encouragement for, collective action. They play a central role in the regeneration of social capital'.

Social capital is the trust, tolerance and non-commercial values and networks in a civil society. Lyons adds that 'Non-profit organisations also sustain and shape a democratic political system. They are the "elementary schools of democracy".'

This view is not confined to the soft left. The economically super-dry federal Industry Commission said in a report on NGOs:

'The charitable sector underscores many basic values in Australian democracy. It exemplifies the principles of pluralism, free choice and the rights of citizens to participate in and take responsibility for their community. It helps ensure that no government has a monopoly on the way society deals with its citizens – especially those who are most vulnerable because of economic or personal need.'

Here are three achievements of Australian NGOs:

- BUGA UP and other anti-smoking groups gave us bans on tobacco advertising
- the Wilderness Society helped stop the damming of Tasmania's Franklin River
- UnitingCare provides crisis accommodation, non-profit aged-care facilities and other services to as many as 800,000 Australians.

Now let's ponder their legacy. In the nineteenth century, campaigns by NGOs helped:

- stop slavery
- achieve women's suffrage
- ban child labour
- put in place consumer protection laws.

None of these reforms would have happened without organised community pressure from NGOs – those dangerous 'vehicles for the idea of citizenship'.

For these reasons people are inclined to trust NGOs – often far more than mass-media outlets, multinational corporations or governments. That's what a public relations firm found when it surveyed people in Australia, France, Germany, the US and the UK on the credibility of NGOs a year after the 1999 World Trade Organization meeting in Seattle was disrupted. The survey found that NGOs 'are trusted nearly twice as much to "do what is right" compared to government, media or corporations. NGOs such as Amnesty International, Greenpeace, Oxfam and World Wildlife Fund have greater credibility than such corporations as Esso/Exxon, Ford, Microsoft, Monsanto and Nike' (and donations to overseas aid agencies have been increasing at over 15 per cent a year for the last few years – a phenomenal growth rate).

The Australian Election Study (a mail survey of voters after each federal election, conducted by the Australian National University) asked this question following the 2001 election: 'Would you say the government is run by a few big interests looking after themselves, or that it is run for the benefit of all the people?' Just under half of the public (48 per cent) thought the government was run for big interests – and only 17 per cent thought it was run for all the people. A third thought governments were half run for big interests, and half for all people.

No wonder certain types are anxious about alternative avenues of participation in democratic life.

But what to do?

John Howard's response has been to pursue a whole range of government strategies to minimise organised dissent to the values of neo-liberalism – most publicly and spectacularly through his assaults on the union movement. The NGO elements of his plan, however, are more intricate and have taken longer to become clear. As Eric Sidoti, of the Human Rights Council of Australia, wrote recently:

'Over the latter decades of the 20th Century the role and importance of NGOs had grown to the point that we had assumed a general recognition and acceptance of their activism as a necessary ingredient in a healthy democracy. We had come to think that we had reached a point of maturity in working with successive Australian governments whereby differences could be put on the public table and robustly debated without jeopardising access or incurring retribution. While we always knew that major differences remained as to how Human Rights would best be realised and protected, we had believed that our shared commitment to Human Rights principles and norms was beyond serious question. We were wrong.'

John Howard has a very rigid view of who does – and doesn't – have a right to work with and lobby governments. Churches should stick to 'religious issues' – meaning that they should shut up about wars or whether a GST on food is fair. Charities should quit talking about the causes of poverty and stick to doling out soup and blankets.

Non-profits that stay out of 'politics' – or toe the government's policy line – are fine. For those who don't, Howard has a five-phase plan to shut them up or shut them down.

Phase One: stop funding NGOs that speak out, thus intimidating others into silence

In 1998 Howard's government stopped its direct funding of the Australian Youth Policy and Action Coalition, a small peak organisation bringing together youth groups around the country to create one voice in the corridors of political power, after it criticised the government's youth policy before the election. The government then channelled big money into a government-controlled, government-censored annual youth round-table – made up of government-selected young people.

Also defunded after critical comments: the Australian Pensioners' and Superannuants' Federation, National Shelter, the Association of Civilian Widows of Australia and the Coalition of Australian Participating Organisations of Women (the last after an unflattering NGO report to the United Nations). In January 2004 the United Nations Association of Australia sent out an urgent national appeal for funds, following the withdrawal of its grant from the Department of Foreign Affairs and Trade.

Other government scrutinisers such as the Australian Council of Social Service (ACOSS) have had their funding severely cut, with what remains coming with strings attached: a requirement to provide the government with twenty-four hours' notice of any media release, and a demand that studies and submissions be provided to government two weeks in advance of release. The result: NGOs that do manage to retain government funding inevitably self-censor.

And the heat is rising. In late 2003 David Kemp, the Minister for the Environment, drastically cut funding to politically active groups, redirecting money to politically benign bodies such as Landcare Australia and Greening Australia.

Don Henry, Executive Director of peak environment group the Australian Conservation Foundation, says his organisation has had its funding cut severely every year under the Howard government, with the result that annual funding of about $200,000 six years ago is now down to about $20,000. And the ACF experience is consistent with that of other environment groups that dare to speak out, including Friends of the Earth and the Wilderness Society.

The government has also progressively abandoned recurrent or core funding for NGOs, preferring to fund only specifically targeted projects or programs. It means that many groups that rely on public funding are now living hand-to-mouth financially and cannot plan ahead at all, much less adopt fearless, free-ranging strategies.

To do a good, honest job, therefore, any NGO that does not agree with government policy and wants to advocate for change must operate largely free of government funding. There are still plenty with the independent fundraising firepower to manage this, and so . . .

Phase Two: strip activist NGOs of charitable status

Many non-profit groups such as Greenpeace and Amnesty International refuse government funding to maintain their complete independence, but almost all NGOs depend on the financial concessions afforded by their status as charities to remain viable: exemptions from income and fringe benefit taxes and the GST, and – crucially – the tax deductibility of their supporters' donations. (Australians claim half a billion dollars a year in deductible gifts.)

Strip an NGO of its charitable status and you cripple it financially.

After the GST came into force, the government set up an inquiry to 'define' what a charity was. Its members were the former head of ACOSS, Robert Fitzgerald, businessman David Gonski, and former NSW Supreme Court judge Justice Ian Sheppard. They agreed that a charity was a group that had altruism as its primary purpose. They also agreed that 'charities should be permitted to engage in advocacy on behalf of those they benefit. Conduct of this kind should not deny them charitable status, even if it involves advocating for a change in law or policy.'

Peter Costello rejected this unanimous finding. His draft legislation, released in July 2003, instead denied tax relief to any charity that had as one of its purposes advocacy of a 'political cause' or 'attempting to change the law or government policy'. And who would make the critical subjective assessments? The Australian Taxation Office, a body under the control of the Treasurer.

Father Peter Norden, Policy Director of Jesuit Social Services, fumed that:

'[The government] had to learn that it is a central mission of charities such as ours not only to do good, but to ensure that harmful legislation and regulations are changed to protect the vulnerable members of our community – a responsible and mature government encourages open and independent public debate and does not try to gag its critics as part of the democratic process.'

Francis Sullivan, chief executive of Catholic Health Australia, which represents 680 Catholic health and aged-care organisations and services, warned that 'The job of charities is to provide services and to speak up for people who haven't got a voice for themselves, and if charities can't have that role, then low income people and people who need a just outcome are in trouble.'

Even the *Australian Financial Review* ran a stiff editorial chiding Costello for proposing a measure that could 'silence any charity' at a time when the government was downsizing the public sector and contracting not-for-profit groups for welfare service delivery: 'Since the government is asking not-for-profit organisations to share more of the load, it can hardly restrict their right to comment if they think its policies are not working.'

Democrats spokesman John Cherry summed up the politics:

'If you agree with Government policy, the Government is saying you can stay a charity, but if you attempt to change Government policy you cease to be a charity for the purposes of tax law, and that's . . . using the Tax Act to censor people from actually trying to advocate a better deal for the under-privileged, the environment, even animal welfare.'

Groups the government loves to hate, such as Oxfam Community Aid Abroad, Amnesty International and Green-peace would be in BIG trouble.

Yet as he was savaging the NGO sector, Costello was busily cultivating a softer, more caring personal image, pro-claiming he wanted to promote a 'culture of community engagement and volunteerism'. He told the *Sydney Morning Herald*'s Deborah Snow that 'Important things in life grow out of values, faith, relationships, family, voluntary associations, culture. I think there are run-downs in these areas, and the run-down has been slow and gradual, and the run-up has to be slow and gradual – through personal leadership, inspiration, through the non-government insti-tutions of society.'

As I write Costello had not announced a final decision on the definition of 'charities'. But his plan was already silencing many charities, with some – including commu-nity legal centres – backing away from projects that could be seen as advocacy.

Enter John Howard.

Phase Three: set up a government 'non-government organisation'

In 1999 Howard set up the Prime Minister's Community Business Partnership to advise him on 'community and business collaboration'. He made all appointments to the board personally: one of them was Rob Gerard, a major Liberal Party donor and an invitee to the Bush barbecue. Howard has since used this body and the funding he gives it to co-opt and control NGOs. In November 2003 he announced that $50,000 from 'Partnership' funds would set up a Howard-approved NGO peak body, the Not For Profit Council of Australia, with the promise of more money later.

If you think a government non-government organisation is a contradiction in terms, you're right.

What Howard really wants is *his* peak body.

Professor Mark Lyons told the *Sydney Morning Herald*'s Adele Horin that beleaguered NGOs feared Howard would use his 'NGO' to 'legitimise' whatever it wanted to do about the non-government sector.

Howard was torpedoing a *real* NGO initiative of the previous year – the formation of a grassroots organisation to 'present to the Australian community the valuable contribution of the non-profit sector in Australia, and to raise and deal with shared issues concerning that sector'. Robert Fitzgerald had chaired the round-table, saying its aim was 'to build the capacity, reputation and respect of the non-profit sector in this country'.

NGOs would subscribe to this new body, which would

in turn speak for NGOs when it came to complicated issues such as the GST. It was similar to what's been done in Canada and the UK. In Canada a voluntary-sector representative body deals directly with the Cabinet Office, and holds annual meetings with the PM, treasurer and other senior ministers. In England the Blair government in 1998 signed a compact on relations between government and the voluntary and community sector.

Unlike Howard's NGO 'council', the genuine article aimed to represent 'the full breadth of the nonprofit sector which comprises the arts, sports, health, environment, churches, welfare, education, overseas aid, consumer protection and many other parts'. The nineteen-member body included Artspeak, the Australian Conservation Foundation, the Australian Consumers' Association, the Australian Council of Social Service, the National Council of Churches in Australia, the National Council of Independent Schools' Associations, Philanthropy Australia, Sport Industry Australia, Volunteering Australia and the Australian Council for International Development.

And Howard's? On the board of his hand-picked Not For Profit Council are the Art Gallery of South Australia, the Benevolent Society, the Jewish Community Council, Odyssey House, the Salvation Army and the Smith Family. The list speaks for itself. The Salvos and the Smith Family basically stick to on-the-ground welfare. All are traditional organisations that largely stay out of political debate. There is no environment or overseas aid organisation.

The man behind the council was businessman John Dahlsen of Southern Cross Broadcasting, owner of leading commercial talk radio stations in Sydney (2UE) and Melbourne (3AW). Accepting a Voltaire Award from Free Speech Victoria, Stephen Mayne, publisher of the political website crikey.com.au, said Dahlsen was a 'connecting factor' in many of his toughest free speech trials and tribulations:

'Dahlsen is from a wealthy Gippsland family and was chairman of the Herald & Weekly Times when it ran its vicious campaign against the Hawke–Keating capital gains tax regime in the mid-1980s. Labor was so furious they devised some media law reforms that cleared the way for Rupert Murdoch to buy H&WT, and move to 70 per cent of the Australian newspaper market – something the nation has been lamenting ever since. After the takeover, Dahlsen concentrated his efforts on Southern Cross . . . Former National Party federal minister Peter Nixon was chairman, and they have recreated their conservative, right-wing brand of media into a $600 million giant.'

What chance that Dahlsen wants to promote a strong, free-thinking NGO sector? Zero. It's called co-option.

Phase Four: use public service and intelligence assets to spy on awkward NGOs

While John Howard plays Machiavelli, Tony Abbott plays hit man. What to do with NGOs that aren't charities and don't get government funding?

In December 2003 Melbourne's *Herald Sun* reported
that former health minister Kay Patterson had investigated
the alleged 'infiltration' of the Defend and Extend Medicare Group by the Socialist Party of Australia. Reporter
Keith Moor – who told me his reports were extensively
'legalled' before publication – published the names of six
people Abbott had his eye on, and reported that an Australian intelligence agency was also investigating the group.
The paper was careful to make no connection between the
Health Department's investigation and the intelligence
agency's. Here's an extract.

**Government accuses DEMG of having anarchist agenda:
left hijack health fight**

Anarchists and extreme socialists are hijacking the health
debate, a confidential government report reveals.

The Federal Government also alleges professional
protesters are using the proposed $2.4 billion Medicare reforms
to mount political campaigns aimed at causing disruption.

It came to these conclusions after checking key identities
behind the recently formed 'Defend and Extend Medicare
Group' (DEMG) . . .

An internal report prepared by the ministerial officers
responsible for investigating DEMG members and supporters
has been obtained by the *Herald Sun*.

The *Herald Sun* has also discovered intelligence officers
have been monitoring DEMG and have attended some of
its rallies.

A senior intelligence official recently briefed the *Herald Sun* about the activities of DEMG. He said intelligence officers had been aware of serious recruiting by DEMG for several months and are closely monitoring its activities.

'Several of the organisers are well-known to us as serial activists with connections to anarchist groups and socialist organisations,' an intelligence source said.

Staff from former Health Minister Kay Patterson's office are believed to have initiated and carried out the probe into DEMG.

Current Health Minister Tony Abbott was recently briefed on the findings of the investigation, and it convinced him some DEMG members had a dangerous hidden agenda. He yesterday claimed DEMG was attempting to hoodwink people into believing it was a true community group with the sole aim of improving health care standards.

'This is a classic unity ticket. Classic rent-a-crowd,' Mr Abbott told the *Herald Sun*.

'These people are foisting a form of false advertising on the Australian public by pretending to be grass-roots community activists when they are the dribs and drabs of the extreme Left' . . .

Intelligence agents have attended recent DEMG rallies in Melbourne, including one last month at the Victorian State Library . . .

Herald Sun, 5 December 2003

As a reader wrote:

'I am no fan of Socialism or Anarchism but I do believe in a right to democratic participation. I fail to see why any person or group in our democracy should be subject to investigation for publicly trying to mobilise political action around any issue they feel strongly about so long as they are not advocating the breaking of laws or engaging in any illegality.

Why are intelligence officers investigating a group opposed to government policy? Who authorised them to do so? Under what legal authority has this occurred? Why is a "senior" intelligence officer providing briefings to the press on such investigations? Do they now have a mandate to attempt to sway public opinion? If there is illegality involved why isn't it a matter for the police? If no illegality is involved why is the investigation occurring at all?

What of the future? Will the government be gathering dossiers on members of the local women's cooperative for lobbying for federally funded child care? Will "grey power" groups find themselves subject to investigation for expressing public dissatisfaction with pension benefits?

I find this occurrence very disturbing and feel it can only undermine the democratic process if dissenting voices are to be subject to background checks for publicly opposing government policy.'

(In reply to a parliamentary question on notice by Greens Senator Kerry Nettle in March 2004, Tony Abbott said he had no knowledge of any intelligence investigation.)

Phase Five: require NGOs to qualify for a 'licence' to talk to government

In a complicated series of largely secret manoeuvres, again using Howard's Community Business Partnership, the government has paved the way to effectively 'license' NGOs as a precondition to them talking to or getting funding from it. Howard's very own 'NGO', the Not For Profit Council, funded through the Community Business Partnership, is expected to oversee the licensing process, under which the government would access an NGO's membership list, structure, community links and donors. Howard could thus get information to better persecute his policy opponents and discourage citizens from contributing time or money to charities the government doesn't like.

The idea was born in United States neo-liberal think tanks – invariably funded by big business – and quickly got taken up by Melbourne's Institute of Public Affairs, a neo-liberal think tank also funded by big business.

Alexander Downer's Department of Foreign Affairs sponsors the 'Fulbright Professional Award in Australia–US Alliance Studies': in 2002 IPA Fellow Gary Johns got $15,000 from taxpayers for a tour of the US to talk to US academics who, he said, 'share my concern about the NGO challenge to the formal institutions of democracy'.

In his August 2002 speech Johns proposed a 'protocol' whereby an NGO would not have access to government unless it filed documents with the government detailing:

- its structure, office holders and accountability mechanisms
- its complete, 'verifiable' list of members, both voting and non-voting, its offshore affiliates and associated parties and its offshore funding
- its election process, and the ability of its members to 'access all decisions of the governing body'
- its complete finances – the statement to include all fundraising and administrative costs
- all its 'solicitation and informational materials', which must include 'a clear description of the programmes and activities for which funds are requested'
- the qualifications of its spokespeople, the research undertaken, and whether it has been assessed by independent peer review.

This material would then be put on a public register.

Johns's proposed 'protocol' claimed only to be demanding of NGOs full disclosure in advertising, membership lists, organisational links and funding – that is, transparency, accountability and honesty. If only political parties were so open!

In fact his requirements would be disastrous for smaller, localised NGOs (the time and administrative costs would be prohibitive for most grassroots groups, just for starters). Why on earth should there be new bureaucratic hoops to deny access for NGOs seeking to promote the public good when business, motivated by private profit, walks freely through the back door to lobby government? 'It's unfair, and inconsistent,' says Don Henry of the Australian Conservation Foundation. And for many people requirements such as public disclosure of membership would mean they would drop out for fear of losing their jobs. Fancy being a public servant in the Department of Industry donating to Greenpeace? A military officer who supports Amnesty International?

Johns's prescription for horrific state invasions of privacy and civil rights was adopted by Amanda Vanstone, then minister for Family and Community Services, whose department is a paid-up member of the Institute of Public Affairs. At her request, Johns submitted a sketchy proposal to produce a 'protocol'. In December 2002 the Community Business Partnership, despite the irrelevance of the matter to its stated goal – to advise on 'community and business collaboration' – agreed to pay Johns $47,450 through the IPA to do the job, 'subject to some discussion regarding what the study will provide'! There was no tender, and no public announcement.

How blatant can the 'in crowd' get? As blatant as we let them. The guidelines of the citizen's watchdog on government spending, the National Audit Office, state that when the government engages consultants it must 'determine the selection criteria and document the evaluation to ensure that the chosen consultants are of appropriate quality and that the process is transparent'.

The red-light ironies escaped the government. The IPA

is an NGO with close ties to Howard's government, acting as Howard's attack dog in his anti-ABC, anti-Stolen Generations and welfare privatisation agendas. It claims on its website that 'we do not accept government funding' and does *not* disclose its *own* donors. Yet it contracted *in secret* to ensure NGO accountability and transparency. In answers to questions on notice in the Senate from Democrats Senator John Cherry, Vanstone's successor, Kay Patterson, admitted the government was aware of the IPA's secrecy about its donors and its promise not to accept government funding. She also admitted that Johns's contract required *no* consultation with other NGOs.

Sensitive to accusations of hypocrisy following news of the IPA's NGO project, its Executive Director, Mike Nahan, told the *Sydney Morning Herald*'s Brad Norington in August 2003 that the IPA would for the first time publish a full list of sponsors and contributions in its 2002–03 annual report. As I write the IPA has not published this report or disclosed its donors. It did not respond to a request to advise when it planned to do so.

The contract, formally signed in May 2003, came to public attention when revealed by Dennis Shanahan in the *Australian* newspaper in August 2003. In the meantime the IPA engaged in the public debate on tax concessions for charities in June 2003 without revealing the contract. Asked on Radio National's *Background Briefing* in March 2004 to justify such lack of transparency, Johns replied, 'Look, you want to know what I had for breakfast this morning?'

Sunday Age journalists Brendan Nicholson and Gary Hughes drew the connection between Johns's 'protocol' and the Costello definition of charities. The IPA's submission to Costello's draft legislation had urged that charities be narrowly defined 'with a strong emphasis on direct relief action'. Nicholson and Hughes wrote that 'The IPA is quick to point out that its [NGO] project and the draft [charities] legislation are "quite separate". But the result is that suddenly the two primary sources of funding for NGOs – tax-deductible donations, and government grants or payments for carrying out consultative work – are under simultaneous attack.'

Francis Sullivan, chief executive of Catholic Health Australia, said the IPA contract 'gives more credence to the view that there is an agenda to restrict charities either through less benefits or through "big brother" tactics to gain compliance rather than permitting strong public advocacy'.

Guess what? The IPA's unreleased interim report on its NGO project, which I obtained just before this chapter went to press and is due to be considered by the PM's inaptly named Community Business Partnership in June 2004, recommends a protocol in almost precisely the terms proposed by Gary Johns in 2002 after his taxpayer-subsidised trip to the US to get the line right. We, the people, have paid the IPA through a Howard slush fund and the 'Fulbright Professional Scholarship' nearly $65,000 to tell the government what it wanted to hear. Of course the IPA, an NGO, saw no need to comply with its recommended transparency requirements for NGOs whose views it and Howard's government are trying to bury. Sums it up, really.

What is the Institute of Public Affairs?

The Melbourne-based think tank has traditionally derived 85 per cent of its funding from subscriptions, and says it has more than 2000 private donors. Its private funding has declined by about a third since Howard took office, partly due to some big businesses distancing themselves from its extreme agenda on native title and its obsessive rejection of 'corporate social responsibility'.

Big business is said to provide at least a third of the IPA's income. Reported IPA donors over the years have included the Western Mining Corporation, BHP Billiton, Clough Engineering, Telstra and Dick Pratt's Visyboard. Many companies write their donation off as a business expense rather than make tax-deductible donations. Big business-men sit on its board. Big names involved with the Institute have included Hugh Morgan, Rupert Murdoch and IPA board member Harold Clough – you'll meet him again as a donor to Tony Abbott's Honest Politics Trust.

Robert Manne, La Trobe University professor in politics, columnist and a former editor of the conservative journal *Quadrant*, believes the IPA is now less influential in business circles than in the 1990s after Western Mining's Hugh Morgan – also a director of the Liberal Party's Cormack Foundation, the biggest donor to the Liberal Party in 2002–03 – poured in money to fund campaigns against native title. There was a swathe of high-profile director resignations in the years 2001 and 2002, and Rio Tinto and BHP Billiton have reportedly recently stopped donating.

But Howard's government has stayed loyal. The two Kemp brothers, David and Rod, now Cabinet ministers, were members of the IPA's research committee throughout the Hawke–Keating years (and Rod was IPA director for a while). Many of the IPA's active members are part of a Melbourne conservative network that grew out of the Samuel Griffith and H.R. Nicholls societies – of which Peter Costello and Liberal powerbroker Michael Kroger were part. Howard has appointed IPA staffers to government bodies.

There are strong links between the IPA and the US neo-liberal movement, via America's Republican Party 'new right' and its supporting think tanks, such as the Bradley and Olin foundations, which would be considered far right in an Australian context. These two are among the largest in the USA and are massive funders of neo-conservative initiatives, including the now-notorious Project for the New American Century, which produced the blueprint for George Bush's post-September-11 'pre-emptive strike' unilateralism. Together the Bradley and Olin foundations donated US$348,000 to Australia's IPA between 1987 and 1995, according to the US research site www.mediatransparency.org.

In June 2003 Gary Johns delivered the opening speech to a Washington conference co-sponsored by the American Enterprise Institute, a key neo-liberal NGO, and the

IPA. The AEI has close connections to the Bush administration and many Bush staffers formerly worked for it. Johns defined which NGOs are the threat: 'indigenous, feminist, gay, environmentalist, civil libertarian, socialist'. He kept a straight face when he told his audience – members of some of America's most powerful, educated and well-connected elites – that he feared 'a dictatorship of the articulate'.

Johns's real paranoia – one he shares with the American Enterprise Institute – stems from a kind of reverse anti-globalisation agenda: fear of the ability of international NGOs to test the claims and actions of the transnational businesses increasingly ruling the world – to hold them accountable to the people. 'It feels much better when you want to change the system and change the world, than it is to directly help someone who lives across the road,' he said.

He was preaching to the long-converted. In 2001 the AEI published a book, *Hijacking Democracy*, which highlighted the links between the United Nations and NGOs, claiming that these 'circumvent traditional democratic and diplomatic channels' to create a 'global parallel society'.

Those traditional democratic channels – which include such unscrutinised, elite and unaccountable groups as the American Enterprise Institute and the Institute of Public Affairs – are selflessly fighting back. The June conference launched the AEI's NGO-Watch website, one very similar to the IPA's NGO-Watch project.

Their attacks on activist NGOs have become particularly pressing following the war on Iraq. The Bush administration was mightily offended when a number of overseas aid NGOs, including Oxfam Community Aid Abroad, not only opposed the war itself, but also refused to be party to it by accepting and distributing US aid afterwards. USAID head, Andrew Natsios, has proclaimed that NGOs providing humanitarian aid in Afghanistan and Iraq must accept that they are 'arms of the US Government'.

Indeed.

Democracy v. the Beast

*Her appeal was simply that she represented something authentic
in a culture of artefact. She was transparent in an era during
which the political class have become expert at concealment. She was
a still point in a culture of spin. She advanced our politics even if it
was only to the extent of showing us what we might be up against if
we chose to get involved as she did. Maybe others will learn
from her mistakes*

Webdiarist Dr Tim Dunlop, an opponent of Pauline Hanson's policies

*I do not believe that the real life of this nation is to be found
either in the great luxury hotels and the petty gossip of so-called
fashionable suburbs, or in the officialdom of organised masses.
It is to be found in the homes of people who are nameless and
unadvertised and who, whatever their individual religious conviction
or dogma, see in their children their greatest contribution to the
immortality of their race*

**Robert Menzies, 'The Forgotten People', from *The Forgotten People*
radio broadcasts, 1942**

Last year a woman named Pauline approached me at a café in Marrickville and thanked me for a talk I'd given on refugees at the Marrickville town hall. She sat down for a chat and mentioned that she and her sister in Wollongong had long been at loggerheads over the boat people. Now they were in dispute over the recent jailing of Pauline Hanson – to her dismay, her sister believed that Pauline Hanson should not have gone to jail. For her sister, Ms Hanson represented the little people, who had virtually no influence in society and whose voice the politicians did not hear.

The women's family had grown up dirt poor in a housing commission house in Wollongong, and Pauline said she'd always voted Labor because no kid should have to endure such a deprived childhood. She was gay and had left her church when it refused to accept you could be gay and Catholic. But after attending the refugee meeting, Pauline – an alternative dispute resolution officer – had wanted to help the cause and approached the priest at Marrickville's Catholic church. He had invited her to join the church, and she became involved in its refugee activism.

How could her own sister feel such anger at refugees, Pauline asked in wonder. How? I asked why her sister supported Pauline Hanson. She had recently separated from her husband, Pauline said, and one of her sons had been a drug addict. She was desperate for help but there was none. Pauline Hanson had provided the scream she needed.

That scream wasn't really about refugees – but that's the part you wanted to hear, John.

These two sisters seemed loving and compassionate women; the kind of Australians you'd reckon would instinctively open the door and help someone less fortunate than themselves if and when the crunch came. They

> Of course I will be called racist, but if I can invite whom I want into my home, then I should have the right to have a say on who comes into my country.
>
> **Pauline Hanson's maiden speech, 10 September 1996**
>
> We will decide who comes to this country, and the circumstances in which they come.
>
> **John Howard unveils his unofficial election slogan, October 2001**

were both, in their own way, lamenting the lack of justice for the world's strugglers. To me it was easy to see them working together instead of turning their backs on each other or simply agreeing not to talk about politics.

A memory flashed into my head, and I suddenly understood its meaning. During Pauline Hanson's Queensland campaign in 1998, in a shopping centre in Mareeba, a far north Queensland town economically devastated by the closure of its timber mills, an Aboriginal man of about 50, wearing an Akubra, diffidently shook her hand. 'Thank you, Pauline,' he said. 'I'm with you.' I asked him if he knew what he'd done: that Pauline Hanson was against funding for special Aboriginal services to address their disadvantage. 'I know, but ATSIC is real corrupt, and nothing gets to us here. She's promised to stop that.'

Pauline Hanson's core appeal was never about race. Sure, she attracted racists to her cause. Sure, she made

I was told I was part of a [Liberal Party] team, and the trouble is I'm too much of an individual and I tend to speak my mind at times. If I really believe in something I will speak up. So I'm quite happy now to be that individual, and I can have my own voice now.

Independent Member for Oxley Pauline Hanson, 17 March 1996, on why the Queensland Liberals disendorsed her – a decision Howard backed

I come here not as a polished politician but as a woman who has had her fair share of life's knocks . . . I won the seat of Oxley largely on an issue that has resulted in me being called a racist.

Pauline Hanson's maiden speech, 10 September 1996

In a sense, a pall of censorship on certain issues has been lifted . . . I welcome the fact that people can now talk about certain things without living in fear of being branded a racist.

John Howard, to the Queensland Liberal Party, 22 September 1996

repellent statements about 'Aboriginal states', and framed some ugly policies on immigration – policies Howard later ran with for all he was worth. But these were just the surface symptoms, not the underlying disease. What Hanson and her supporters suffered from wasn't a disease anyway, but a very rude case of democratic good health.

Hanson's scream mattered because it was authentic and timely. Her mobilisation of the disaffected, most of whom had never been involved in politics before, saw the resurrection of the passionate town hall political meeting. These people – like Bob Brown and the Greens – were frustrated with the loaded Big Party rules and wanted some honest answers, *now*.

Hanson's catchcry – 'Please explain' – was heartfelt.

The government was terrified by that virulent outbreak of grassroots democracy. In the beginning John Howard hoped that if he stroked it, it would be soothed. Then he thought he could get away with only treating the superficial manifestations.

Every time Hanson's voters screamed about a social issue, Howard sought not to explain or even engage – but to appease. Then, after One Nation devastated the conservative vote at the 1998 Queensland election anyway, he knew he had to do more to hold the battlers' vote he'd so assiduously cultivated. Soon after, a young Howard protégé named Tony Abbott signalled a shift in tactics when he wrote that 'the only viable Coalition strategy is to find ways of undermining support for the Hansonites'.

Yet five years, many more policy thefts and a lot of 'undermining' later, and even after Pauline Hanson had been disgraced and jailed, her supporters were *still* screaming at John Howard – and this time they were joined by a hell of a lot of Australians who couldn't stand most of her policies. A Brisbane poll on the weekend following Hanson's successful appeal against her conviction in November 2003 revealed that nearly one in three Queenslanders would have given her their primary vote in an immediate election.

What about smug progressives like me?

When Hanson first arrived on the scene I was among the many who thought that if the media ignored her, her scream would soon die out. Next, we overreacted to her growing popularity, helping stoke bitter divisions over issues such as race and immigration – the ones that would drive the Marrickville alternative dispute resolution officer and her sister apart – while ignoring what lay behind that scream as wilfully as the conservatives. These were mistakes I still regret today, for into the mainstream vacuum that greeted her 1996 election to Parliament as a representative of the people of Oxley stepped the worst kind of exploiters: those who heard in her scream only political opportunity.

Dick Morris, former spin doctor to President Clinton, says in his book *The New Prince: Machiavelli Updated for the 21st Century* 'The media play the key role in bringing the private pains and needs of real people to public attention.' This role, along with its corollary – to scrutinise the powerful to ensure they are telling the people the truth – is the reason the media have a privileged role in a democracy. The Hanson phenomenon exposed it as unfulfilled.

Eight years later we're still not bringing the private pains and needs of those who once supported Hanson to public attention, and we're still not scrutinising the powerful to ensure they are telling the truth. Not by a long shot.

The scream was always about money, power and democratic exclusion, John.

If this government wants to be fair dinkum, then it must stop kow-towing to financial markets, international organisations, world bankers, investment companies and big business people.

Pauline Hanson, 10 September 1996

So far the Trust has raised nearly $100,000, almost all of which is committed to supporting the action brought by Mrs Barbara Hazelton in the Queensland Supreme Court to test the validity of the Queensland registration of One Nation – which may not have been brought but for the Trust.

Tony Abbott explains the purpose of a new trust to the Australian Electoral Commission, 20 October 1998

Pauline Hanson's political career represented the first poeple's revolt against what both Labor and Liberal governments were doing to our core Australian value: the fair go.

A fair share in our growing national wealth.

A fair say in the way we shape our collective future.

A fair degree of access to power and privilege.

A fair shot at a decent job, a decent home and decent health care.

And – one of Hanson's key messages never taken up by the media – a fair education for our kids.

A fair bloody go, John.

Hanson's scream was never an articulate or informed one, but it was loud, real and made on behalf of many of Australia's powerless and disfranchised, and unlike many such screams it was expressed in the *right* way: using our democratic institutions. That's what made it so frightening to *all* the elites – Labor and Liberal, left and right, progressive and conservative – and Big Party, Big Money and Big Media. Pauline Hanson was screaming at the three-headed Beast of Australian power not from some wacky fringe, but from right at its heart.

Of course the Beast was going to destroy her.

August 1998

Imagine this.

You're a fly on the ceiling at Bistro Moncur, Damien Pignolet's splendid French bistro in the fashionable Sydney suburb of Woollahra. How fashionable? Paul Keating himself lives not far away. The clientele on any day at Moncur might be as famous as its Sirloin with Café de Paris butter, which melts in your mouth. You can't book a table – patrons must wait in the Woollahra Hotel bar for a nod from the staff. They reckon it's first come, first served – no 'queue jumpers' here.

Although being a Sydney MP known to be close to the PM probably doesn't hurt.

From your position on the ceiling you can see that the table below is occupied by four stalwarts of the neo-liberal scene, including a couple of associates of its most influential intellectual forum, *Quadrant* magazine, published from another fashionable Sydney suburb, Balmain. There's former NSW Liberal leader and ex-federal MP Peter Coleman, a

Woollahra resident, father-in-law of Treasurer Peter Costello. There's former Whitlam minister turned economic
ultra-rightist John Wheeldon. The third bloke, who's just
selected another bottle of crisp chardonnay, is the *Daily Telegraph*'s fervently pro-Howard columnist Piers Akerman. The
last man is the Member for Warringah and Parliamentary
Secretary.

The reason for this lunch – the first of several – is to
create a new private trust. Its purpose? To nail Pauline Hanson through the courts. One Nation is riding so high on
its recent Queensland election successes that it now threatens John Howard's chances at the upcoming federal poll,
and these neo-liberal power-players have decided upon a
dual strategy: let John woo her voters in public while they
destroy her party in private.

There's at least two One Nation dissidents up in
Queensland willing to go after Hanson with civil actions.
Abbott's already convinced Terry Sharples to seek an injunction stopping One Nation getting the cheque for $500,000
in public funds due after her Queensland success, to deprive
her of resources for the coming federal campaign. He's
given Sharples two top Liberal lawyers who'll do the work
for free, and a guarantee he won't be out of pocket – but it's
getting messy and Abbott's already misled the public about
what he's up to, as we'll see.

He now wants a more formal arrangement to fund
the injunction application of another dissident, Barbara
Hazelton.

Some top Liberals down in Melbourne – Jeff Kennett, and even Coleman's son-in-law Peter Costello – have been calling for the party to take on Hanson the honest political way: preference her party last while arguing the case against her policies out on the voting stump. Jeff even went north to eyeball her in a shopping mall during the Queensland election campaign. But John Howard isn't having any of that democratic nonsense. 'Speaking freely and openly' in public about 'certain subjects' with Hanson voters?

No one at this exclusive restaurant table today wants that.

Instead Howard has long been publicly empathising with Hanson's voters on the strictly social issues – land rights, refugees, family breakdown, law and order. And especially on the way our nation's cherished fair go is being destroyed by those damned elitists – the kind of moralising lefty hypocrites who chatter on endlessly about doing good for the battlers, while enjoying an excellent steak and a crisp chardonnay in some flash restaurant in some fashionable suburb.

The trust's money-men – there are twelve wealthy donors lined up, for the law is an expensive business – know that what they're about to fund is just business as usual from the three-headed Beast of Australian politics: Big Party, Big Money, Big Media.

The details will come together quickly, but there's an early snag: nobody can think of what to call this new trust. We imagine Piers – who, despite later claiming to crave 'greater transparency' in politics, will not write a word about these lunches for five years – suggesting another bottle while they think on it some more.

Tony Abbott brightens. He's got it! Three heads turn his way and Tony grins his trademark grin. You're gunna love this, fellahs: let's call it 'Australians for . . .'

Their laughter hasn't stopped when the waiter arrives with the Moet five minutes later.

It's just a silly, made-up conspiracy theory, of course. Or is it? Let's have a look at what actually happened.

The whole process of political funding needs to be out in the open so that there can be no doubt in the public mind – Australians deserve to know who is giving money to political parties, and how much.

Kim Beazley commends new laws requiring disclosure of political donations, 2 November 1983

There are some things the public has no particular right to know.

Tony Abbott explains why the laws don't apply to his trust, 5 September 2003

---

13 October 1997

Pauline Hanson applies to register in Queensland a political party she calls Pauline Hanson's One Nation. A major benefit of registration is that election costs are recoverable from the public purse. To satisfy Queensland electoral law a party without a sitting MP in the state Parliament must have at least 500 members. She lodges more than 500 names and addresses and the constitution of a very unusually structured and centralised party.

4 December 1997
The Queensland Electoral Commission, having confirmed the membership in the standard manner, accepts registration of Pauline Hanson's One Nation.

John Howard's party raises no objections.

10 May 1998
On the *Sunday* program Peter Costello states that One Nation will be preferenced last in his Melbourne electorate at the next federal election.

12 May 1998
John Howard argues in the party room against placing One Nation behind the ALP on Liberal how-to-vote cards at the federal election. He says he would prefer to work with One Nation than the Democrats in the Senate. Tony Abbott agrees, advocating the Voltaire approach: 'I disagree with what she says, but I'm happy to defend her right to say it.'

13 June 1998
After the Coalition in Queensland gives its preferences to One Nation above Labor, Brisbane liberals desert the Liberal Party

for Labor, and One Nation decimates the Nationals' vote, gaining eleven seats. The ALP wins office in Queensland.

Mid-June 1998

Tony Abbott begins attacking the legality of One Nation's registration in Queensland. He tells the House of Representatives on 2 July, 'I am not a lawyer, but it seems to me that . . . One Nation, as registered in Queensland, does not have 500 members, it is not a validly registered political party, and it cannot receive any public funding.' He personally lobbies the Queensland electoral commissioner to investigate One Nation's legality. He travels around the country encouraging One Nation dissidents to take legal action.

7 July 1998

Abbott meets One Nation dissident Terry Sharples in the Brisbane offices of establishment solicitors Minter Ellison to nut out the legal and financial support needed for Sharples to launch a Supreme Court injunction to stop One Nation getting $500,000 in public funding due after its strong vote in Queensland before the impending federal election. Abbott brings with him two top lawyers with Liberal Party connections – one is Queensland Liberal Party President Paul Everingham – who will run the action for free.

Sharples later claims that Abbott tells him that any Liberal Party connection should be kept secret, but that he will financially underwrite Sharples' intended civil action testing the legality of One Nation.

11 July 1998
Abbott gives Sharples a signed and witnessed 'personal guarantee that you will not be further out-of-pocket as a result of this action'. Sharples issues his Supreme Court writ for an injunction. Abbott has obtained the financial backing of someone – who he still will not name – to stump up $10,000 to meet that guarantee.

31 July 1998
Tony Abbott and journalist Tony Jones have the following exchange in an interview for an ABC *Four Corners* broadcast on 10 August.

JONES: So there was never any question of party funds —
ABBOTT: Absolutely not.
JONES: Or other funds from any other source —
ABBOTT: Absolutely not.
JONES: — being offered to Terry Sharples?
ABBOTT: Absolutely not.

21 August 1998
In the witness box during what will be an unsuccessful action for an injunction, Terry Sharples is cross-examined on his funding relationship with Abbott. Asked whether Abbott ever talked to him about 'providing an indemnity

for this action or any action you may bring', he replies 'No, he didn't.'

(Later, on 11 March 2000, in an interview with *Sydney Morning Herald* journalist Deborah Snow, Abbott will recount his reaction to Sharples after the August 1998 cross-examination: 'Terry, this thing is out of control, you have perjured yourself, you should just terminate this action and there'll be a costs order against you and I'll look after it.')

Soon after 21 August 1998
Abbott disassociates himself from Sharples' civil action.

24 August 1998
Tony Abbott establishes the Australians for Honest Politics Trust. Its stated objective is 'to support actions to challenge the activities of a political party or association within Australia which is alleged to conduct its affairs in breach of the laws of Australia'. First cab off the rank is former secretary and estranged friend of Hanson, Barbara Hazelton, who duly issues a Supreme Court writ also seeking an injunction against payment of the $500,000 before the federal election.

29 August 1998
The *Sydney Morning Herald*'s Marian Wilkinson reports Abbott's Australians for Honest Politics Trust under the headline 'Lib MP Backs Trust to Attack Hanson'. Abbott denies any Liberal Party involvement in AHPT, and says he

I saw One Nation as a threat not so much to civilisation as to the Coalition. It had brought down the Borbidge government in Queensland and was defeating Coalition MPs and candidates all over the country . . . [Tony Abbott] deserves a medal.

Peter Coleman reminisces in the *Australian*, 28 August 2003

Peter Coleman and . . . John Wheeldon used to hold their irregular meetings over lunch at the Bistro Moncur in Woollahra . . . I know, because I joined the gathering for a few pleasant meals. Conspiratorial? Hardly . . . Those attempting to demonise Mr Abbott, however, would be better employed arguing for an overhaul of the nation's electoral laws to ensure that all political parties are forced to operate with greater transparency.

Piers Akerman reminisces in the *Daily Telegraph*, 28 August 2003

is acting 'as a citizen and a democrat, because One Nation is a fraud on the taxpayers and must be exposed'. Hanson's senior adviser, former Liberal David Oldfield, who'd worked for Abbott before defecting to Hanson, claims that AHPT 'is a clear example of big business money being used to stop Pauline Hanson's One Nation. It is the filth of the Liberal Party at its worst, and Abbott's involvement in such nefarious activity is appropriate and understandable.'

3 October 1998

John Howard is returned to government with a reduced majority. One Nation polls 8.4 per cent of the national vote, but only has one senator elected. The result earns One Nation about $3 million in public reimbursement.

20 October 1998

Tony Abbott's response to a request from the Australian Electoral Commission on 18 September 1998 to disclose the trust's donors is to say that he is not required by law to do so.

10 June 1999

The AEC writes to Abbott accepting his assurances that the trust is not an 'associated entity' with the Liberal Party and therefore need not disclose its donors.

18 August 1999

Justice Roslyn Atkinson of the Queensland Supreme Court finds for the plaintiff in the Sharples civil action. (Barbara Hazelton had dropped her action.) She rules that Electoral Commissioner Des O'Shea's decision to register Pauline Hanson's One Nation was 'induced by fraud or misrepresentation' because the people on the membership list were 'supporters', not 'members'. One Nation is ordered to repay the $500,000 of public funds. A police investigation commences.

Although victorious, Sharples is considerably 'out of pocket as a result of this action'. He pursues Abbott to honour his indemnity pledge.

Late 1999

Abbott's lawyer writes to Sharples asking him to accept $10,000 to call it quits, maintaining this is not 'an admission of liability'.

24 September 1999

In Victoria Jeff Kennett's government suffers a stunning 4.5 per cent statewide swing against it, rising to 10–15 per cent in rural and regional seats, and is ousted. The backlash is attributed to voter anger after seven years of neo-liberal economic reform. Labor, which had made it its business to promise better services to regional voters, and Independents poll strongly in rural and regional seats. One Nation wins only 0.3 per cent of the primary vote.

January 2001

After extensive fundraising drives, Pauline Hanson finishes reimbursing the $500,000 owed by One Nation to the Queensland Electoral Commission under Justice Atkinson's judgement.

10 February 2001

One Nation polls 10 per cent of the primary vote in the WA state election, and up to 30 per cent in some rural seats. Its decision not to preference sitting members is crucial in the ousting of Premier Richard Court's Coalition government.

17 February 2001

One Nation polls 9 per cent in the Queensland state election in which the ALP is returned with a record majority and the Coalition Opposition is further devastated. Twenty-three per cent of Queenslanders abandon the main parties, mostly fleeing the conservative side to vote for One Nation, the One-Nation-derived City Country Alliance or ex-One-Nation Independents.

27 May 2002

Pauline Hanson is committed to stand trial on one count of fraudulently registering a political party, and two counts of fraudulently obtaining public funds.

22 March 2003

Hanson is narrowly unsuccessful in her bid for an Upper House seat in the NSW election.

15 July 2003

Hanson's trial commences before Judge Patsy Wolfe.

20 August 2003

After nine hours' deliberation, a jury convicts Hanson on all charges. Judge Wolfe sentences her to three years' imprisonment, noting that the publicity surrounding the case has severely damaged any chance of her resurrecting her political career.

22 August 2003

John Howard tells Neil Mitchell on Melbourne talkback radio:

'Like many other Australians, on the face of it it does seem [to me] a very long unconditional sentence for what she is alleged to have done. And you're dealing here with a breach of a law which is not based on something which is naturally a crime . . . Can I talk generally about the issue of registering political parties? . . . I've always had some reservations about whether the requirement that you register political parties is justified as necessary . . .'

28 August 2003

In an article for Sydney's *Daily Telegraph* Tony Abbott writes, 'I'm sorry that Pauline Hanson is in gaol. I believe that the sentence she received was too severe. But I'm not sorry for trying to expose the fact that One Nation was never a fair dinkum party. It was a company with three directors, not a party with 500 members.'

6 November 2003

The Queensland Supreme Court upholds Hanson's appeal and orders her release. Chief Justice Paul de Jersey writes, 'The preponderance of available evidence points to the conclusion that the applicants for membership became members of the political party.'

Pauline Hanson's One Nation was a fair dinkum party in Queensland, after all.

7 November 2003

Outside prison Hanson agrees with a Channel Seven reporter who suggests that the inmates with whom she has just shared eleven weeks have 'obviously touched you deeply':

'The whole thing has. I've learnt a lot from it. I was a person that had my opinion and, yes, I thought I knew everything – as a Member of Parliament to go and look through the prisons you know nothing, and these politicians and bureaucrats that make the legislation have no idea. And, yes, it's been a very daunting, distressing time. I could never explain what it's done to me, but in so many ways I've learnt so much from it . . .'

15 January 2004

Hanson announces that she is quitting politics:

'I'm sick and tired of seeing people elected to Parliament who haven't got the determination or the integrity, and who sell their souls to get their positions. I'm not feeling sorry for myself. I'm just really angry for the system we have, because I've seen the breakdown in many aspects of Australian life – education, the family unit, health, Australian ownership, even the Australian way of life.'

The Beast – Big Party, Big Money, Big Media – has finished off Pauline Hanson's political career. Tony Abbott is being called an underhand thug by some and a future prime minister by others. John Howard has already moved on.

16

Australians for Honest Politicians

*There is no reason to believe that large parts of any population
wish to reject learning or those who are learned. People want
the best for society and themselves. The extent to which a populace
falls back on superstition or violence can be traced to the
ignorance in which their elites have managed to keep them, the
ill-treatment they have suffered and the despair into which a
combination of ignorance and suffering have driven them*

John Ralston Saul

Pauline Hanson's jailing pinched a dangerous democratic nerve for our two Big Parties, and particularly
for the Prime Minister.

It triggered a re-examination of some recent political
history that Howard hoped would stay buried, exposing his
government's covert strong-arm tactics *and* the lame performance of our primary democratic watchdog, the Australian
Electoral Commission, to greatly unwanted scrutiny. It also
gave us a chance to prise open the door on who really bene-
fited from his regime – a door Howard desperately needed to
stay closed to protect the myth that he governed 'for all of us'.

The nerve pinched was the fair go: Australian society's
traditional defining, non-partisan value.

Whatever the rights and wrongs of the process that led to Pauline Hanson's conviction, an overwhelming number of Australians – including many who hated her policies and surprised themselves with their response – felt her jailing symbolised something rotten in our democracy. The little person who'd had a go without big money or big corporate or big union connections was in jail. The politicians with the dough, education, experience and clout had got away with blue murder.

A Moir cartoon in the *Sydney Morning Herald* told the story: politicians holding a 'Too harsh' sign bayed 'We're very concerned about the precedent.'

Hanson was jailed – after an exhaustive, expensive pursuit – over a registration technicality: a ruling that paid-up members of her Pauline Hanson Support Group were not members of her political party. It was a differentiation that would have been easily avoided with good legal advice. And as Bob Bottom wrote in the *Bulletin* on 12 November 2003: 'Even a cursory examination of other political parties . . . discloses different classes of members, who are all deemed to be part of the party. For example, the Liberal Party (Qld) specifies three classes of member: members, party supporters and corporate members.'

The Big Party politicians were rabbits in the spotlight. On the day Hanson was jailed, Howard had let Wilson Tuckey stay on his frontbench despite revelations that Tuckey had aggressively lobbied the South Australian government using ministerial letterhead to get his 45-year-old son – who he falsely claimed was his constituent – off a traffic fine. Tuckey had then lied about the matter to Parliament. Penalty? Howard called him 'stupid'.

Pauline Hanson never used her position to try to help her children avoid Australia's laws. Judge Patsy Wolfe sent her to jail for three years because her crimes 'affect the confidence of people in the electoral process'.

Just days before, Howard himself had been caught redhanded misleading Parliament over a meeting with Dick Honan, ethanol near-monopolist and Big Party donor (2002–03: Liberal Party $200,000, National Party $110,000, ALP $50,000). Our fervent 'free trade' PM had ignored Treasury and Finance Department advice and delivered mega-bucks to Honan through a taxpayer subsidy – in the process knowingly causing massive financial loss to two other Australian companies. Howard denied having the meeting to our Parliament. Penalty? Nothing.

Hanson never threw taxpayer money about in this way and then misled Parliament about it. Hanson went to jail as a public funds rorter.

In that same week, Labor announced that its new national assistant secretary would be Mike Kaiser, who had confessed to electoral fraud in 2000 but had never been charged.

Hanson's political career was over after she was charged with electoral fraud.

Australians laughed, bitterly. Whatever one thought of Hanson's policies, her rise was a *response* to disillusionment with the electoral process, not the *cause* of it.

The Big Party politicians who had started the ball rolling bolted for electoral cover as Hanson went down for three. Howard immediately opposed the length of her sentence, and suddenly declared that he did not even agree with the law under which his protégé had relentlessly pursued her in 1998. Abbott was 'surprised' by the conviction and 'shocked' by the sentence. Howard refused to answer all questions on whether he had approved Abbott's campaign in the courts. Abbott said, 'I don't know whether I specially discussed it with the PM, and when I might have done it.'

Again the cartoonists told the story: Leahy in Brisbane's *Courier-Mail* drew Howard as a crying crocodile, begging Abbott, standing atop Hanson with money bags in his hands, to 'Remember Tony, nobody told me anything, OK?'

The Libs' Bronwyn Bishop called Hanson a political prisoner and blamed Queensland Premier Peter Beattie. Labor's Craig Emerson blamed Abbott. NSW Premier Bob Carr thought the sentence was 'excessive', while Australian Conservation Foundation Chairman Peter Garrett said he thought 'Mr Abbott has actually done us a favour.' Conservatives and progressives alike groped for the 'right' response, while in Brisbane Beattie was unimpressed with everyone: 'I have never seen so many gutless wimps in my life, running around like scalded cats trying to position themselves for political gain.'

Some commentators called anyone who saw Abbott as less than a saint a hysterical conspiracist. Polls gauging public response to his behaviour suggested that if that were so, 70 per cent of Australians were loonies.

Abbott is accused of 'shedding crocodile tears' over Hanson's jailing. Yet it's not inconsistent to lambast One Nation as an undemocratic shambles while sympathising with Hanson's tough three-year sentence . . .

Matt Price, *Australian*, 28 August 2003

Arsonists are part and parcel of Australian life today, and no less so in the political sphere. Mr Abbott has had opponents trying to light flames under him since he was elected to represent Warringah at a by-election in 1994.

Piers Akerman, *Daily Telegraph*, 28 August 2003

Hanson's love–hate biographer and journalist Margo Kingston [is] putting Abbott in the dock and fuelling One Nation sympathies.

Dennis Shanahan, *Australian*, 29 August 2003

Abbott told the *Herald* he was acting as 'a citizen and a democrat because One Nation is a fraud on taxpayers and must be exposed'. Abbott was right.

Alan Ramsey, *Sydney Morning Herald*, 30 August 2003

How should one judge Abbott? He made some blunders along the way, but his strategic judgment was correct and validated. From what is known of Hanson's demise, Abbott is more hero than villain.

Paul Kelly, *Australian*, 30 August 2003

> The Workplace Relations Minister [Abbott] has been the most forthright player in this episode. He disagreed with Hanson and her policies and went after her. His methods were legal. His guiding principle, the maintenance of the integrity of the electoral system, sound.
>
> **Glenn Milne, *Australian*, 1 September 2003**
>
> In this unpleasant but enlightening episode, while he has been viciously attacked by almost every progressive with access to a word processor or a cartoonist's brush, Abbott has shown the kind of grit, determination, equanimity and, above all, concern for a purpose larger than himself, that marks out a future Prime Minister.
>
> **Greg Sheridan, *Australian*, 4 September 2003**

It was true that Abbott's Australians for Honest Politics Trust had been briefly publicised back in 1998 in the broadsheet newspapers, but very few Australians knew about it. Dramatic shots of Pauline Hanson disappearing behind bars made people sit up, scratch their heads and say 'Hang on a minute.' They began asking questions and demanding answers.

Many more Australians now learnt what only *Sydney Morning Herald* readers who'd read a Deborah Snow profile in 2000 had known: that soon after writing his indemnity guarantee for Terry Sharples in the lead-up to the 1998 election, Abbott had lied to Tony Jones about it on *Four Corners*, and lied about it *again* to the *Herald* eighteen months later – until Snow produced the document with Abbott's signature that exposed his dishonesty:

'When the *Herald* first put to him Sharples' claim that he'd promised money at the outset to be paid into a solicitor's trust account, Abbott said: "No, it's not correct." But when shown his signed personal guarantee, Abbott recants: "I had secured the agreement of a donor to provide up to $10,000, if necessary, to cover any costs award made against Sharples." Challenged about the conflict between this and his denial on *Four Corners* [10 August 1998], Abbott initially replies: "Misleading the ABC is not quite the same as misleading the Parliament as a political crime."'

Suddenly the public were hopping mad, and on 27 August they cheered the journalist for once when the *7.30 Report*'s Kerry O'Brien forensically dismantled Abbott's attempts to use every semantic trick in the book to avoid acknowledging his deceit.

Abbott then expanded his list of Australians *not* to lie to in an interview with Paul Kelly for the *Australian*: 'I shouldn't have been flippant about the ABC, certainly not to the *Sydney Morning Herald*.'

Perhaps worst of all, for the first time we got to note the contempt he'd expressed to Deborah Snow in 2000 for the One Nation dissidents he'd so assiduously cultivated in 1998: 'Do priests want to mix with sinners? Do doctors want to mix with people with terrible diseases?' People such as Terry Sharples and Barbara Hazelton were a pox on our democracy that brave Saint Tony had held his nose and endured for Australia's sake. As the awkward truth about Abbott's behaviour began to crystallise in the national mind, John Howard washed his hands.

Should Abbott be sacked for misleading the public, Prime Minister?

'Abbott has answered for that, and you go and talk to Abbott.'

Did the public have the right to know the donors to the Sharples legal action and the Australians for Honest Politics Trust back in 1998?

Of course. It was relevant information to voters casting an informed choice. Had the methods, motivations and individuals behind both legal moves been widely known, many One Nation voters might have suspected the sincerity of Howard's oft-stated empathy with their views. Other people might have thought the AHPT was a legitimate tactic, given the danger One Nation posed to their values, although as the belated outpouring of sympathy for Hanson showed, many voters might not have liked the idea of a rich, well-connected party using the law – an expensive and complicated business – to destroy a fledgling competitor. Many might have reckoned that it wasn't quite playing by the democratic rules; that there were more honest ways to defeat One Nation.

When the scandal finally broke after Hanson's jailing, Peter Costello joined the Labor Party in espousing just that view while, unlike some colleagues, pointedly refusing to criticise Hanson's sentence out of respect for the legal process: 'I don't think that the way to resolve political disputes is through the courts. I think the way to solve it is at the ballot box. It is a point that I have always made in relation to One Nation; I was always prepared to argue why its policies were wrong, and let's determine that at the ballot box.'

Suddenly, with Hanson behind bars, democracy was beginning to look like a sick insider's joke: a quiet little 'Honest Politics' club formed over a few lunches in an exclusive Sydney restaurant, headed by the same man who had just lied to the Australian people over Sharples; Abbott whipping up a cool $100,000 in less than three weeks from twelve anonymous donors whose identity he was determined to keep secret; Abbott courting One Nation dissidents in 1998; Abbott sneering at them in 2000; and now Abbott crying crocodile tears over the ultimate fruits of his own work.

There were deeper democratic questions, too.

When Abbott's AHPT had got that minuscule coverage in the broadsheets in August 1998 no reporter had thought to request its donors' identities, despite the implicit claim to transparency in its eye-catching name. That was disturbing in retrospect.

Why had no one checked with the Australian Electoral Commission about whether disclosure was required?

Why had no one queried the ethics of a wealthy party using its muscle to harass through the courts a new democratic entrant without disclosing its financial backers?

The answer was simple, really. Back then most of us in the political mainstream *had* reckoned it was justified or at least not worth scrutinising – or something weak and undemocratic like that – especially given that many of us were making careers out of scrutinising every twist in the internal dramas of the One Nation story.

Abbott wasn't the only one who had demeaned our democracy with his AHPT. The least the media could do, I thought, was atone for *our* professional failure to scrutinise *everyone*'s Electoral Act dealings, regardless of our own biases. Besides, I'd harried Hanson for five weeks during that 1998 election race trying to make her accountable for what she said – so much so that she'd accused me of destroying her entire campaign. The least I could do was apply the same standards to Tony Abbott.

It was only fair.

The Australian Electoral Commission has two vital roles in our democracy: to manage the electoral rolls and conduct our elections, and to enforce our donor disclosure laws.

In a Webdiary piece during the Honest Politics Trust scandal, Australia's most experienced electoral law expert, Graeme Orr of Queensland's Griffith University, described the democratic purpose of the latter role:

'Disclosure laws are meant to provide two related types of transparency. One, to inform interested voters about "who supports who" (on the assumption that this in itself provides clues about the real intentions/ideologies of political actors); and two, to allow the media, in particular, to shine light on possible "quid pro quo" corruption of political actors.'

The AEC was converted from a government department to an independent statutory watchdog in 1983 when the Parliament gave it responsibility for upholding new laws requiring the disclosure of large donations to political parties. Before 1983 Big Media and Big Business financed political parties in secret. Compulsory disclosure was a trade-off for the introduction of public funding for election campaigns, under which all candidates polling more than 4 per cent of the votes in the seats they stood for would be paid a certain sum per vote.

The Labor government that introduced the public-funding laws argued they would reduce the parties' dependence on private funding, both directly through the compensating public subsidy and indirectly due to the scrutiny of donations. The two Big Parties would in future be able to count on a guaranteed base 'public income' to fund their campaigns, and so the private fundraising pressure, with all its associated 'temptations', would be eased.

Twenty years later it still sounds like a damned good argument. In a system such as ours there's always scope for wealthy businesses and individuals to use their economic power to gain disproportionate political influence, and thus subvert democracy's bedrock promise: that each citizen shares equally in political power. It's an insidious anti-democratic threat that can be hard to avoid.

The then special minister of state Kim Beazley, who stewarded the 1983 reforms, said the new laws would minimise that threat: 'There is no greater duty upon the representatives of the people in a democratic society than the duty to ensure that they serve all members of that society equally. This duty requires government which is free of corruption and undue influence.'

As it turned out, our politicians, as usual, just wanted to eat *our* public cake *and* gobble every other private one they could get their hands on.

Since 1983 the Big Parties have used taxpayer money to secure their financial bases while massively *increasing* the corporate donations they collect. After the 1984 election 60 per cent of the Big Parties' revenue came from the new, vote-based public subsidy. After the 2001 election – by which time Labor and Liberal were together 'earning' around $38 million in taxpayer reimbursement – this had fallen to *20 per cent*.

Far from spurning private dough since 1983, the Big Parties have gone berserk: a rich voter can now buy superior access to political heavyweights – framers of policy, national executives, ministers, prime ministers – in all kinds of ways. Special lunches and dinners, expensive 'forums', one-on-one meetings and inside briefings – parties even get Big Money to *sponsor* their annual national conferences. La Trobe University's Joo-Cheong Tham, a leading electoral law expert, argues that we citizens should be under no illusion about these arrangements: 'Such sale clearly involves undue influence of politicians, because access to and influence on political power are secured through the payment of money.'

The stranglehold that large corporations now have on our government-forming parties – the Big Money, Big Party nexus – is tightening, and it isn't confined to the conservative side. Since 1999–2000 corporate donations have outstripped those from both wealthy individuals *and* big unions, with results that would almost be funny if they weren't so sad. A conservation group in Byron Bay recently called for donations to help it campaign against a major development – not to fund a demo or knock up some flyers, but with a view to offering money to NSW Premier Bob Carr to listen to its point of view, just as the developer, Becton, had done!

At the ALP's 2004 national conference in Sydney – Mark Latham the headline speaker – a cool $11,000 would have bought you a 'Platinum Table of 9' complete with its own 'senior Labor representative', *plus* a 'full-page advertisement in the evening's program'. All this while you and I pay these people every time we vote for them.

The AEC, as an *independent* statutory authority equipped with strong investigative powers, was supposedly going to allow Australians to keep a close eye on such excesses. It was to be answerable only to an *independent* board and overseen by a part-time chairman selected from a shortlist of three judges *independently* recommended by the judiciary. Those 1983 disclosure laws were meant to be as unambiguous as the AEC's democratic duty: to inform us, the Australian people, about who gives how much money, or donations in kind, to whom and when – and to remain impartial and apolitical while doing so.

In practice the major parties have treated these reforms with contempt. Just how much – and the depth of disdain shown by our politicians for the AEC's role as a public watchdog – would become clear during the controversy over the Australians for Honest Politics Trust. As Kathy Mitchell, head of the AEC Funding and Disclosure branch, would tell Senate Estimates in February 2004, 'It has become apparent to the AEC that what people expect the legislation should achieve is not what it is achieving.' Asked to explain why investigating a funding mechanism such as Abbott's was taking so long, she lamented that 'When you open one door, you potentially find several more doors to be opened after that . . .'

Disclosure laws cover donations to political parties and any 'associated entity':

'Commonwealth Electoral Act (1918) – Section 287 – Interpretation

(1) In this Part, unless the contrary intention appears: *associated entity* means an entity that:

(a) is controlled by one or more registered political parties; or

(b) operates wholly or to a significant extent for the benefit of one or more registered political parties.'

Here's where the citizen's game of cat-and-mouse begins. Or cat-and-Beast.

Where did Tony Abbott's AHPT fit in?

We learnt of Abbott's fellow trustee Peter Coleman's motivation for setting it up when he wrote in the *Australian* on 28 August 2003 that 'I saw One Nation as a threat not so much to civilization as to the Coalition.' John Howard had already made the reason for the trust even clearer in a doorstop exchange with a reporter on 27 August.

HOWARD: . . . but the important thing is that [Abbott's trust] was disclosed in the media in August of 1998, and he made no secret of it.

REPORTER: Are you happy with ministers of your Government being involved in destabilising other parties like that?

HOWARD: Well it's the job of the Liberal Party to politically attack other parties, there's nothing wrong with that.

So here we have the parliamentary leader of one 'registered political party' describing an entity's attacks on an opposing 'registered political party', in the lead-up to an election, as the Liberal Party doing its political job. This is a public admission by Australia's senior Liberal that the AHPT *was* an 'associated entity' operating 'wholly or to a significant extent for the benefit of' his own party.

So Australian voters could be told the identity of the trust's donors, right? Wrong.

On 27 August 2003 Abbott, through the *Sydney Morning Herald*'s Mike Seccombe, told the Australian people something else they'd been kept in the dark about. The AEC *had* asked him, in a letter dated 18 September 1998, to disclose his donors. He released the reply he had written on 20 October 1998 – but not the trust deed enclosed with it – and the AEC's response, to the *Australian Financial Review*. (The AEC had refused to release the correspondence to the media.) In the reply Abbott had advised the AEC that 'Before seeking donations to the Trust I spoke with one of Australia's leading electoral lawyers who assured me that the Trust would not be covered by disclosure provisions.'

When the AEC eventually wrote back – on 10 June 1999 – it accepted Abbott's word: 'On the basis of the information provided, I am of the opinion that the Trust does not constitute an associated entity at this time, and accordingly is not required to lodge a disclosure return.'

Once that was out Mike Seccombe contacted experts in electoral law, who expressed surprise that the AEC had backed down, said the AHPT looked like an 'associated entity' of the Liberal Party, and urged the AEC to release any legal advice to the contrary. Please explain!

And anyway why would Abbott want to keep secret the donors who'd helped him act 'as a citizen and a democrat' to expose 'a fraud on taxpayers'? And why wouldn't those donors be glad to out themselves if, as Abbott now claimed, they were acting in the public interest 'for all of us', not just the Liberal Party?

For the same reason Howard hadn't wanted the public to know about the donors he'd invited to the Bush barbecue perhaps?

Would the outing of Abbott's money-men be the people's first glimpse of how business really gets done in John Howard's Australia?

Would it embarrass Howard's rich mates?

Were media or National Party figures involved?

Were any of Saint Tony's twelve faceless donors linked to the PM's office?

Two were quickly exposed. *The Age's* political editor, Michael Gordon, outed millionaire businessman Trevor Kennedy, the former Packer executive, who'd kicked in $10,000. Once a Labor man, he was later strongly pushed by the Liberals to become the ABC's managing director when Jonathan Shier got the sack. Kennedy's motivation? He said he was proud to donate because Hanson 'was not only a great menace to this country, but a crook as well'.

Soon after his remarks Kennedy resigned his many directorships amid revelations of Swiss-account tax-dodging and the exposure of his long-denied involvement in Offset Alpine, a controversial company under investigation by the corporate regulator the Australian Securities and Investments Commission. As I write, Kennedy's crack legal team has just lost the first round of their legal fight to exclude certain documents from being used as evidence.

Terry Sharples outed another trust donor: Western Australian construction magnate, major Liberal Party donor and board member of Melbourne's neo-liberal Institute of Public Affairs, Harold Clough. Clough is generous to neo-liberal causes, and the IPA is appreciative enough to hold an annual chat in his name. At the 2002 Harold Clough Lecture Gary Johns spoke on 'Corporate Social Responsibility: Democracy or an Assault on Stakeholders?' The latter, of course.

Worth about $120 million in the early 1990s, Clough had helped finance a legal persecution of the WA Democrats by businessman John Samuel, who'd been expelled from that party after trying to seize control of his branch. The long, expensive legal action had nearly destroyed the WA Democrats.

Funnily enough it turned out that Samuel had since shifted his 'support' from the WA Democrats to WA One Nation – and had promptly begun legally attacking them, too. (Abbott admitted that the same John Samuel had been a 'close collaborator' in stumping up the cash to fund Sharples.)

On 5 September 2003 WA Democrat Senator Andrew Murray sent details of the Clough–Samuel Democrats party hijack attempt to the AEC. 'This is why you need disclosure and transparency – that's why people need to drive the connections hard,' Murray said.

An ugly pattern was beginning to emerge. Destroying the competition through the legal system was starting to look like no mere one-off tactic aimed at One Nation, but part of a systematic 'anti-competition' campaign by Liberal power-players to stop new parties gaining a foothold in the political 'marketplace'. It was beginning to seem as if John Howard the free marketeer was after a 'democratic monopoly' – squeezing out 'consumers' of 'minor brand' parties by using Big Money and our courts behind the scenes.

Who were the ten remaining mystery donors? Why was Tony Abbott so determined to keep their identities a secret from the people? And where was a public servant with the strength of Professor Allan Fels, our former competition watchdog and people's champion, to tell him to do the right thing?

In his letter to the AEC Abbott had said the Australians for Honest Politics Trust sought to 'preserve and strengthen the integrity of the electoral process'.

OK, Tony, I thought. Let's see whether *you* have been, and would continue to be, the recipient of favoured treatment under Australia's electoral laws.

First I checked out the AEC's track record.

Way back in May 2002 Labor Senator John Faulkner had asked the AEC's officers in Senate Estimates whether the Liberal lawyers' donation of services to Sharples for his

Supreme Court case and Abbott's indemnity should have been disclosed to the Australian people. The AEC replied that it would seek legal advice and advise further 'as soon as possible'. Fifteen months later it was yet to do so, and when Faulkner gave it a nudge after Hanson's jailing, the AEC promised to get back to him! In a 28 August 2003 brief to the Special Minister of State, Eric Abetz, obtained under FoI laws, the AEC claimed it had not replied to Faulkner 'as its inquiries to date have been inconclusive'. (It would become apparent that *no* fresh inquiries had been undertaken after receiving the legal advice.)

Not a bunch of movers and shakers, then.

On Monday, 1 September 2003, I questioned AEC Director of Communications Brien Hallett, who'd been handling Abbott queries for several days.

'On what basis did the AEC decide not to require disclosure of the donors to the Honest Politics Trust?'

He said he didn't know.

'Did it consider the trust deed before making the decision?'

He said he didn't know.

'Did it receive a copy of Abbott's legal advice?'

He said he didn't know.

'Did the AEC take its own advice before making the decision?'

He said he didn't know.

'Would the AEC release its correspondence with Abbott?'

No.

'Why not?'

That wasn't 'usual practice'.

'When did the AEC receive its legal advice?'

He said he didn't know.

'Would the Commission release that advice?'

No.

'Why not?'

It was 'privileged'.

When I pointed out that legal privilege belongs to the client, and that the AEC could therefore freely release its legal advice, the Director of Communications again refused to do so, saying he would get back to me later that day. He didn't.

Hallett was behaving exactly like a political media-minder whose boss had something to hide; if he really didn't know those answers it meant he deliberately hadn't been briefed. Politicians play that game with their mouthpieces when their aim is to kill an issue. For an independent statutory body whose explicit duty was to the *voters*, not ministers or government, this was untenable. The AEC's job was to keep our democracy clean, and to be seen to be doing so.

It was supposed to be on *our* side.

I decided to report the story on Webdiary transparently, declaring questions I had asked and answers I had got so that readers could see the games being played for themselves. I also decided to supply all the information they needed to participate directly in my attempt to get the truth. So I published the AEC's charter, which – on orders from John Howard's Department of Finance – it now calls its 'corporate goals':

'**Our Purpose:** The AEC's purpose is to help our primary customer, the eligible voter, have a say in who will represent him or her in the government of Australia.

Our Values: Independence and neutrality, integrity and accuracy, mutual respect, respect for the law, service, transparency.

What We Want to be Known for: The AEC wants to be recognised by its customers and stakeholders for providing leadership and expertise in electoral management.'

I added: 'If you are a voter, and thus the AEC's "primary customer", you may wish to communicate with your service provider on this matter. Ph (02) 6271 4411, National 13 23 26, Fax (02) 6271 4558.'

It was the first day of spring, and Pauline Hanson's twelfth in prison.

The next day began with a ring from a reader to report the results of his call to the AEC. By day's end I realised that the Australian people's democratic right to know who financed our political parties was a polite fiction. I also knew that many Australians were angry, engaged and trying hard to make it a reality.

Jim Mangleton said he worked in a real-estate agency

on the NSW North Coast. First thing that morning he'd rung the national AEC hotline to ask about the AHPT and was put through to Michael Avery, his local returning officer.

'He told me he didn't know what I was talking about!' Jim complained. 'He said he didn't have time to sit around looking at the newspapers.'

I rang Michael Avery, who agreed that he'd had an unusual start to his day: voters didn't usually 'ask for information on such matters', he said. '[Jim] rang first thing this morning, and said he'd read your article and wanted to know what was going on with Tony Abbott. I didn't even know what he was talking about ... I told him funding and disclosure was a national matter ... and gave him the expert's contact number.'

I complimented Michael for doing what he could for Jim.

'We try to help all our clients,' he replied. 'It doesn't matter what walk of life they're from, or who they preference.'

At least AEC people on the ground believed voters were more than 'customers'.

And their bosses? Brien Hallett rang later that day, after issuing a bland press release by AEC Electoral Commissioner Andy Becker stressing the AEC's statutory independence, its political neutrality, its earnest intention to address the 'complex issue' in a 'measured and deliberate' way, blah blah blah. Yet again Hallett stonewalled. He was playing political spinner and I copped the requisite 'prepared line': 'We made a decision in 1998 and are monitoring it, and if new information comes to hand it might change but we do not yet have enough information to form an opinion.'

Here we go again.

MARGO:	So on what basis did the Commission make that 1998 decision?
HALLETT:	Correspondence with Mr Abbott.
MARGO:	Did that correspondence include his legal advice?
HALLETT:	I'm not going into the details. We don't give running commentary on the specifics.
MARGO:	What was the basis of the AEC's 1998 decision not to order disclosure of donors?
HALLETT:	The evidence before us at the time.
MARGO:	What was that evidence?
HALLETT:	Correspondence . . . among other things.
MARGO:	Did the AEC read the Honest Politics Trust deed Abbott says he sent?
HALLETT:	I can't tell you.
MARGO:	But Abbott has already told us he sent it to the AEC!
HALLETT:	We don't normally comment on such things.
MARGO:	Did the AEC get its own legal advice to check if Abbott's claim that he need not disclose his donors was correct?
HALLETT:	I'm not going to comment.
MARGO:	Why not?

HALLETT: We don't give a running commentary on individual decisions on matters to do with disclosure.

MARGO: Why not?

HALLETT: It's between us and the individual concerned.

I was gobsmacked. So the Australian people the AEC was supposed to be serving didn't have the right to a full report from *their* statutory body!

MARGO: How does that sit with the AEC's duty to its 'primary customers'?

HALLETT: It's between us and the individuals or groups concerned.

MARGO: What is the Commission doing now that its decision is being strongly questioned by independent legal experts?

HALLETT: We're monitoring the situation.

MARGO: Are you investigating, or reading the [news] clips?

HALLETT: We're aware of Abbott's statement last week, and comments made by him and others. If someone brings a complaint, we'll consider it.

I couldn't believe it. In response to serious questions about whether the AEC had done the job, it didn't even see fit to investigate and was relying on the media to do it. And if we asked questions the AEC's spin doctors would stonewall anyway.

MARGO: You're saying you don't investigate, but you're supposed to be the people's representative here. Surely you must investigate this for yourselves, on their behalf? Why won't you release the legal advice you've got now so people can judge for themselves?

HALLETT: We don't give out our legal advice. That's standard practice.

MARGO: Why?

HALLETT: We don't.

MARGO: Why?

HALLETT: We see this as part of our duty to implement the Commonwealth Electoral Act.

MARGO: So why don't you give the people the legal advice, if that's your duty – to implement this Act on behalf of voters?

HALLETT: Because it's standard practice.

MARGO: But the AEC's credibility is on the line – its own press release showed that. Why won't the AEC let the people know what's going on if there's nothing to hide?

HALLETT: These are matters between individuals or groups under disclosure obligations and the AEC.

Got it by now? The AEC was not administering the Electoral Act in accordance with its own stated goals, much less its civic duty. There was nothing in electoral law that obliged it to be at all secretive, yet it chose to impose confidentiality – to suit the politicians. It was playing the game of those who wished to avoid scrutiny and could well be breaking the law! The AEC had become part of the Big Party closed shop. Part of the Beast.

I wondered aloud if the part-time Chairman of the AEC, Justice Trevor Morling QC, would approve, and asked for his phone number. Hallett said he'd get back to me.

By now most reporters who'd taken an interest had moved on. That's the spinner's main aim. First defence: the stonewall. Second defence: meaningless verbiage from the boss. Then more stonewall. These tactics usually kill the story.

Unfortunately for the AEC, Australians were taking matters into their own democratic hands.

Webdiarist Michael Hessenthaler wrote to the AEC:

'Dear AEC,

I am a customer of the AEC because I am an enrolled voter. Could you please advise me on the status of your "further inquiries" in relation to the topical issue of Tony Abbott and your original decision that he did not have to comply with disclosure requirements pertaining to the Australians for Honest Politics Trust. When do you envisage that you will, in accordance with your stated Corporate Goals, be transparent about the outcome of your inquiries?'

Webdiarist Brendan Mooney called Brien Hallett to find out what the disclosure laws demanded, and advised us where to look further on the internet: 'I am very interested in this matter as many other Australians are. We would like to see the AEC come clean and adhere to its own guidelines, which it clearly hasn't done to date. We would like to see who the donors to the Honest Politics slush fund were.'

Joo-Cheong Tham wrote a legal opinion for Webdiary that said the donors must be disclosed by law and agreed to answer Webdiarists' legal questions. In a piercing aside, he warned that 'If political litigation becomes the norm, it will then become another way of insulating the major political parties against less well-off competitors.'

Several other Webdiary 'primary customers' emailed, phoned and wrote to the AEC. The most detailed contribution was by Sue McDonald, of Sydney's suburban belt, who on 3 September sent AEC Chairman Trevor Morling a list of questions about Abbott's trust and a statement of her reasons for believing the donors should be made public. Weeks later, after the AEC wrote a pro-forma reply on Morling's behalf, Sue submitted her 'deluxe case', a comprehensive compilation of cross-referenced press statements, written evidence, AEC aims and electoral law citations. It was an amazing submission, and I emailed Sue asking if she was a lawyer or an activist.

No. She was an ordinary Australian citizen who was finally fed up:

'I entered adulthood as a typical member of the SAP (Suburban Apathy Party), with my social conscience taking me as far as being on my child's school Tuckshop roster. Despite this early detachment and lack of commitment to either the Right or the Left, I am now finding it more and more difficult to adhere to my natural inclination for disinterestedness. I do not like being taken for a fool, nor do I like injustice, intolerance or racism, or being fobbed off. My grandmother always told me to go to the top of the tree, and she also believed in over-explaining and asking questions until she arrived at the truth.'

Sue McDonald – Australian CITIZEN!

The breakthrough came on 3 September 2003 courtesy of a tip-off from a concerned insider. The bloke who'd decided to let Abbott off the hook was named Brad Edgman, I was told, the head of the AEC's Funding and Disclosure branch at the time. I gave him a call.

Brad Edgman does not have legal qualifications. Despite the complexity of disclosure law – due to the Big Parties' use of disclosure avoidance schemes – he'd neither asked for a copy of Abbott's legal advice nor sought his own in 1998–99. He said he'd read Abbott's letter, looked at the trust deed and was 'of the opinion that the Trust does not constitute an associated entity'. Can you imagine the ACCC asking a company questions about price fixing, then closing the file on the basis that the company *says* its lawyers *say* its activities are legal? The Tax Office doing the same when it queried your deductions? How convenient for Tony Abbott.

And would Pauline Hanson – or any other non-establishment politician – have got the same treatment? My AEC sources said *no way*.

Public pressure was having an effect. The day after I published the Edgman story – Hanson's second week in jail completed – I interviewed AEC Chairman Trevor Morling. He began, 'I'm a non-executive chairman. I don't work in the Commission, and can't possibly know the day-to-day operations.' (AEC Electoral Commissioner Andy Becker is effectively the managing director, with oversight by a board comprising the Chairman, Becker and another non-executive person.) Morling said he had 'arranged to have sent to me today all our records'. Why? 'Because of the level of public concern.'

He said the AEC had sought new, urgent advice from the Australian Government Solicitor that very day, adding that after Faulkner's 2002 query about Sharples' legal services the AEC had also sought advice from the AGS and the Director of Public Prosecutions. He was reading the first AGS advice as we spoke and described it as 'inconclusive'.

Morling said, 'I wish it had been referred to me then', and seemed nonplussed that the Commission had not investigated further. 'I may refer this to a senior counsel for an opinion,' he added.

Trevor Morling has now retired as chairman, and since

that conversation the AEC has strenuously denied that he *did* intervene in the case, but neither the AEC nor Morling has complained to my editor for reporting to the contrary. Documents since extracted under a Freedom of Information request also show that Morling refused to sign a draft AEC letter denying that he had criticised the Commission or intervened in the AHPT case. Morling returned another call some time later, leaving a message saying that since he'd left the job it was now inappropriate for him to make further comment.

While still in office, however, Morling had told me that the AEC 'must stay outside politics – you'd be surprised at the ways we have to fend off politicians and political parties trying to get what they want implemented. That applies whatever government is in power – I've been in the job for fourteen years.'

Brien Hallett suddenly became more expansive. Of the AEC's failure to provide the Senate with the legal advice relating to Sharples' case, he said, 'It was an oversight. It's regrettable.' (Sound familiar?)

So would the AEC now investigate Abbott's trust? 'I'm not in possession of all the facts yet. Steps are being taken, and I believe a discussion is being held today with the AGS.'

Hmm, I thought. Tony Abbott reckons he's an honourable man. Why not ask him to disclose his donors directly to take the pressure off the AEC and restore people's trust in the democratic process? I lodged some questions with his spokesman the next day.

Abbott left a return message: 'Margo, it's Tony Abbott here, the object of your derision and ridicule. I'm returning the call that you put in to Andrew Simpson yesterday.'

We spoke late on Friday, 5 September. Hanson was spending her third week in jail.

MARGO: Had you given intending donors to the AHPT a guarantee of confidentiality?

ABBOTT: No. I did not tell them that their names would be publicised.

MARGO: Why didn't the public have the right to know the identity of the donors?

ABBOTT: There are some things the public has no particular right to know.

MARGO: Such as?

He asked whether I had publicly disclosed my salary.

'Yes,' I replied.

He asked whether I had criticised Fairfax in public.

'Yes,' I replied. I asked him again what things the public had no right to know.

Abbott: 'Where do you start? I don't propose to nominate a list. I don't propose to enumerate them. Short of the AEC changing its mind, they are not entitled to know who those donors were unless the donors choose to volunteer that information.'

He said the donors had done 'a good thing' for Australia. So why did he design the trust to ensure that donors would remain secret?

Abbott: 'I didn't design the trust so that donors weren't required to disclose. I set up the trust to support legal action.'

So why did he take legal advice on secrecy before soliciting the donations?

Abbott: 'I didn't take legal advice on disclosure till after I got the AEC's letter. I sought legal advice and got oral advice from a senior lawyer.'

Who was his lawyer?

Abbott refused to answer.

Why?

He had not advised the lawyer that 'by the way, in five years' time I'm going to dob you in to Margo Kingston'.

'I just believe private conversations should be private,' Abbott said.

Then why did he reveal the content of this private conversation in his letter to the AEC and why had he now released the letter to the media?

Tony Abbott did what certain politicians do when they're cornered – attack the questioner.

ABBOTT: I think your problem is, Margo, that you support One Nation. That's your problem.

MARGO: Why would you think that?

ABBOTT: You're Pauline Hanson's best friend. You're

delighted at the prospect of Hanson coming back. You'd be delighted.

MARGO: Did your lawyer see the Honest Politics Trust deed before giving advice?

ABBOTT: I'm not going to disclose that.

MARGO: Why?

He said he'd given me enough time and hung up.

It took a while for it to sink in. Over the weekend I read his 1998 letter to the AEC again, not quite believing what I was reading. But there it was in black and white: 'Before seeking donations to the Trust I spoke with one of Australia's leading electoral lawyers who assured me that the Trust would not be covered by disclosure provisions.'

If what he'd just told me on the phone were true, then had he lied to the AEC in writing? If he had that was a very different matter, as Pauline Hanson now knew, from lying to the ABC, the *Sydney Morning Herald* or, in Howard's government, to our Parliament. Hanson was in jail. Abbott was a Cabinet minister. A future prime minister, some reckoned.

I read it again.

On 20 October 1998 Abbott told the AEC in writing he had sought legal advice on donor secrecy *before* collecting donations. On 5 September 2003 he told me he got his legal advice *after* the donors had paid up, in response to the AEC's letter of demand.

So what?

There's a big persuasive difference, for starters. His letter to the AEC intimated that he'd structured the AHPT specifically to avoid disclosure, on expert legal advice, and had then guaranteed confidentiality to his donors. His story to me now was that he had not given assurances of confidentiality and had not taken legal advice on disclosure until after hearing from the AEC: meaning he had misled the Commission to bolster his case against disclosure.

But the legal implications were more disturbing. The authority of 'legal advice' is worthless unless lawyers are prepared to put their name to it. So given Abbott told the AEC he'd got legal advice the question is not simply *when*, but also *if*.

Did he really get legal advice? Or did he just relay a few off-the-cuff observations from a lawyer mate – observations not made with intent to be represented as legal advice?

Why wouldn't Abbott say whether he briefed his lawyer with the AHPT deed? I'm a lawyer myself and self-respecting lawyers would *never* give advice without considering the relevant material if they knew clients intended to present it as authoritative.

Did Abbott's lawyer know that his 'assurance' would be used in this way? IF not, is that why Abbott wouldn't name his lawyer? IF so, why the problem in naming his lawyer now? Why would his lawyer be professionally unwilling to stand publicly by it?

Question: had Tony Abbott misled the Australian

Electoral Commission not only about the timing of his 'legal advice', but also about its very *existence*?

Section 137.1 of the Uniform Criminal Code Act (1992) states that providing (materially) false or misleading information or documents in 'compliance or purported compliance with a law of the Commonwealth' is a criminal offence carrying a penalty of imprisonment for twelve months.

On Tuesday, 9 September 2003, I phoned Brien Hallett to inform him of Abbott's admissions. He said he would 'send it up the line'.

Was the AEC finally asking Abbott the questions it failed to ask him in 1998?

'I can't give you a running commentary on what we're doing,' Hallett said, because the AEC didn't want to broadcast its strategy. But he gave an assurance that the AEC was no longer just reading media reports and was actively investigating.

'We do take our accountability [to voters] very seriously,' he said.

I asked what penalties there were for misleading the AEC. He checked with the experts and confirmed that misleading the Commission would come under the Uniform Criminal Code.

'We don't have a view on whether he has misled,' Mr Hallett said. 'We don't have enough evidence. If you have particular information you can put that before us.'

I wrote up the Abbott interview and published it on Webdiary. That was my evidence. The next day a fax arrived:

'September 10, 2003
Dear Margo,

I've just been given your latest online piece.

The important facts remain: the Honest Politics Trust did not endorse candidates, support candidates or fund campaigns. I did not tell donors their names would be revealed when seeking donations because I had no reason to think they would be. I did not tell the lawyer whose advice I sought that his name would be revealed. I have always been upfront about my role in Australians for Honest Politics but don't intend to say anything about other people's roles except as required by law. To do otherwise would be to break faith with people who supported a good cause at a difficult time for Australia.

Yours sincerely, Tony Abbott'

Tony, the identity of your donors, and the purpose and activities of the AHPT, were no longer the only 'live' question. It was your lawyer we'd like to have heard more about. Still would.

The AEC went quiet after that.

I understand that it has demanded access to more documents and, as I write, is in protracted correspondence with Abbott's lawyers. I also understand that a passionate internal debate is underway within the AEC about the need to assert its independence.

The AEC is, in theory, in a strong position. Abbott has said over and over that if the AEC tells him to 'I will be happy to disclose the donors'. But if there were nothing politically embarrassing in their identities they themselves would have come forward to defuse things by now. I think Abbott *would* argue the matter in court if push came to shove, and that his assurances to the contrary were for public consumption in the belief the AEC would not call his bluff.

Why not bring it on? The potential abuse of such trusts to destroy or exhaust new democratic players through the courts, for the benefit of the Big Parties, is obvious. If the AEC won in court it would have a legal precedent of enormous value for forcing disclosure from reluctant political parties. If it lost it could recommend strengthening the law. The ACCC does this all the time.

And what if the AEC doesn't bring it on? The only citizens who can ask the Federal Court to order disclosure are Pauline Hanson and David Ettridge. Other citizens could ask the Federal Court to order the AEC to do its duty. Perhaps citizens could form their own AHPT to fund their own court action to, in Tony Abbott's words, 'preserve and strengthen the integrity of the electoral process'.

On 25 January 2004 I emailed Abbott some questions, which he replied to on 4 February.

MARGO: Was your lawyer briefed with the trust document before giving his or her legal advice?

ABBOTT: No.

MARGO: You say in your letter to the AEC that your lawyer 'assured me that the Trust would not be covered by disclosure provisions'. Was that assurance given without reservation or qualification?

ABBOTT: Yes.

MARGO: Was your lawyer aware that you would use this advice for the purpose of representations to the Australian Electoral Commission?

ABBOTT: To the best of my recollection, yes.

MARGO: What is the basis on which you describe your lawyer as 'one of Australia's leading electoral lawyers'?

ABBOTT: My judgement.

MARGO: Why did you advise the AEC by letter that you had sought legal advice *before* seeking donations to the trust, when you sought the advice *after* receiving the AEC letter requesting disclosure?

ABBOTT: I had more than one conversation with the lawyer in question.

MARGO: Has the AEC sought further information from you in relation to the trust and the content of your letter to it?

ABBOTT: You should ask the AEC.

Thanks, Tony. Oh, yeah, just one more thing. It's been bugging me for months.

MARGO: How did the [Australians for Honest Politics] trust get its name?

ABBOTT: I chose it.

In his letter to the AEC Abbott had said that 'I very much doubt whether the framers of the Electoral Act would have wished to discourage those seeking to test and strengthen the electoral law.'

Yet while reporting this story I learnt that Abbott's own government has done precisely that for years, starving the people's watchdog of the funds to do its job on donation disclosure and thus intimidating it out of doing its job. This suits both Liberal and Labor, helping them avoid party politics interfering with their mutual donor 'sins', and such has been its progressive atrophy that the AEC now plays along. Even if the Big Parties are caught not disclosing – overwhelmingly by chance – the AEC never prosecutes.

There's also the question of leadership. Throughout the Abbott controversy Commissioner Andy Becker refused all interview requests. Neither the way Becker was appointed nor his career so far inspires much 'confidence in our electoral process'. Becker was a political appointment: Howard's Cabinet overruled the selection committee's view that he was unsuitable to be assistant commissioner in 1997, and again when it did not recommend him for the top spot in 2002.

Two months after Becker got the top job the AEC

admitted that he had agreed to supply our 8 million electoral roll names, complete with our birth dates and gender, to the Australian Taxation Office – so that John Howard could send us all a personalised covering letter with ATO information about the GST. Becker misled Senate Estimates on his knowledge of what would be sent to voters and had to correct the record twice. Privacy Commissioner Malcolm Crompton found that Becker was in breach of his legal duty not to hand over our private information without our permission.

Business as usual from top-level bureaucrats in John Howard's 'frank and fearless' public service.

There are, however, early signs that the AHPT fiasco has had some cleansing effects. At Senate Estimates in February 2004 the AEC announced a change in policy – it will now publish its decisions on disclosure and the reasons for them on a new web page to 'provide the client service people are looking for'. It's also investigating six organisations 'fronting' donations to the National Party, which the last returns revealed were all on the same floor of the same Sydney building.

One factor may be the increased media scrutiny the AHPT has inspired. Politicians are less inclined to 'heavy' statutory bodies when they know the country is paying attention. If we want the AEC to watch the politicians effectively for us, then perhaps we – and especially the media – must watch the watchdog in return.

But there's a long way to go before the original intent of the

1983 legislation is realised. Fifty-one AEC recommendations to tighten disclosure laws remain unheeded, while as far back as 2000 the AEC had told a parliamentary committee examining root and branch reform that disclosure laws were a farce because 'full disclosure can be legally avoided'. That committee lapsed at the 2001 election and John Howard did not revive it. (The Senate did so in the wake of the AHPT scandal.)

Howard and Tony Abbott believe in a certain kind of politics for those parties that have the power and money to do whatever it takes to avoid our electoral laws, and another kind of politics for the battling ones that can't.

Soon after Pauline Hanson was sent to jail, I wrote a Webdiary piece called 'Mother of the Nation in Jail, It's Father in Charge':

'The big brand names of politics and the big media – with all their considerable assets – worked tirelessly to silence the scream of the Hanson disfranchised. I wrote in my book about [Hanson's] 1998 election campaign that Australia had been lucky that our brand of far-right nationalist politics had been amateur, unresourced, and too-quickly put together by carpetbaggers like David Oldfield and David Ettridge. What if a professional had captured the masses' imagination – where would Australia be now?

Now we know. A professional has stepped in. His name is John Howard.'

The 'anti-democratic' threat posed by Pauline Hanson inspired seven years of bitter division among those who, like Pauline, the battling Marrickville refugee activist, and her sister, the single mum who could get no help for her addicted son, should have been natural allies. As we all bickered the real enemy savaged Australia's fair go, while stoking our resentments of outsiders to stop us looking closely at who was really causing our pain, anxiety and fear of what lay ahead.

Today, to gaze back upon 1996 from Howard's post-GST, post-*Tampa*, post-Bali Australia – with its dog-eat-dog economics, its contempt for non-economic UN covenants on the environment and for international law, its destruction of our hard-earnt global reputation in human rights and its normalisation of intolerance and mistrust – is to wonder, almost nostalgically, what it was about the redhead from Ipswich we could ever have been so scared of.

On 20 January 2004, just a few days after she'd announced her retirement from politics for good, Pauline Hanson sang a duet version of 'I am Australian' in Tamworth's Oasis pub. Singing along beside her was 10-year-old Indigenous schoolgirl Nellie Dargan, who had opened up her heart to write to the woman who'd once declared that, while an MP, she would happily represent everyone in her electorate except Aborigines and Torres Strait Islanders.

Nellie had written 'I know you will get lots of mail. My mum has been in jail, too.'

After they'd celebrated our way of life together in song,

Hanson hugged the child and said, 'I'm so very proud to be able to stand beside Nellie, who I think is a precious, darling child who has a big future in country music.'

Unyielding progressives might call that a belated, chastened and much-needed public apology. Unyielding conservatives might call it practical reconciliation in action. But, like so many of us now, I'm tired of the old arguments and the exhausting divisions, and prefer to call it something optimistic and forward looking.

Australian. Honest. Not politics. Hopeful.

Postscript: the quest to reveal the ten remaining mystery donors goes on. I finished this chapter while the AEC dragged its feet on my Freedom of Information request for material on Abbott's Australians for Honest Politics Trust. The legislative deadline for handing over the documents passed, and then two extensions the AEC itself specified. The Commission gave no explanation for the delays. Finally it released some documents, including an extraordinary email from the decision-maker Brad Edgman in 2003, after I lodged an FoI request for documents on my FoI request! Even later the AEC finally released the trust deed. The witness to the signature was blanked out and the last two pages, including what looks like a receipt for stamp duty, were illegible. The AEC did not even ask for legible copies to be sent before letting Abbott off the disclosure hook. It then told Senate Estimates it sought legal advice before releasing relevant documents – something it failed to do when exempting Abbott from disclosing his donors to the Australian people. The AEC's actions remain at odds with its charter.

Edgman sent the damning email to Brien Hallett and the AEC's executive group on 26 August 2003 after journalists asked why the AEC had run dead on the AHPT:

'The letter Abbott is talking about [exempting him from disclosure] was signed by me. Back in FAD [the AEC's Funding and Disclosure Branch] in 1999 we considered whether his trust might be an associated entity. The bottomline conclusion was that, on the scant information available at the time, it couldn't be concluded to be such . . .

The basis of this conclusion, as Brien [Hallett] and I discussed earlier this afternoon, was that the trust's operations were aimed at causing a political party harm rather than to benefit any particular party/ies. In other words, it does not meet the Act's definition of associated entity. This is no real surprise, as the provision was introduced to cover front organisations that were being used to launder party donations and transactions (ie "benefits") . . .'

You can only wonder what form Edgman's 'considered' attention took, as there is absolutely nothing in the AEC's file in 1998 or 1999 evidencing any consideration at all. No memo, no email, no file note, no record of discussion – nothing came to light after my FoI request. And why did it take the AEC eight months to reply to Abbott's letter seeking exemption from disclosure? Yet another 'unfortunate oversight', according to Edgman in another email.

The AEC has extensive powers to get the information it needs to make an informed decision. It did not do so, and reached its decision on the basis of 'scant information'. Why?

Edgman's reasoning is logically as well as legally untenable. To say a group dedicated to destroying one party can't be doing it to benefit another – in this case the Liberal Party – is ludicrous.

Electoral law expert Joo-Cheong Tham said of Edgman's decision:

'Disturbingly, the email indicates that the AEC's 1999 conclusion was made without adequate information. Further, it suggests that no serious attempt was made to obtain such information. More generally, it reveals an artificially narrow approach to the "associated entity" provisions that risks hollowing out these provisions. With such an approach, front organisations engaged in negative campaigning would, for example, fall outside the definition of "associated entity".'

Edgman's email of 26 August 2003 also shows that Hallett misled me on 1 September 2003 when he said he did not know why the AEC had let Abbott off in 1999.

And other documents show that at the same time the AEC was refusing to release its 1998–99 exchange of letters with Abbott to the Australian people it was charged with serving, it jumped to attention when Abbott – the alleged law breaker – asked for copies at the height of the scandal. The AEC delivered them on the same day.

We're talking dereliction of duty by the AEC, followed by a sustained and determined cover-up. Howard has presided over the collapse of the AEC as a credible watchdog of democracy, at least when it comes to political donations. A root and branch overhaul is urgently required.

Over to you, Mark Latham.

Part Five

Our Australia

17

Harry Heidelberg was born in Lismore on the NSW North Coast and grew up in Brisbane's Indooroopilly. He graduated from the University of Queensland in 1986 with a Bachelor of Economics. His first job upon graduation was in Sydney working for a global accounting firm, and Harry says one motivation was to open up opportunities to work overseas. He's since done just that and at present lives in Switzerland, where he works at the European headquarters of a US multinational.

Although Harry likes to consider himself a 'citizen of the world', his Australian identity remains of central importance to him, and he is vitally engaged in Australian political and cultural debate.

M.K.

Ever More Democratic

By Harry Heidelberg

*If liberty and equality, as is thought by some, are chiefly
to be found in democracy, they will be best attained when all
persons alike share in the government to the utmost*

Aristotle (384–322BC)

*To stand erect and say, 'I am one of the rulers of my country' –
there is a position of dignity and of responsibility. Yet,
they are a dignity and a responsibility which democracy,
properly understood, gives to every grown man and
woman in this nation*

**Robert Menzies, 'The Nature of Democracy',
from *The Forgotten People* radio broadcasts, 1942**

Four years ago I started an extraordinary online conversation. At first it sounded like a conservative yelling at a rabid lefty journalist. The conservative being moi, and Margo Kingston being the rabid lefty journalist.

When Margo started her Webdiary I offered a small bouquet – swiftly followed by an overwhelming denunciation of the witch of Fairfax! Bloody Fairfax as usual in cahoots with the bloody ABC.

While the beginning was inauspicious and predictable, the course of the next four years was less so. The conversation became a political journey where certainties were questioned and sometimes overturned. Out of a new ambiguity I found unexpected common ground with a diverse group of Australians. Together we were able to distil the values that really mattered.

Part way through the journey I even changed my name!

Right from the start of Webdiary, Margo did something different. She short-circuited a ritualised, Canberra-style debate, where slogans are tossed back and forth in mindless synchronicity.

Not that I realised this at first. I was still dancing on Keating's political grave, and I began by making a generalised smear against all the 'politically correct'. You could understand my sense of triumph and unmitigated glee: after all I was a committed Liberal voter and it was back in 2000, four years after the Howard landslide.

I found it a tasty blood sport to dismiss the so-called chardonnay-quaffing media-agenda-monkeys of inner Sydney and Melbourne – and yet I'd long held many of their views myself. I thought Keating's minimalist republic was ideal for Australia: we'd emerge with our own head of state but not put at risk an entire constitutional system that, to quote John Howard, 'had served us so well'.

Another example was reconciliation with Indigenous Australia. I believed that practical and symbolic reconciliation were intertwined, not mutually exclusive, and that both needed to be addressed urgently.

If it seemed like a contradiction to despise the cultural

elites while holding some of their views, I never saw it that way. I'd been listening to mainstream Australia and had watched the rise of Hanson. The mainstream felt denigrated and excluded by the political correctness of the 1990s: Keating could not have done a better job of creating an environment ripe for Hansonism.

In 1996 Howard had said he wanted government 'for all of us' and that he 'believed passionately in the things that unite us as Australians rather than the things that divide us'. This had excited me and I was looking forward to the emergence of a more inclusive Australia.

My dream was an Australia where the dignity and needs of the mainstream would sit comfortably beside the advancement of the key cultural and social issues of the time. I thought a more 'ordinary' leader such as Howard, who was a self-confessed cricket tragic rather than a French antique-clock collector, would be able to take Australia to the next level. My view was that Howard would do the right thing by the economy (which he has) and the rest would surely follow. In common with many moderate liberals, 'the rest' was no small matter for me: it was important that the country embrace the full implications of its past and look forward to a future in which we would lead the world in social development. I didn't expect a conversion to republicanism on Howard's part, but I did expect that his ability to identify with the mainstream would allow him to lead in areas where leadership was surely needed.

I didn't blame Howard for tolerating Hanson, I blamed Keating for creating her.

Times change, though, and mindsets, too. Dramatic events have transformed the world, and with it Australia. *Tampa*, 9-11 and Bali stand out as the markers of this era.

The leadership I'd wanted and waited for has never come.

The conservative John Howard has emerged as a constitutional radical, wanting to detooth the Senate by abolishing its power to veto legislation: an extraordinary grab for power. I could never have predicted that he'd turn on our democracy – and that consequently I'd turn on him.

Now even my attack on Margo is ancient history. For the past four years I've been responding to her challenge to explain my views. In the process I've accepted that things were not as black and white as my original emails had suggested. Of course I knew about shades of grey, but they didn't fit into my style of debate. I wasn't interested in common ground and thought consensus with Margo's ilk was a waste of time.

However, given that I wasn't a member of the Liberal Party or involved in politics it became a bit silly to adopt a ruthlessly partisan approach against the left. The Webdiary trip taught me that early on. If both sides adopt a take-no-prisoners style of debate we end up with a barren, sterile discussion in which the language may be strong, but the blows are as meaningful as those we see in World Championship wrestling. Denunciations become hollow and laughable.

I've found that the meaningful blows are the ones you land against yourself or the ones where you let your guard down and give your opponent a free go. Brutally honest feedback is one of the most intellectually cleansing things you can have. I'd recommend it to anyone. Opening up, engaging and accepting the complexity of modern Australia comes with rich rewards.

It's easy to say that we believe passionately in the values that unite us as Australians, but it's an odyssey to discover what those values are. In my Webdiary trip I've contributed a quarter of a million words on the subject and read millions more words from other engaged Australians.

I've formed the view, shared by many Webdiary participants, that some of our core values are under attack – and that Australian democracy itself is threatened.

At the most basic level of politics we all embrace democratic values. That's easy to say but what we mean by it grows ever more complex. Our Australian system of democracy is akin to a complex ecosystem such as a rainforest or a coral reef, rich in diversity. Its vibrancy stops you in your tracks: you're excited to be part of it.

We know now that rich ecosystems are not invincible. You'd think there would be an immense strength in all that diversity, but in fact what we have are interdependencies so intricate that the whole system can collapse if we take a small part out of it. And if we introduce a species alien to the system we can so upset its delicate nature that it collapses.

I'm not suggesting our democracy is going to collapse, but I am suggesting that it is more delicately balanced than the government would have us believe. I'm also suggesting that some of the government's current agenda will surely result in a material weakening of our system.

As citizens we have a duty to fight threats to our democracy.

The attack on the remaining diversity in our media is the first threat to our democracy, as Margo has shown. We're not going to get the information we need for the proper functioning of our democracy unless it's independent. Independence requires diversity, and we'll never have that in the barren media world that John Howard plans. Under the proposed legislation Packer and Murdoch – or Telstra and Murdoch – could own all the influential arms of the media.

Packer is a fine businessman. He inherited a fortune and made it a lot bigger. There's nothing wrong with that. The Packer family interests span media, entertainment, banking, retail, publishing, gaming and more. Packer is an extraordinarily influential figure on the Australian landscape.

Murdoch is the man who started out at the *Advertiser* in Adelaide and went global. I was in Italy a couple of weeks ago and his reach even extends there. Whichever region of the world you go to, Murdoch will be waiting. His satellites hover in low earth orbit. He's at one with the

Bush administration. Murdoch's world is a potent cocktail of power and influence.

Packer and Murdoch are already joined in Foxtel, and there's no reason to believe they wouldn't carve up the rest of the market in a cosy way. Their sons, Jamie and Lachlan, went in together on One.Tel. (What a disaster that was.) If Packer and Murdoch owned even more of the media than they do now, you'd never get such a story reported properly.

More than that, you'd never be able to expect proper reporting of the diverse business interests of the moguls. If you lived in Sydney you could pick up the *Sydney Morning Herald*, the *Daily Telegraph*, the *Australian Financial Review* or the *Australian* and you'd get exactly the same story.

In an economy where business has a larger and larger share of national life, the reporting of it becomes more important not just to the efficient functioning of the market but also to the survival of the democracy.

When the government does favours for the moguls – and vice versa – it is reasonable for citizens to assume there will be a quid pro quo. Power is not given for free, and power should never be redistributed like that without our prior permission.

The moguls need to be reminded that in a democracy the people run the joint.

We delegate our power to our political representatives, but we don't do so without caveats. We know they can't be

trusted with unlimited power so the Senate was designed
to mitigate the power of the House of Representatives. We
elect both Houses in different ways to more evenly distribute power in our country. The original thinking was
to avoid a dominance of NSW and Victoria by giving all
states equal power in the Senate. But it is also a house of
review and a brake on the House of Representatives, and
the people understand this. That's why a large number of
people habitually vote one way in the House of Reps and
another in the Senate.

John Howard seeks to undermine the balance by detooth-
ing the Senate, but he won't get away with it because the
framers of the Constitution were smart enough to write us
into the equation. Sadly for Howard we need to approve his
power grab, and that will never happen.

It won't, however, stop him getting his mogul legislation
through, in time. A coalition of government and moguls
is forming to conspire against our democracy. Once the
power is handed over to the moguls we'll never get it back,
and we'll never be sure what's really going on in Canberra.
You'll look towards Capital Hill in Canberra and you'll
see the searchlights crossing over Parliament House. Our
government will be brought to us by 20th Century Fox in
collaboration with Kerry Packer. We'll have become passive
observers in the theatre of our democracy.

Snarling guard dogs at the base of Capital Hill and
searchlights above.

In the twenty-first century we can do a lot better than

that. We have the means at our disposal to distribute more power to the people, not less.

The second basis of our democracy under attack is education. The health of our democratic system is dependent on the people maintaining power. To do this we need to not only protect our citizens from an overreaching government and businesses, but also to actively empower them.

Compulsory voting and our present parliamentary system offer the most obvious protection, but the best way to empower people is to educate them. An intelligent, knowledgeable citizenry will have the skills to perform their duties and assert their rights. Each will understand the responsibility we have to regulate the powerful, in the interests of all of us.

We don't have different classes of citizenship in our country. There's only one class and we have a right to expect it to be first class. Australian citizenship is not a no-frills affair. It's the full-service deal. That means every citizen should be entitled to a free education, up to and including an undergraduate degree at university.

Of course the core of *liberal* philosophy is empowerment of the individual – but this is not achieved by creating inequities and denying young Australians their right to education on the basis of material circumstances. Introduced by a Labor government, HECS has become an insidious influence on education. We should be continuing with the more liberal Menzian tradition of encouraging higher participation in tertiary education. Rather than progressing in line with our increasing prosperity, we've lost ground in the high-tech era and the present government needs to be held accountable for this.

My commitment to equality of access to education found common ground with Webdiary contributors. Carmen Lawrence was one of several unexpected fellow travellers I had on my journey. In one of her columns she said:

'Rising inequality, especially in a society accustomed to seeing itself as fair, creates a nagging sense of unfairness and threatens social solidarity and stability. It undermines the perception that we are all equal. It can lead to bitter divisions and increase the psychological and social distance between the haves and the have nots.'

The Hawke–Keating government instituted the deregulation that opened up the Australian economy. These reforms were reinvigorated and extended under the Howard–Costello regime. Howard and Costello have undoubtedly set the framework for a more prosperous Australia. I strongly believe the neo-liberal economic agenda results in a richer and more vibrant economy.

But what's it all for?

Any society that has grown demonstrably more prosperous, as Australia has, is duty-bound to deliver the fruits of that prosperity to the next generation. This is not about being Robin Hood or donning socialist garb. It's about providing young Australians with more opportunity than any of us ever dreamt of. They have to take the opportunities and make of them what they will, but it is up to us to provide the environment in which they can.

It's all about the fair go and there's nothing more Australian than that.

French philosopher Jean Jacques Rousseau maintained that people are basically good but institutions and society corrupt them. He's probably right. I wouldn't want to believe that people are basically bad, otherwise I'd find life a chore rather than an inspiration.

This brings me to the third threat to our democracy: the failure of ethics in both business and government. If you assume Rousseau is right, it follows that you have to look at society and institutions to see why we have had an apparent ethical crisis.

The topic has often been addressed in Webdiary. I'm intensely preoccupied with it not because I'm a saint, but because I believe civil society and business life will collapse unless we address the question of ethics.

Two years ago I was given the freedom in Webdiary to express my views on the subject. So that I could be frank Margo let me use a nom de plume to reflect on my experiences in business situations where ethical considerations had become critical.

I became Harry Heidelberg and was given my own column. I've enjoyed being Harry! One of the funniest experiences was when my mother recommended an SMH online article by Harry. 'Ah, Mum, that's actually me!'

Behaving ethically can be immensely challenging. I've worked only in multinational organisations and it is a feature of them that people in good positions are confronted by ethical dilemmas.

Being delinquent in your ethical duty may only involve something as simple as saying nothing, and this makes the correct path even harder for some to take.

Yet the system need not be that way, and if you have the guts and determination to take it on you can prove that ethical behaviour will ultimately be rewarded. The US multinational I work for has a crystal-clear code of conduct and a structure of nominated business ethics officers. Staff are trained in ethics and it's fully recognised that in some situations the distinctions between principled and unprincipled conduct become blurred. I'm thinking of 'nuanced' areas such as conflict of interest, the duty to report wrong-doing, and the 'appearance' of independence (people may be independent in fact but not appear so). That is why my colleagues are encouraged to discuss ethics, and it has become a source of company pride. We have a structure that even allows someone to go to an independent outsider to report and discuss concerns – and staff do.

This is corporate governance at its best. It demonstrates that if people are provided with a structure in which they can act ethically, they will.

I recently passed through Parma, in Italy, and was reminded of Parmalat, the latest monumental corporate scandal. Parmalat has joined Enron and Worldcom in infamy.

We should not forget the nature and scale of scandals such as Enron, Worldcom and Parmalat. In each case scores of executives were involved. We need to think about what that says about the type of people who have been promoted in such companies and what it says about company culture more broadly. Even worse, the companies relied on so-called professional accountants, lawyers and auditors to attest to shams and form over substance at the outset. The end result was outright fraud. When these scandals started there were only five global accounting firms. Now there are four. Ex-Andersen employees are ashamed to have that name on their CVs. The tragedy is that the ethics of thousands of them were no doubt beyond reproach.

The ramifications of the collapses were enormous: thousands thrown out of work; suppliers screwed; markets manipulated; investors' retirements ruined; and, in the case of Parmalat, even a crisis in Brazil. A dairy-product multinational in Italy commits fraud and farmers in Brazil go hungry. That is our interconnected world.

In Australia the insurance market was totally stuffed by the collapse of one of the largest players, HIH. We can't allow insurance companies, or banks, to collapse like that. They are too fundamental to the overall system. Where were the regulators when ethics went on holiday?

Never forget the actual money involved either. Parmalat:

$20 billion. Compare this with Kim Beazley's 'black hole' legacy of $8 billion back in 1996, when the Labor deficit was considered an unimaginable amount placing the entire Australian economy at risk.

The perpetrators of corporate crimes should be shown no mercy. An essential feature of market capitalism is that risks are taken and from time to time businesses fail. That part is fine. The part that's not fine is the lying and cheating. The issue is not that a business fails, it is that the watchdogs were asleep or in cahoots with the perpetrators. Governments and media have a responsibility to prevent and uncover these scandals by promoting a rigorous and open environment where all pertinent information is shared on time, all the time. The survival of the system rests on transparency.

Which brings me again to the moguls: we will never be able to maintain piercing financial journalism if they are allowed to take over. There will be so many conflicts of interest that the financial pages will be rendered meaningless. Our democracy and our economic system cannot afford such weaknesses.

The government has ethical problems of its own. There's the tawdry lack of ethics that you find in instances such as the Telecard scandal of Peter Reith. Labor does this kind of thing equally well when it's in power. Instant dismissal is the only proper treatment. It restores the faith of the people and puts the fear of God into would-be perpetrators.

There is a worse ethical issue, though: the Big Lies.

I believe I was lied to by my government over the 'Children Overboard' affair. This was part of a wave the Coalition rode to win the last election. The stakes could not have been higher and the lie could not have been more serious.

The next case was the Iraq war. I supported that. I was told that weapons of mass destruction existed and that action was urgent. I didn't find this hard to believe and even now, when I analyse all the data from the years leading up to the war, the existence of WMD seems a reasonable proposition. Yet now we're told that WMD probably didn't exist and it's explained as, Oh, well, that was the intelligence at the time.

I belittled Baby Boomers who still seemed traumatised by the Vietnam War. I didn't think I was being naïve over Iraq.

It turns out I was, and I've grown tired of the lies.

As I write, it's a week since the Madrid bombing and the Howard government is saying Iraq had nothing to do with it. There are constant games of semantics and distortions of meaning. We deserve better.

Governments, corporations and all institutions are on notice. We're no longer simply disillusioned. We're going to take control back. We, the people. We're not switching off, we're turning on. They've sown the seeds of an enormous backlash. Light will be shed on every sordid, lying and cheating corner in our country.

It's time for us to return to our concept of the real

Australia. As voters, the government is ours. As consumers, investors and employees, the companies are ours.

I'm in Switzerland. It's six on a Sunday night and as I write I can hear the church bells ringing in this gorgeous old town of Bern. I'm one of the million Australians who live overseas. We're an enormous but poorly understood group. Thanks to our expatriate status many of us can't vote in Australian elections even though our commitment to Australia couldn't be stronger.

Senator Nick Bolkus has launched a Senate inquiry into the Australian diaspora. The government had no interest in us, but Bolkus was able to launch this important inquiry via the Senate. I wrote to him as a grateful expatriate and he said he'd look forward to my submission. A Liberal in Switzerland communicating directly with a senator from Labor's left. The intended beneficiary? Australia.

That's my kind of country. That's the Australia we've dreamt of in the Webdiary: a place where the individual is empowered, connected and engaged.

Our Australian system of federal government designed at the end of the nineteenth century is delivering for us in the twenty-first century. The framers would never have foreseen the diaspora phenomenon, but the system was so well conceived to cater for *all* that it extends its reach beyond Australia's shores to reflect the reality of globalisation.

The internet has been so over-hyped that some have

forgotten how truly revolutionary it is. The Webdiary concept wouldn't be possible without the internet and, as a small example, I wouldn't have been communicating directly with a senator before its advent. A letter would not have been my style.

I was very attracted to the recent US campaign by Howard Dean to win the Democratic Party's presidential selection. Firstly because he was using a new and confident language to take on George Bush. Secondly because he has proved the power of the internet. It is now history that Dean crashed and burned early in the primaries. In one sense, though, this is unimportant because he's already delivered. He's managed to mobilise the grassroots of the Democratic Party and change politics. Before Dean, the Democrats were compliant. Dean had the courage to say that the 'war president' betrayed the people and ought to be booted out. Leaders change agendas, and the other contenders are now adopting his leadership qualities.

We will change politics in Australia. We will bring the people back into our democracy.

We will do this because we have the power and it makes us happy. Touchy, feely nonsense? Not at all.

The proof that democracy makes you happy lies here in Switzerland. Professor Bruno Frey and Alois Stutzer, economists at the University of Zurich, conducted landmark research in 1999 that showed that the more opportunities citizens have to participate in democracy, the happier they are. Switzerland is a democrat's paradise and a perfect environment in which to test various democratic models because it has a weak central government and is made up of twenty-six powerful cantons, with widely differing democratic systems. All the cantons are far more democratic than most countries, but some are much more so than others. Frey and Stutzer found that those living in the cantons with the most scope for participation had the highest proportion of happy people!

It's not surprising that people are happier when they feel they are in control. The control starts in people's backyards and goes all the way up the political structure. When the people at the base of a democracy feel powerful and connected democracy itself becomes more robust and secure.

Our political leaders speak of security but we'll never have the kind of security and contentment people really want unless, at the most local level, people feel involved in our democracy.

Threats to media, education and ethical conduct are but three of the road blocks on the way to a better democracy. There are more threats than these, but tackling these issues will get us much closer to the place we'd all rather be: a fair and ever more democratic Australia.

Postscript: this chapter wouldn't have remained in *Not Happy, John!* without Margo letting me include a 'disclaimer'. As the Liberal voter in the book, I found the focus of the cover and the title on John Howard totally partisan, and not a reflection of the search for a common ground.

It's my view that most of the concerns raised in the book will still be present long after John Howard leaves office, so the presence of my writing is a compromise. But I don't believe it's a token: Margo wanted the chapter because it represented the shared values we had searched for in the Webdiary. I remain a Liberal strongly committed to the ideas conveyed in the chapter, and my hope remains for an Ever More Democratic Australia.

18

Democrazy: Ten Ideas for Change

We will never achieve what we can't imagine,
so what are we hoping for?

Stephanie Dowrick

If we believe in democracy you have to believe in
the power of the citizen – there is no such thing as
an abstract democracy

John Ralston Saul

The premise of this book is that just about every citizen, whatever their political colour, can unite on the need for an honest, open, fair and representative democracy. If we get that, then we all have a chance to have a say, and the representatives of all of us have a chance to debate and decide the policies our society believes to be in its interest.

What's happening is that our governments no longer see themselves as trustees for the common good – the stewards of our shared future – but as business executives. Their job is to manage the books, make a profit (surplus) and secure their own financial futures. Unlike most executives, however, they seek to make their company smaller, by handing its assets and many of its duties to the private sector – usually to make a short-term profit. They sell this to us by claiming that the sold-off services will be cheaper. For most people they're almost always not, of course. Worse than that, we lose our rights as citizens.

That's a bloody big price to pay.

Gara LaMarche, the Vice-President of the Open Society Institute in the US – a think tank for democracy sponsored by billionaire financier George Soros – said in a recent speech:

'[Progressives] have been in the posture of criticism for so long, have had to spend so much time fending off attacks on hard-won gains, and on values and institutions we hold dear, that we have virtually lost the capacity for critical imagination. We can't see the forest we would like to dwell in because we are trying to protect tree after tree from the buzz saw.'

It's time to get on the front foot. Jack Robertson, Antony Loewenstein, Harry Heidelberg and I have come up with some ideas.

Idea One: stop the public-funding rip-off

Here's Labor Minister Kim Beazley back in 1983 explaining why *we* should help pay for *their* operating costs: 'The price of public funding is a small insurance to pay against the possibility of corruption.' I'd say our insurance premiums since then have been wasted money. Time to take our *own* steps.

First step: let's tweak *their* hip-pocket nerve

When we vote at the next federal election we'll each have nearly two bucks to spend. That's because any party or Independent who gets more than 4 per cent of the vote is entitled to $1.91 for each first preference vote they receive.

The Parliament agreed to public funding in 1983 on the clear promise that it would reduce the Big Parties' reliance on corporate donations. The politicians also promised that the law would require full disclosure of private donations so we'd know who was paying the piper. The precise opposite has occurred. As John Menadue, former head of the Department of the Prime Minister and Cabinet under both Gough Whitlam and Malcolm Fraser, said in November 2003:

'Money has replaced membership as the driving force of political campaigns. In the USA it is called donocracy. In NSW the state office of the ALP is so successful in raising money from the corporate sector, and particularly property developers, that it can largely ignore party members. Corporate donations are a major threat to our political and democratic system, whether it be State governments fawning over property developers, the Prime Minister providing ethanol subsidies to a party donor, or the immigration minister using his visa clientele to tap into ethnic money.'

OK, so the politicians betrayed our trust and take our money under false pretences. What can we do about it? Easy. Don't give the Big Parties your first preference! Give it to an Independent, or if you'd like smaller parties to get a fairer go, preference them first in the hope they'll reach the 4 per cent threshhold. Only give your preferred Big Party your second preference – your (eventual) vote – not your financial backing.

If enough of us 'consumers' use the 'market force' of our $1.91 to protest the public funding Big Con, the con-artists will get the message all right. Big time.

Second step: let's demand some concrete reforms

As I write, Mark Latham is making a splash about how he wants to clean up 'our democracy'. Let's challenge him to match his rhetoric with substance.

Suggestion one: this idea comes from Webdiarist and insurance investigator Michael Hessenthaler, who was incensed that Tony Abbott thought he could so brazenly dodge questions about his Australians for Honest Politics Trust:

'I'm struck by something so obvious that I am ashamed not to have recognised it earlier – this fellow Abbott is NOT FRANK AND OPEN! It struck me what a painstaking, drawn-out process [getting information] is . . . But why? Why should it have to be so painful?

As a factual investigator well versed in insurance policies and insurance law, I often face tricky claimants trying to care-fully word their answers (à la Abbott, Reith, Howard, etc) so that maybe, just maybe, they can get away with their false claims. Some of them feel quite smug at how clever they are in the use of the English language. I face them with the obvious, that is written into law and into the policy (being a "contract" between two parties) – YOU HAVE AN OBLIGATION TO BE FRANK AND OPEN. I explain to them that I am not paid to outsmart them with trick questions – that I don't have to play cat-and-mouse games – but that they must tell me the information relevant to their claim in a frank and open manner. No misleading, no double-meaning terms, no reversing sentences.

If it's good enough for insurance companies (and later, courts) to knock back claims and even prosecute claimants for fraudulent actions, why should it not be good enough for the Abbotts of this world?'

Yes! How about turning the tables? Instead of the major parties getting their tricky lawyers to find ways to *avoid* disclosure laws, put the obligation on *them* to be frank and open in order to qualify to get our money. Private donations that are not transparent would simply be subtracted from their public funding total. Won't tell us exactly who was behind $100,000 in largesse? Fine – that's $1.91 per primary vote *minus* $100,000 for your lot, then.

Suggestion two: we should ban all selling of political schmoozing and lobbying opportunities. Cash for access is obscene, and it's indefensible.

Suggestion three: and while we're at it, how about legislatively limiting private donation revenue to the proportion it was for the Big Parties when we started giving them our money – 40 per cent of their total revenue, not the 80 per cent it is now? Anything over 40 per cent would again be lopped off any party's public-funding total. Let's at least get back to the way things were in 1984, just after these wonderful new 'democratic' laws were foisted upon us. (Or, better still, ban corporate donations altogether, as Canada has done.)

Such reforms would make the job of the Australian Electoral Commission a lot easier, and the parties would actually have to deliver the benefits they promised us we would get if we paid them. They would reduce the 'undue influence' exerted by rich companies and individuals, and with less money to slush around we'd suffer fewer manipulative, dishonest TV ads and might end up with a more level political playing field. Beazley in 1983 again:

'Public funding ensures that different parties offering themselves for election have an equal opportunity to present their policies to the electorate. Without it, worthy parties and candidates might not be able to afford the considerable sums necessary to make their policies known. In this way, public funding contributes to the development of an informed electorate.'

It was *your* idea, Big Parties – how about you finally implement it?

Third step: let's get a meaner watchdog

Finally, the AEC itself – for all its lower level employees' good intentions – is clearly not the body to do the job on political donations. Its traditions are of cooperation and consensus because it's primarily there to empower people to vote and to help candidates fulfil the legal requirements to stand. Since our pollies ignore the spirit of their own disclosure laws we need a separate body to aggressively enforce them, including prosecuting breaches as a matter of course.

Idea Two: make them accountable

Since successive federal governments began outsourcing and privatisation in the early 1980s it's become increasingly obvious that we need a corruption watchdog in Canberra. The state of play today is that comparatively low-paid public servants – under orders from governments beholden to the private sector – dole out multimillion-dollar public contracts to business. It hardly takes a rocket scientist to spot the danger, yet governments now routinely avoid *any* accountability in such transactions by seeking refuge behind another neo-liberal Big Con: 'commercial-in-confidence'. Absurd. All you have to do is to wave the magic 'private sector' wand and suddenly, where once we had a right to see exactly how our politicians spent our money, now it's none of our business.

The potential for 'Banana Republic' corruption is immense and growing, especially as the public service *itself* is privatised and its low-level workers' conditions are squeezed. The threat is insidious: as the line between 'public' and 'private' blurs, the normalisation of previously unthinkable practices accelerates, so much so that last year public service commissioner Andrew Podger had to issue an explicit order to all public servants not to accept 'freebies' from companies seeking to woo them.

Our public servants need to be *told* this?

It's now imperative that we have a federal equivalent of Queensland's Crime and Misconduct Commission and the NSW Independent Commission Against Corruption. I suggest that enforcement of donation disclosure become one of the duties of this new body. Just as the Australian Competition and Consumer Commission maintains competition and fair play in business and protects consumers, the new body – let's call it the 'Australian Honest Politics Commission' – would be charged with maintaining competition and fair play in politics and protecting voters.

Like the ACCC it would have strong investigative and prosecution powers. The head of the Australian Honest Politics Commission would be a 'consensus' figure selected by a two-thirds majority of both Houses, and would also report directly to Parliament on its investigations.

At the moment, the Australian Federal Police, a body vulnerable to government pressure, does the job – unsurprisingly, not very well. Here's just one of many examples where the AFP appears to have run dead on 'politically sensitive' matters. In June 2003 someone leaked a top-secret Office of National Assessments report by ex-intelligence officer Andrew Wilkie to pro-Howard columnist Andrew Bolt, to undermine Wilkie's credibility as a whistle-blower of the Iraq WMD scandal. That's a serious criminal offence, yet when the ONA referred the matter to the AFP it procrastinated for *nine weeks* before deciding to investigate, and decided to do so only after the scandal broke in Parliament. Months later Bolt had still not even been interviewed.

Alexander Downer has refused to guarantee that his staff didn't leak the report, while in February 2004 the ONA admitted in Senate Estimates that its records showed it was given to an unnamed authorised person in the week of the leak. As I write, we're told the AFP is still on the case, whatever that means.

Successive governments have come to believe they can get away with a hell of a lot of dirty business simply by controlling the state apparatus of investigation or rubber-stamping 'In Confidence' on government contracts.

NOT GOOD ENOUGH!

A strong Australian Honest Politics Commission would keep our politicians on their best behaviour while giving our public servants – increasingly pressured by politicised department heads – an independent mechanism to stay frank and fearless and impartial on *our* behalf.

What about it, Mark Latham? How serious are you about cleaning up politics? Peter Costello?

As part of our new corruption watchdog, why not appoint an 'Ethics Ombudsman', too – someone above reproach, like Allan Fels? Public servants with concerns about corruption, cover-up or misdemeanour – such as the sexing up of intelligence reports or a failure to tender for public contracts – could pass on information 'in confidence' and with full legal protection. The Ethics Ombudsman could refer matters to the Australian Honest Politics Commission for investigation.

Consider this example from Britain: public servant Katharine Gun received a US request for British assistance to illegally bug members of the UN Security Council before the vote on war with Iraq. She leaked the document – and was charged. Her defence was that she was acting to stop an illegal war, and in February 2004 Tony Blair's government dropped the charges rather than produce its own legal advice on the war.

It emerged that the UK Foreign Office had warned that the war would indeed be illegal without UN approval, and that the head of the Foreign Office legal team, Elizabeth Wilmshurst, had resigned in protest at the Attorney-General's advice to the contrary (reportedly after pressure from Blair). An honourable public servant was forced to break the law or resign to act honourably. Wilmshurst and Gun are the sort of public servants you want to *keep* in the system, and an ethics ombudsman would have afforded both less daunting outlets for their concerns.

Our Australian Honest Politics Commission watchdog and the Ethics Ombudsman might even 'encourage' governments to eschew illegal and unethical acts of governance – such as lying to their own people to get them to support the invasion of another nation.

Idea Three: make them protect our civil rights

John Howard himself makes the best case for this idea. He told the High Court at celebrations of its centenary on 6 October 2003:

'There is frequent debate as to whether or not this nation should endeavour to in some way entrench formally in its law a Bill of Rights. I belong to that group of Australians who is resolutely opposed to such a course of action. It is my view that this nation has three great pillars of its democratic life. A vigorous Parliamentary system, robustly Australian, responsible for the making of laws; a strong, independent and incorruptible judiciary; and a free and sceptical media.'

As I've shown in this book, two out of three are in serious trouble, John, and you and your sidekicks also consistently undermine the judiciary.

Howard is also pressing to erode the power of the Senate, with its long tradition of protecting individual civil rights against encroachment by the state (most recently in the ASIO and anti-terrorism law debates, in which the government proposed to outlaw political and industrial protests as 'terrorist acts').

Australia is the only Western country where citizens don't have some civil rights protection in law, and it's showing. I like Professor George Williams's idea: that Parliament pass a law guaranteeing our right to free speech, freedom of association and assembly, our right to equality before the law, and our right not to be arbitrarily detained by the state. These rights would prevail over contrary laws unless those laws specifically overrode them. That would mean we'd at least get advance notice when our rights were about to be curtailed and could debate whether the cost was worth the benefit.

Professor Williams says there is 'strong community support for a Bill of Rights, with one survey showing 72% for, 7% against and 21% undecided'. And why wouldn't there be? We need all the help we can get to preserve our rights as citizens these days.

We'd be following the UK's precedent, too – the source of all our parliamentary traditions, John.

Idea Four: empower our Parliament

A resolutely independent Speaker of the House of Representatives is a must-do starting point.

Mark Latham has now promised us one under a Labor government, but political insiders reckon it will never happen. Speaker is a cushy job and if Labor wins Latham will have to farm it out to the boys – business as usual. We need a Latham promise written in political blood.

Latham has also promised to clean up Question Time by introducing new rules giving the Speaker real power to force ministers to actually answer questions, allowing his own backbenchers to ask real ones, too – not merely preplanned dorothy dixers – and strengthening Freedom of Information legislation. These improvements would bring us much closer to our British parliamentary model, where the Speaker is independent and Labour backbenchers are able to ask questions that Tony Blair would prefer he didn't have to answer.

In fact why not follow the British example further, with a regular Prime Minister's Question Time, during which *both* sides of politics can directly question our leader?

Radical words are all very well, but in 1996 John Howard also promised to improve our parliamentary democracy – and promptly delivered the opposite result when he got into power. So I'd say we need Mark Latham's signature to a 'Charter of Parliamentary Empowerment' *before* the election for his rhetoric to mean anything.

Other elements could include the referral of allegations of ministers misleading Parliament (which the independent Speaker decides aren't frivolous) to a parliamentary committee to investigate and report back to Parliament. No more self-serving decisions by prime ministers to let lying ministers off the hook without the people knowing exactly what's happened.

ALP President and MP Carmen Lawrence detailed more ideas for giving our elected representatives clout in Parliament, and to make it a genuine curb on the executive, in a Webdiary piece called 'Ideas to Save Our Withering Democracy':

• establish joint Estimates and Legislation committees with power to question public servants and ministers

from either House, take submissions and commission independent research
- give parliamentary committees the power to put up legislation arising from their inquiries – especially if the government has refused to respond to its recommendations
- allow private bills with the backing of a set percentage of voters to be brought on for debate by a sponsoring MP
- commission citizens' juries or deliberative polls on contentious and complex policy matters – getting together cross-sections of 'ordinary Australia' to hear the arguments and discuss the merits of issues as wide-ranging as water conservation and free trade agreements
- invite expert and community representatives to address the chambers in session and engage in debate with members.

Carmen wrote:

'As well as engaging the general public and their representatives more fully in the democratic process, I believe such initiatives could transform politics in the way that many have dreamt about, into a more engaged and active democracy. The goals of greater participation, more civil and co-operative parliamentary conduct and an informed public debate are worth striving for.'

Idea Five: enhance our Senate – vote 1 watchdog

Throughout this book you've seen how Senate Estimates has proved the only way the people can get the facts on many issues of government policy and practice. Unlike Britain and the United States, we don't have a strong parliamentary committee system with solid powers that require ministers and their advisers to front up, and Question Time is a sick farce.

Senate Estimates has become a vital accountability mechanism *because* the government doesn't have the numbers there, and the big Opposition party (Labor or Liberal), the minor parties and the Independents invariably vote together when it comes to democratising and scrutinising the government. In late 2003, for example, the Senate decided that Estimates would no longer tolerate government attempts to hide information from voters by using 'commercial-in-confidence as a blanket excuse', even on the financial state of our publicly funded universities.

In the so-called people's House – the House of Representatives – virtually the only parliamentary committees are ones set up to politically damage the Opposition. Again because of the numbers, only the Senate can create viable, genuine inquiries – although it has limited powers – and the Senate president, unlike the Reps' Speaker, must be fair because he or she is dependent on the Senate majority to keep the job. Result? In Senate Question Time ministers actually have to give meaningful answers!

There's a lot riding on the next election. Political

statistician Malcolm Mackerras notes that if Howard maintains the Coalition Senate vote the Coalition will have thirty-eight of the seventy-six Senate seats. This means that if the Coalition wins government again, it need only seduce *one* other senator to its side – with the bribe of the Senate presidency perhaps? – to kill off the Senate's watchdog role. Howard would be able to push through his cross-media legislation, along with all the other neo-liberal, authoritarian reforms he's craved for so long.

So Liberal voters have a huge decision to make when casting their Senate vote. It's clear that Menzian liberalism has long collapsed in Howard's party, and that the conscience vote is dead as a point of differentiation from Labor. Not one MP or senator has defied Howard to cross the floor in three terms! So much for the individual being more important than the collective.

What Senate choices remain for Menzian Libs? The traditional alternative, the Democrats party, formed by disillusioned Liberal Don Chipp, has suffered a debilitating split on whether it should be centre right or centre left, but is now reverting to its traditional role: brokering deals with whatever government is in power. It's one choice for Liberals. In the Senate the only other one I see – for true Liberals – is if a ticket of 'Independent Liberals' stand pledged to support a Coalition government but also to exercise their conscience rights when necessary.

Since the battle for liberalism is lost within the Liberal Party, its supporters have no real choice but to buttress it from the outside. A strategic Senate vote is a no-lose for Menzian Liberals this time around: maintaining watchdog numbers there would be a brake on Dishonest John if he wins, and constrain Crash-Through-or-Crash Mark II if *he* gets the top job.

Either way, centrist liberal democracy wins.

Such a tempering of ideological rigidity could also work in the Lower House. Since Hanson, rural voters have increasingly moved towards respected local Independents to protect their electoral interests and stiffen the National Party's spine within the Coalition. The same strategy is possible for true Liberals. Tony Abbott's Sydney seat of Warringah is ripe for such action – his Independent opponent Dr Peter MacDonald gave him a real scare in 2001. And I'd love to see former leader John Hewson stand as an Independent Liberal in his old seat of Wentworth against the born-to-rule plutocrat Malcolm Turnbull.

One potential focus for a movement like this is the Reid Group (http://reidgroup.org/) formed in 2003 by ex-Democrat, ex-Labor and Independent NSW state MPs to resurrect Australian liberalism – free-trade economics meets social progressivism. I met one of its founders, former NSW Democrats officeholder Cameron Andrews, at a forum on cross-media laws in August 2003, and he wrote for Webdiary on the new group:

'Australia has a fine tradition of genuine liberalism. In the late 1800s it was the dominant paradigm in Australian political life. Our country led the way in introducing liberal reforms like extending suffrage, creating public education and health systems, improving working conditions, and encouraging religious (though, sadly, not racial) tolerance. We were seen as a laboratory for democracy to which other liberal-minded nations should aspire.

The Liberal Party of Australia, its modern incarnation having been reformed by Menzies in the 1940s, has now left any pretence to true liberalism far behind. As a party of social conservatism and market fundamentalism it is more closely aligned with the conservative English Tories and American Republicans than any true liberal party. Indeed, Prime Minister Howard is the Chairman of the International Democrat Union: a conservative and Christian alliance of which arch-conservatives Ronald Reagan and George Bush Snr were founders. A century on, there is no party, or group, in Australia occupying the true liberal position.'

At the Reid Group launch Kim Beazley's former chief of staff Syd Hickman hit the nail on the head:

'Understandably, it is taking liberal Australians a fair while to appreciate the alarming reality that faces us. After all, liberalism for a long time represented the political middle ground. For much of the past thirty years small-l liberals have had the luxury of being the swinging voters who decided who would win federal elections.

What we thought about key issues used to matter. Quite frankly, in political terms, now it doesn't. And that's why core liberal issues like the future of the ABC, the secular education system and universal health care get such meagre attention.

The war on terror has made great cover for the quiet dwindling of our key national institutions. We can complain loudly but that won't change things. Quite frankly, things will not return to that long-standing idea of normal. We cannot seriously believe a) that Peter Costello will become Liberal leader and b) that as Prime Minister he will suddenly discover his inner Moderate. Surely no one seriously thinks Labor will suddenly regroup around progressive and forward-looking ideas?

People who hold liberal values must demand their own place in the political spectrum. To get it they are going to have to work outside the old frameworks. They should stop telling themselves that it's good enough to be the wets or progressives in political parties which are now openly dedicated to illiberal ends. This is not virtue, it's self-delusion.'

Idea Six: the big call – direct democracy
By Harry Heidelberg

As an Australian I'm proud of our relatively old system of parliamentary democracy. From preferential and compulsory voting to the protection provided by the Senate to the balance of powers in the federal system, I see much to like.

It is a system that has provided great stability and prosperity in the 103 years since Federation.

I've always viewed the system as being self-balancing: excesses of power and any dynamic that causes an imbalance will be corrected by the people at the appropriate juncture. Throughout this book, though, we've identified excesses that show no sign of correction. The system itself is now under attack and at risk.

What do we do about it? We change the system. In an ever more democratic Australia we should not be afraid to progress to the next level: direct democracy. If we really want the people to have power let's give it to them in a far more direct way. The dynamics of the current system are no longer sufficient to regulate the powerful. The people need another lever to pull.

In Australia if you can get a proportion of people to agree to an idea through a recognised process of petition you should be able to initiate a referendum at the federal level. I'd set that number at 300,000 based on a national population of 20 million. I'd then want to do the same thing at the state and local levels, at a similar ratio based on population.

I am no longer comfortable with the existing checks and balances in a two-party state such as Australia. Voting for a minor party in the Senate is nowhere near enough. I want to have more direct power in situations where I feel it is warranted.

In the normal political process of a general election there

are always some issues, such as media diversity, that appear to be secondary to hot issues such as health or education. On a superficial level this is understandable, but deciding everything based on the manic, compressed and artificial nature of a political campaign is not sufficient.

I don't think that direct democracy in Australia is unrealistic.

In Switzerland, where I live, this kind of system works well. The obvious advantage is that it provides a further check on the powerful and an additional guarantee that the people will always remain sovereign. It also provides less obvious advantages in that it allows complex issues to be fully debated. Recently there was a debate in Australia about superannuation. The contributions were good but the debate died because there was nowhere further to take it. Our system is designed around the short term. Direct democracy enables the people to tackle and debate thorny, long-term issues.

In Switzerland these issues have included train tunnels through the Alps, pension reform and harm-minimisation measures for drug victims. The format of the referendum tends to create sensible rather than hysterical debate. It's a grown-up way of governing that embraces the people rather than defining them as the 'mob', to use John Howard's term.

If you take people out of the system they will feel disconnected. Funny about that. If you put them back into it they will participate. In the US you hear people railing against Washington for this and that. Australians do the same with Canberra. The Swiss don't say such things about their federal government and their capital because they feel more at one with them.

In a more perfect democracy it gets harder and harder to blame someone else for problems. In a more direct democracy the people know they have the power, and they use it.

We're not the mob; we're citizens, and we should be given more tools to prove it.

M.K.: If we don't want to go all the way with Harry, 'deliberative democracy' is a great alternative. The idea is to bring together randomly selected Australians with different views on, say, Reconciliation or the health system, and have experts and practitioners on all sides of the debate lay out the topic. The group can raise questions and have a go at agreeing on ways to go forward. Check out Issues Deliberation Australia at www.l-d-a.com.au for more information: it ran 'The ACT Deliberation on an ACT Bill of Rights' before the ACT government became the first in Australia to introduce a Bill of Rights.

Idea Seven: a more open free press
By Jack Robertson

We're deep into the information age now and technology has torn up all the old media rules, so whether you old-school editors and journalists like it or not you're going to have to develop a far more interactive relationship with us, your information-consuming public, if you want to remain relevant. And you *must* remain relevant.

Unqualified media amateurs like me can set up a very slick 'journalism' website in about ten minutes, and we don't have to play by *any* rules. We can surf the net, access your wire services, cut 'n' paste (and viciously undermine) *your* painstaking reporting work, present gossip as fact, and fantasy as reality, as we please – and we do.

You have to fight to hold your audience now, and you must because what we web-amateurs can't do is what you professionals can do: interview powerful people, attend press conferences, key events and Parliament, investigate behind the scenes and get at the truth in person. Only professionals can really sort out the information-age wheat from the chaff.

If nobody reads you (or trusts you) any more, we all lose.

So you mainstream journalists need to start utilising the internet's interactive capacities to maintain your relevance, offering something closer to participatory journalism than the current dinosaurian, one-way arrangements of most newspaper and broadcast outlets.

One example: the specialist reporters – on economics, defence, foreign policy, education – among you could start up an ancillary weblog for your media's paying readers, with a database to supplement your daily reportage. We readers could ask technical and background questions and suggest ideas on developing stories.

It's about rebuilding what is a pretty battered relationship between you and us. We both only need to consider how crucial an element of political reportage Stephen Mayne's crikey.com.au website has become to recognise the online potential. Some older hacks accuse Mayne of journalistic anarchy, yet if there's one thing that defines his site it's transparency.

Crikey.com.au is recklessly courageous and always upfront about the basis of its posts; errors are *always* corrected and – mainstream journalists take note – mistakes admitted, retracted and apologised for. Perhaps paradoxically, each admitted stuff-up nurtures a readership that is not less but *more* confident that the Crikey team has no hidden agenda except to be as honest as they can.

Let's subscribe now! Eighty bucks a year will help Crikey keep the media, politicians and business honest and people informed. It gives people a chance to say what they think of the job our leaders are doing in a no-holds-barred forum that most Canberra insiders read religiously.

I'd also give this process of media reconnection a collective focus via a radically expanded Press Gallery Committee – a feisty public body, not merely an in-house rubber stamp for press passes and parties. A more vigorous committee could become the national touchstone on press freedom issues; I'd like to see a high-profile spokesperson – Michelle Grattan, say – who could argue the case for the professional role of you journos in the defence of our democracy.

The beefed-up Press Gallery Committee would have a

website stating its goals and principles; archive members' articles on the free press, ethics, defamation laws, cross-media ownership and other relevant issues; provide links to international groups; and give the public information about how the media works, such as the difference between 'on-the-record', 'background' and 'off-the-record' information, and why such distinctions are necessary to your work.

This would give you some sense of vocational fraternity (via a neutral body that doesn't impinge on your duties to your individual employer) and us non-journalists a window into your working world.

Your Press Gallery Committee website could have members-only sections, too; a bulletin board with upcoming events and trade news; journalists' cyber-forums for discussion, debate and bagging editors and proprietors; and updates on any ongoing Committee campaigns in support of individual journalists.

The case of the *Australian*'s Patricia Karvelas, trampled by a police horse while reporting on World Trade Organization demonstrations in Sydney in November 2002, is just the sort of unacceptable treatment of our media that a more focused – and permanently resourced – Press Gallery Committee could follow up on. NSW Police Minister Michael Costa assured state Parliament he was seeking a 'full report' on the matter. It didn't happen – Patricia was not interviewed and Costa's failure to act was never reported.

Who's looking after you guys? Who's arguing your case and defending *your* rights?

We punters like to whinge endlessly about the 'arrogant media' these days, but deep down we recognise how important you are in safeguarding our democratic freedoms. You need to give us a better opportunity to get behind you. Show us that you're serious about crafting a healthier relationship with us and we'll stop regarding you with such jaundiced scepticism. We're supposed to be on the same side, right?

Idea Eight: internet activism

By Antony Loewenstein

The *New York Times* journalist John Markoff says that 'anyone with a modem is potentially a global pamphleteer'. From Iran to Russia, America to Australia, an ever-increasing number of people across the political divide are talking, debating and connecting in ways unimaginable only a decade ago.

The invasion of Iraq is a prime example. Relying on Australian media alone for information and analysis became unthinkable due to its capitulation to government control and unquestioning regurgitation of government propaganda. The internet allowed newspapers from across the globe to be read and military briefings studied, with independent journalists in Iraq filing from satellite phones and bloggers such as Salam Pax, based in Baghdad, writing about the invasion on the ground.

But the web's strength is increasingly in the realm of participatory organisations dedicated to change on a national and global level, with the US leading the charge. In a country so often derided as anti-democratic and controlled by corporate interests, more and more US citizens are becoming aware of the growing connection between government and big business, and they're sick of it.

Take MoveOn.org. Started at the height of the Clinton–Lewinsky scandal by two Silicon Valley entrepreneurs to convince people to focus on more important issues than the sexual predilections of a president, the movement really started gaining traction during the anti-war campaigns in the lead-up to the 2003 Iraq war. A grassroots movement, linking people across the country who believed that George W. Bush was leading the US into an unnecessary and illegal war, built electronic advocacy groups to pressure key politicians and law makers. Citizens, not getting the answers they wanted from the mainstream media, joined an organisation whose sheer numbers could force accountability from those in power.

Soon enough, over 2 million people had registered on the MoveOn.org website: citizens of many political colours who wanted a more open, tolerant and honest America. In 2003 George Soros gave millions to MoveOn.org because he wanted 'an open society . . . where nobody is in possession of the ultimate truth'. The movement now focuses on environmental issues, campaign finance, media ownership and the future direction of the nation. It held a competition for filmmakers to make thirty-second anti-Bush advertisements, with the winner's ad screened on mainstream media.

MoveOn.org is the most successful online activism in the world. It's time we tried something similar in Australia.

Prwatch.org brings together citizens fighting the war against spin. To 'help the public recognise manipulative and misleading PR practices of secretive, little-known propaganda-for-hire firms that work to control political debates and public opinion', the small US team issues regular email updates on PR companies hired by government and big business to promote everything from supposedly healthy meat uncontaminated by mad cow disease to the testimony of Iraqi defectors on Iraq's alleged weapons of mass destruction.

Powerful interests have to hire others to push their agendas because we don't believe what they're saying any more, but people are starting to fight back.

Adbusters.org campaigns against consumerism, including the US's heavy reliance on oil and the ever-increasing corporatisation of public spaces. Based in Vancouver, Canada, Adbusters is a collection of writers, journalists, environmentalists, artists and businesspeople concerned about the effects of heightened advertising and 'dedicated to examining the relationship between human beings and their physical and mental environment'. Their publication has a circulation of 120,000, accepts no advertising and is active on media concentration, militarism, and Buy Nothing Day and TV-Turnoff Week.

Net activism is no longer on the fringes, but harnessed by citizens to advocate, campaign, lobby and hassle in the name of democratic transparency and change. Australia is just awakening to these possibilities. Together we can lessen the cynicism and find new avenues of connecting like-minded individuals to achieve common goals.

Czech President and freedom fighter, Vaclav Havel, says this about power in society: 'The [net activist] dissident does not operate in the realm of genuine power at all. His actions simply articulate his dignity as a citizen, regardless of the cost.'

Idea Nine: get involved, get interactive, talk, think, act

Individualism . . . disposes each member of the community to sever himself from the mass of his fellows and to draw apart with his family and his friends, so that after he has thus formed a little circle of his own, he willingly leaves society at large to itself. . . . Individualism, at first, only saps the virtues of public life; but, in the long-run, it attacks and destroys all others, and is at length absorbed in downright selfishness

Alexis de Tocqueville, *Democracy in America*, 1835, Second Book, Chapter II

Whatever you do may seem insignificant to you, but it is most important that you do it

Mahatma Gandhi

Since I covered Pauline Hanson's 1998 election campaign and began my Webdiary in 2000, I've become increasingly convinced of four things.

First, that there are thousands of ordinary Australians, of every conceivable political stripe (including none at all), who are interested, enthusiastic, optimistic and bursting with great ideas about the future of our nation.

Second, that there are thousands of ordinary Australians who are uninterested, unenthusiastic, pessimistic and despairing of the future of our nation.

Third, that these two groups of ordinary Australians are one and the same.

Finally, I've learnt that all it takes for our positive energies to swamp our negative ones is for us to get together and do what human beings do best: talk, think, interact, give and take, argue, persuade, be persuaded, agree, disagree, agree to disagree – and then find out what common ground we do all share and fight for it.

Together. All of us.

In so doing, we seek out, find and encourage the better angels in each other's nature, making ourselves, our community and our country greater than the sum of its constituent parts.

All of us. It's the difference between being a citizen and a consumer.

That's been the true underlying impulse of this book. It's not really 'about' the current Prime Minister. I wanted to argue the case for Australian citizenship, and his government and corporate cronies seem determined to make meaningful Australian citizenship impossible.

Not happy, John. Not happy about that at all because I believe we aren't here just to make a buck and look after ourselves and those we love. I want to be a citizen. Australian – and global.

I want to hold that thought beyond the last page of this book, too. It's my hope that the book can help launch a bigger civic movement to defend our democracy, and we've established a website with that in mind. If you're interested in seeing how we're trying to take up where *Not Happy, John!* will shortly leave off, go to www.nothappyjohn.com.

I don't think that I've got all, or even many, of the answers. The whole point of being a citizen in our Australian democracy is that we've all got the same democratic rights and the same democratic obligations, and we're all no better and no worse than the next citizen. So these ideas are just some of ours. No doubt you've got your own – probably quite different ones from mine.

In the end whose ideas turn out to be 'right' and whose turn out to be 'wrong' is far less important than that all of us remain willing and prepared to 'have a go' in good democratic faith.

Need a model? My favourite is the North Shore Peace and Democracy Group in Sydney. Citizens of all political colours have come together to organise community forums on the war in Iraq and its implications for Australian democracy. The group has organised politicians from all sides of politics to front community meetings and answer questions. I'd like to see every community have a 'defend our democracy' group. How can you make it happen? See www.sydneypeace.com and other activist websites in Further Reading.

So *my* final idea for defending our democracy – Idea Nine: get involved, get interactive – could be your starting one.

Idea Ten: insert your own idea here

Whatever it is and however you express it – through a political party, local community groups, schools, sports clubs, business, faith groups, issues-based activism or by simply being nicer to your neighbours – express it as an AUSTRALIAN CITIZEN. With all the rights, privileges, obligations and responsibilities to your fellow citizens that this title entails.

If it was good enough for Robert Menzies, who as our longest-serving democratic leader must have the last word in a book about defending our democracy, then it's good enough.

For all of us

*When the war is won, for every hundred boys and girls who
now pass into higher schools and universities there must be
a thousand. Lack of money must be no impediment to
bright minds. The almost diabolical skill of men's hands in the last
forty years must be supplemented by a celestial skill of
men's minds and a generosity of men's hearts if we are not to be
destroyed by the machines of our creation. In common
with other members of Parliament, I must increasingly realize
that my constituents are not seventy thousand votes,
but seventy thousand men and women for whose welfare and
growth I have some responsibility. To develop every human
being to his fullest capacity for thought, for action,
for sacrifice and for endurance is our major task;
and no prejudice, stupidity, selfishness or vested interest
must stand in the way*

**Robert Gordon Menzies PC AK KT, 'The Task of Democracy',
from *The Forgotten People* radio broadcasts, 1942
Prime Minister of the Commonwealth of Australia 1939–41, 1949–66**

Notes

Robert Menzies' radio addresses in 1942 are quoted from throughout this book with the kind permission of Mrs Heather Henderson. They were published in 1943 as *The Forgotten People*, and are published by the Menzies Virtual Museum at http://www.menziesvirtualmuseum.org.au/transcripts/ ForgottenCont.html.

Introduction : I Am, You Are, We Are Australia

My Webdiary, begun in July 2000, is at www.smh.com.au/ webdiary. Its statement of ethics is at http://www.smh.com.au/ articles/2003/07/23/1058853117710.html. Its charter, at http://www.smh.com.au/articles/2002/04/29/ 1019441338099.html, is as follows.

'I believe:
- that widely read broadsheet newspapers are essential to the health and vibrancy of our democracy
- that they are yet to adapt to a multi-media future pressing on the present
- that there is a vacuum of original, genuine, passionate and accessible debate on the great political, economic and social issues of our time in the mainstream media, despite the desire of thinking Australians in all age groups to read and participate in such debates
- that newspapers have lost their connection with the readers they serve
- that the future lies in a collaboration between journalists and readers.

The mission of the Webdiary is:

- to experiment in the form and content of the *Herald* online
- to assist in the integration of the newspaper and smh.com.au
- to help meet the unmet demand of some Australians for conversations on our present and our future, and to spark original thought and genuine engagement with important issues which affect us all
- to link thinking Australians whoever they are and wherever they live
- to insist that thinking Australians outside the political and economic establishment have the capacity to contribute to the national debate
- to provide an outlet for talented writers and thinkers not heard in mainstream media.'

I disclosed my voting intention at the 2001 election in 'Time to Choose' at http://www.smh.com.au/articles/2003/11/26/1069522666845.html.

Chapter 1: Disclosing John Howard's Elite

Mark Riley's 21 October 2003 story, 'Say What You Like, but Don't Expect Bush to Hear', was published in the *Sydney Morning Herald* and is at http://www.smh.com.au/articles/2003/10/20/1066631356196.html. I published my first take on the barbecue guest list in 'Howard's Elite – the Official List' at http://www.smh.com.au/articles/2003/10/27/1067233100397.html and the complete list in 'Howard's Elite – the REAL Official List' at http://www.smh.com.au/articles/2003/11/05/1068013265769.html, which also republished Mark Riley's 1 November 2003 story on the Liberal Party donors at the Bush barbecue. The Department of Prime Minister and Cabinet's evidence to Senate Estimates on the Bush barbecue is at http://www.aph.gov.au/hansard/senate/commttee/S7052.pdf.

Chapter 2: Yours Not to Reason Why

A (typical) Newspoll over the weekend 18–19 January 2003 recorded 61 per cent against, 7 per cent uncommitted and only 30 per cent for non-UN participation in an Iraq invasion. The full letter of 'Brian Dabeagle' is in 'A Letter from the SAS?' at http://www.smh.com.au/articles/2003/03/07/ 1046826524409.html. John Howard's phone conversation with Bush was revealed in a Greg Sheridan interview published in the *Australian*, 27 September 2003. The letter from elder statesmen and former military leaders was published in most major newspapers. Andrew O'Connell's piece is in 'Spiders Spread in all Directions' at http://www.smh.com.au/articles/2003/03/07/ 1046826524409.html, and Jim Forbes's is in 'The Big Walks: Reader Reports' at http://www.smh.com.au/articles/2003/02/ 17/1045330533116.html. Howard's 'mob' description came during a Channel Nine *60 Minutes* interview with Charles Woolley, broadcast 16 February 2003. John Augustus's poem is in 'Feelings on the Eve of War' at http://www.smh.com.au/ articles/2003/03/19/1047749827286.html. For the Hermann Goering anecdote, from *Nuremberg Diary*, by Gustave Gilbert, see www.snopes.com/quotes/goering.htm. The Mark McKenna essay 'Howard's Warriors' was first published in *Why the War Was Wrong*, edited by Raimond Gaita, Text Publishing, 2003.

Chapter 3: Divided and – Conquered?

Brigadier General John Kelly was quoted by SMH's Lindsay Murdoch, 9 April 2003. My speech 'Could We Start Again, Please?' to the Sydney Institute was delivered 16 April 2003; the full text is at http://www.smh.com.au/articles/2003/ 04/18/1050172751376.html. Hugh Driver's comments are in 'Protecting the Joys of a Free Society' at http:// www.smh.com.au/articles/2003/04/03/1048962867942.html.

Chapter 4: Ordinary Australian Appeasers

The Alec Campbell quote was attributed by Peter
Lewis, editor of *Workers Online*, May 2002, at http://
workers.labor.net.au/137/editorial_editorial.html. *Luck Is
No Accident: Flying in War and Peace 1946–1986*, by Colin
G. King, was published by Australian Military History
Publications, 2001, for whose commemoration of his uncle's
sacrifice Jack Robertson is warmly grateful. (The book is
available via http://www.warbooks.com.au/IndividualBooks/
luckisnoaccident.html.) John Howard's first comments on
Alec Campbell are from a statement released on 16 May 2002
and are at http://www.australianpolitics.com/news/2002/05/
02-05-166.shtml; his eulogy was delivered at the Cathedral
Church of St David in Hobart, 24 May 2002, and is at http://
www.pm.gov.au/news/speeches/2002/speech1665.htm.
Paul Keating's eulogy for the Unknown Australian Soldier,
delivered at the Australian War Memorial, 11 November
1993, was written with Don Watson and is archived at http://
www.keating.org.au/main.cfm. The reply to Jack Robertson
on refugee human rights abuse, 18 February 2003, was signed
by Richard Sadleir, Assistant Secretary International Division,
Department of the Prime Minister and Cabinet, on behalf of
Howard. Len Robertson's *Argus* letter was published either
22 or 23 May 1952. The Melbourne *Sun News-Pictorial* article
of 11 July 1986 was by-lined Jane Roskruge and is reproduced
courtesy of the Herald & Weekly Times Ltd.

Chapter 5: Waiting for the Great Leap Forward

Howard's comment on Fairfax was reported by me in 'Fairfax
off the Christmas Wish List' in SMH on 2 September 1997.
Jack Robertson kicked off the Webdiary journalism debate
in 'Questions to You Journos' at http://www.smh.com.au/
articles/2003/01/16/1042520716364.html. Greg Weilo's

comments on journalism are in 'Journos v. Pollies: The
Tirade Goes On' at http://www.smh.com.au/articles/2003/
11/20/1069027245641.html, and 'Catharsis Complete'
in full is at http://www.smh.com.au/articles/2003/11/20/
1069027245364.html. The Webdiary journalism debate was
in November 2000; see http://smh.com.au/news/opinion/
webdiary/archive/2000/.

Chapter 6: Closing the Door on Your Right to Know

The report of the Kent Commission (Canadian Royal
Commission on Newspapers 1981 – Commissioners Tom Kent,
Borden Spears and Laurent Picard) was published in 1981. The
Charlie Reina quote is from a 31 October 2003 email sent to
Jim Romensko's Poynter Institute website, http://
www.poynter.org/column.asp?id=45&aid=53018. The Fox
News response is at http://www.poynter.org/column.asp?id=
45&aid=53132. Rupert Murdoch's oil quote is from an
exclusive interview with the *Bulletin*'s Max Walsh, 12 February
2003, at http://bulletin.ninemsn.com.au/bulletin/EdDesk.nsf/
ALL/87D6BE4ACBB673C4CA256CC5007E11E2. Max
Moore-Wilton's comments on Murdoch were as a judge in the
Australian Financial Review's 'Overt Power Top Ten' list,
1 October 2003. The press release for the University of
Maryland study on Iraq war misperceptions, released 2 October
2003, is at http://www.pipa.org/OnlineReports/Iraq/Media_
10_02_03_Press.pdf. (The work compares the figures for those
embracing 'one or more misperceptions' based on their stated
primary news source: Fox 80 per cent, CBS 71 per cent, ABC
61 per cent, NBC 55 per cent, CNN 55 per cent, print sources
47 per cent, NPR/PBS 23 per cent.) For details of the Murdoch
play on the Brisbane *Sun* and the *News* in Adelaide, see 'How
Rupert Murdoch Is Helping the Competition', by Andrew
Keenan and Colleen Ryan, in SMH on 30 July 1988; Hank

Spier's quote is in my piece 'TPC Demands Cuts to Links
Between Murdoch Papers', in SMH on 30 May 1989; Bob
Baxt's comments are in 'TPC Asks News to Alter Paper
Buyouts', by me and Catherine Armitage in SMH on 30 August
1989. I noted Richard Alston's cross-media flip-flops in my
piece for SMH, 'Alston Sighs for His Own Victim', slipped in
by Chris McGillion, 15 April 1997. Ian Heads's reason for
resignation, revealed to ABC TV's *Media Watch*, 18 October
1999, is at http://www.abc.net.au/mediawatch/transcripts/
s60974.htm. For the history, industry structure, economics and
politics of media ownership, see the House of Representatives
committee report *News and Fair Facts* (conducted during the
bidding for Fairfax in receivership), Australian Government
Publishing Service, 1992, and the Senate committee report
*Percentage Players: The 1991 and 1993 Fairfax Ownership
Decisions*, Commonwealth of Australia, 1994. For an in-depth
history of the relationship between governments and media
moguls, I recommend *Party Games: Australian Politicians and the
Media from War to Dismissal* by Bridget Griffen-Foley, Text
Publishing, 2003. For the background to attempts so far to
concentrate media ownership, see http://www.xmedia.org.au.
I helped set up the site.

Chapter 7: Unholy Alliances
All quotes from parliamentary speeches can be found in the
Senate Hansard for 24 and 25 June 2003 at http://
www.aph.gov.au/hansard/hanssen.htm. Eric Beecher's media
moguls article was published in SMH, 23 June 2003; Paul
Keating's unpublished response was first publicly aired by
crikey.com.au, 25 June 2003; the full text of Keating's speech is
at http://www.abc.net.au/mediawatch/transcripts/s891529.htm.
The Roger Colman quote is from the *Australian*'s Media
supplement, 3 July 2003. My book *Off the Rails: The Pauline*

Hanson Trip is published by Allen & Unwin, 1999. All quotes
relating to Liberal Party about-faces, along with other
background information, can be sourced in detail at http://
www.xmedia.org.au/. The Hon. Charles Davidson MP, the
Postmaster-General quoted by Brian Harradine, was the
Country Party Member for Dawson, Queensland.

Chapter 8: Outside the People's House

The Joseph Campbell quote comes from *Joseph Campbell and the
Power of the Myth*, published by Doubleday, 1988. *Interpreting the
Art and Design of Parliament House* was written by Douglas Smith.
Parliament House Canberra: A Building for the Nation was edited
by Haig Beck and published by Watermark Press, 1988.

Chapter 10: A Day in the Life of Our House Under Siege

For all parliamentary quotes, including the text of Howard's
presidential welcome and Bush's speech, refer to Hansard
at http://www.aph.gov.au/hansard/index.htm. Details of the
arrangements for Bush's visit are found in the Senate Estimates
3 November 2003 hearings on the Bush and Hu visits at http://
www.aph.gov.au/hansard/senate/commttee/s7048.pdf. The
submissions to the Senate Privileges Committee inquiry into
the Bush and Hu visits are at http://www.aph.gov.au/senate/
committee/priv_ctte/joint_meeting/submissions/sublis.
The Committee's report, released 1 April 2004, is at http://
www.aph.gov.au/senate/committee/priv_ctte/report_118/
report.pdf. The Speaker's statement to Parliament on the Bush
and Hu visits is published in 'Democracy a Hassle? Just Call
the Speaker' at http://www.smh.com.au/articles/2003/11/03/
1067708147410.html.

The press joint conference with Keating and Bush Senior
is archived in the Bush library at http://bushlibrary.tamu.edu/
research/paper.html. The file note of 17 September 2003

('no official state visit') obtained by FoI was prepared by Ms
Carol Cartwright, Head of Events at the Australian War
Memorial; Department of the Prime Minister and Cabinet
representatives in attendance were Jan Fuhrman, Judi Holgate
and Geoff Brough. The leaked White House press briefing
was first reported in Australia by *The Age*'s Annabel Crabb,
4 October 2003; the transcript of the Neil Mitchell interview is
at http://www.pm.gov.au/news/interviews/Interview511.html.
The Bolger report can be obtained from the Senate
Finance and Public Administration Committee at http://
www.aph.gov.au/senate/committee/fapa_ctte/index.htm. The
'POTUS red alert' quote was extracted from internal emails
obtained by FoI request. The Greg Turnbull anecdote is
from Matt Price's *Australian* Media supplement article of
30 October 2003. The Alan Porritt quote is from Malcolm
Farr's 'Submission on Media Issues from Presidential Visits' to
the Senate Privileges Committee, 27 January 2004. Webdiary's
report of the human shield for Bush is in 'Charge of the
Lightfoot Brigade Doesn't Stop Green Protest' at http://
www.smh.com.au/articles/2003/10/23/1066631547601.html.
A video of the human shield and a photo identifying most
participants is on the Webdiary home page. The John
Valder quote is from a conversation with the author. George
Brandis's speech is in 'Nazi Greens an Enemy of Democracy,
Government Decrees' at http://www.smh.com.au/articles/
2003/10/29/1067233222840.html. 'Parliament Greets Bush:
A Day in the Life of Our Faltering Democracy' is at http://
www.smh.com.au/articles/2003/10/23/1066631577337.html.
John Howard delivered the 1997 Sir Robert Menzies Memorial
Lecture on 23 June. It is archived at http://www.pm.gov.au/
news/speeches/1997/menzies.html.

Chapter 11: The Forgotten People

See Hansard for parliamentary quotes at http://www.aph.gov.au/ hansard/index.htm. Details of the arrangements for Hu's visit are found in the Senate Estimates 3 November 2003 hearings on the Bush and Hu visits at http://www.aph.gov.au/hansard/ senate/committee/s7048.pdf.

My article in SMH on 6 September 1995 and the email exchange between the Chinese Embassy and Fairfax are published in 'Howard Humiliates Our Parliament and Betrays Our Democracy for Hu' at http://www.smh.com.au/articles/ 2003/10/25/1066974332090.html. The Senate Procedures Committee report on the legality of the joint sitting, published in December 2003, is at http://www.aph.gov.au/Senate/ committee/proc_ctte/reports/2003/no3.pdf. Chin Jin's 27 October 2003 piece for Webdiary, 'An Excluded Guest's Story', is at http://www.smh.com.au/articles/2003/10/28/ 1067233155899.html; a second piece, 'An Excluded Guest's Account of Hu Day', is at http://www.smh.com.au/articles/2003/ 10/29/1067233234930.html. Paul Bourke's submission and others to the Senate Privileges Committee inquiry into the Bush and Hu visits are at http://www.aph.gov.au/senate/committee/ priv_ctte/joint_meeting/submissions/sublis. Mark Latham's 6 February 2004 suggestions on the future of the Speaker's office were made during an address at Club Banora, Tweed Heads.

Chapter 12: The Girl We (Almost) Left Behind

Parliamentary quotes from Hansard are at http:// www.aph.gov.au/hansard/index.htm. Quotes from Kylie Russell on her snubbing are from a phone interview by the *West Australian*'s Daniel Clery, 26 October 2003, published in that paper the next day. Graham Edwards's letter was first published, 27 October 2003, in 'Snub for War Widow' at http:// www.smh.com.au/articles/2003/10/27/1067233083792.html.

See also 'War Widow's Long Wait for PM's Apology' at http://
www.smh.com.au/articles/2003/10/29/1067233227051.html.
Kylie Russell's letter to the *West Australian*, 24 October 2003,
was not published; I published it in 'Kylie's Statement' at http://
www.smh.com.au/articles/2003/10/30/1067233313765.html.
Gay Alcorn's piece on Kylie Russell in *The Age*, 24 February
2003, 'Why SAS Widow's Quarrel Is a Matter of Honour' is at
http://www.theage.com.au/articles/2003/02/23/
1045935273835.html. John Howard's reply to Graham
Edwards was published in Webdiary in 'Howard's Letter to
Kylie's MP' at http://www.smh.com.au/articles/2003/10/31/
1067597152059.html. My 2 November 2003 *Sun-Herald*
weekend column, 'No Invite, Dismissed as an "Oversight"',
which quotes Webdiarists Greg Carroll and John Boase, is at
http://www.smh.com.au/articles/2003/11/01/
1067597205105.html. Howard's comment on our soldiers in
Iraq, made during an interview with 3AW's Neil Mitchell,
31 October 2003, is at http://www.pm.gov.au/news/interviews/
Interview552.html. Howard's answer to Edwards's question in
Parliament is published in 'Andrew Russell's Legacy' at http://
www.smh.com.au/articles/2003/11/03/1067708140653.html, as
is a tribute to Andrew by Robert Sadleir. The evidence of the
Department of the Prime Minister and Cabinet in Senate
Estimates is at http://www.aph.gov.au/hansard/senate/
commttee/S7052.pdf.

Chapter 13: Taking Back the Power: Hanan Ashrawi
The George Brandis speech is in 'Nazi Greens an Enemy of
Democracy, Government Decrees' at http://www.smh.com.au/
articles/2003/10/29/1067233222840.html. Brandis's *Lateline*
comment is at http://www.abc.net.au/lateline/content/2003/
s980044.htm. The quote from Professor Juan Cole is from
'Informed Comment', 3 February 2004, at http://juancole.com/

2004_02_01_juancole_archive.html. The Webdiary pieces by
Ian Cohen and Antony Loewenstein were published in 'The
Battle for Minds' at http://smh.com.au/articles/2003/11/05/
106798607649.html. An example of the Webdiary debate is
Jane Doulman's 'Howl of the Despondent Historian' at http://
www.smh.com.au/articles/2003/10/30/1067233313759.html.
The 7.30 Report interview with Ashrawi is at http://
www.abc.net.au/7.30/content/2003/s983009.htm. Margo
Kingston's email questions to Colin Rubenstein and his replies,
January to March 2004, are published in 'Mel, Colin, George
and Miranda' at http://www.smh.com.au/articles/2004/03/02/
1078191317738.html. The 'racist conspiracy' quote is from the
article 'Award Overboard' by Tzvi Fleischer in AIJAC's
December 2003 Review at http://www.aijac.org.au/review/2003/
2812/ashrawi2812.html.

Ashrawi-related Webdiary entries, with detailed sourcing of
quotes, can be found at http://www.smh.com.au/articles/2003/
11/05/1067989607649.html; http://www.smh.com.au/articles/
2003/11/06/1068013332607.html; http://www.smh.com.au/
articles/2003/11/10/1068329476527.html; http://www.smh.
com.au/articles/2003/11/14/1068674374750.html; http://
www.smh.com.au/articles/2003/11/18/1069027111273.html.

Baruch Kimmerling's quotes may be found via his website
(see Further Reading) and his book listed below; a full copy
of his letter to Carr, published in 'Ashrawi and Brandis: The
Great Debate' at http://www.smh.com.au/articles/2003/11/06/
1068013332607.html, was sent to Webdiary by Scott Burchill,
Lecturer in International Relations at Deakin University's
School of Social and International Studies. The Hanan Ashrawi
quote comes from her speech at a public meeting at the
Petersham Town Hall, Sydney, 8 November 2003, recorded
by Antony Loewenstein in 'Real Sydney People Meet Hanan
Ashrawi', SMH, 10 November 2003. Loewenstein's interview

with Premier Bob Carr was conducted over an hour and a quarter, 26 November 2003, in Carr's Sydney office. Colonel Kelly's letter was published in the *Weekend Australian*, 1–2 November 2003. Private correspondence between Carr and General Peter Cosgrove was contained in an Ashrawi file given to Loewenstein by Carr's Communications Director, Walter Secord. The interviews for the chapter were conducted between November 2003 and January 2004. Alan Ramsey's 'Here's Lucy, Caving In, Taking Flight' and 'From Great Hall to Messy Brawl' appeared in SMH on 25 October 2003 and 8 November 2003 respectively. (Sydney University denied the claim it had refused, saying it had a clash of bookings for the Great Hall.) An earlier piece by Ramsey, 'Lost Even with a Map', on 30 August 2003, covered the ALP's internal debate on the Israel–Palestine issue. The Jewish community's funding of political parties was recorded by Michael Cavanagh in 'Most Funds Went the Liberals' Way' in the *Australian Jewish News* on 13 February 2004. The Sydney Peace Foundation's Stuart Rees published an article (rejected by the *Australian*) in Webdiary at http://www.smh.com.au/articles/2003/11/19/1069027166746.html. Tony Abbott's words at the Victorian Zionist Council's annual general meeting were reported in the *Australian* 30 October 2003 and crikey.com.au. Alexander Downer's opinion was expressed on ABC TV's *Insiders* on 26 October 2003, Howard's in a Sky TV news report on 6 November 2003. George Soros's words were quoted by Uriel Heilman in 'In Rare Jewish Appearance, George Soros Says Jews and Israel Cause Anti-Semitism' in *JTA* on 9 November 2003; Isi Leibler's comments were reported in 'Self-hatred Spurs Antisemitism – Isi Leibler' in the *Australian Jewish News* on 12 December 2003; Michael Visontay's words appeared in SMH on 14 November 2003. The Hanan Ashrawi interview with Jon Elmer, recorded in 'Hurtling Towards the

Abyss', 23 November 2003, is from OccupiedPalestine.org.
Antony Loewenstein's piece on Ashrawi for US website ZNet is
at http://www.zmag.org/content/showarticle.cfm?SectionID=
44&ItemID=4387. The UK *Independent*'s Robert Fisk article
noting his stance on Ashrawi, 4 November 2003, is at http://
www.counterpunch.com/fisk11042003.html.

The following books provide information on and the
context of the politics behind the Ashrawi affair and the
Israel–Palestine conflict: Roane Carey and Jonathan Shainin
(eds), *The Other Israel: Voices of Refusal and Dissent*, New Press,
2002; Noam Chomsky and Edward Herman, *Manufacturing
Consent*, Vintage, 1988; Alexander Cockburn and Jeffrey
St Clair (eds), *The Politics of Anti-Semitism*, AK Press, 2003;
Norman Finkelstein, *Image and Reality of the Israel–Palestine
Conflict*, Verso, 2001; Norman Finkelstein, *The Holocaust
Industry*, Verso, 2003; Robert Fisk, *Pity the Nation*, Oxford
University Press, 2001; Amira Hass, *Reporting from Ramallah*,
Semiotext(e) Active Agent Series, 2003; David Hirst, *The
Gun and the Olive Branch*, Nation Books, 2003; Christopher
Hitchens and Edward Said (eds), *Blaming the Victims:
Spurious Scholarship and the Palestinian Question*, Verso, 2001;
Baruch Kimmerling, *Politicide: Ariel Sharon's War Against the
Palestinians*, Verso, 2003; Ephraim Nimni (ed.), *The Challenge
of Post Zionism: Alternatives to Israeli Fundamentalist Politics*,
Zed Books, 2003; Tanya Reinhart, *Israel/Palestine: How to End
the War of 1948*, Allen & Unwin, 2002; Rafi Segal and Eyal
Weizman (eds), *A Civilian Occupation: The Politics of Israeli
Architecture*, Verso, 2003; Raja Shehadeh, *When the Bulbul Stopped
Singing: A Diary of Ramallah Under Siege*, Profile Books, 2003.

For Antony Loewenstein's detailed report on media
coverage see www.nothappyjohn.com.

Antony Loewenstein wishes to thank the following (many of
whom were interviewed) for their support, information, insights

and belief in the truth: Ephraim Nimni, Stephen Rothman, Peter
Manning, Noam Chomsky, John Docker, Ian Cohen, Gerard
Noonan, Barbara Bloch, John Pilger, Tony Stephens, Stephen
Crittenden, Marcus Einfeld, Robert Fisk, Michael Gawenda,
Phillip Knightley, Baruch Kimmerling, Sari Kassiss, Ihab
Shalbak, Vic Alhadeff, Violet and Jeffrey Loewenstein, Stuart
Rees, Bob Carr, Walter Secord, Virginia Gordon, James Cumes,
Uri Avnery, Caroline Ayoub, Jozef Imrich, Scott Burchill, Greg
Philo, Kate Bice, Amira Hass, Gideon Levy, Alan Ramsey,
Vivienne Porzsolt, Ian Head, Rob Thomas, Danny Gilbert,
James McLaughlin, Randa Abdel-Fattah, Mark Forbes, Mary-
Anne Toy, Peter Kerr, Stephen Mayne and Lyn MacCallum.

Chapter 14: Keeping Democracy in Its Place
Peter Costello's 16 July 2003 'Building Social Capital' speech,
delivered to the Sydney Institute, is published at http://
www.smh.com.au/articles/2003/07/16/1058035070852.html.
Gary Johns's speech 'Government and Civil Society: Which Is
Virtuous?' was delivered as part of the Senate's Occasional
Lectures series, 23 August 2002, and is published at http://
www.aph.gov.au/Senate/pubs/occa_lect/transcripts/
230802.pdf. Margaret Thatcher's words come from an
interview with *Woman's Own* magazine, 3 October 1987, quoted
in Christopher Scanlon's essay 'What's Wrong with Social
Capital' in *Arena*, Feb.–March 2004. 'Laureates Say Bush Is
Twisting Science' appeared in SMH, 20 February 2004. Aban
Contractor's scoop on censorship in the federal Department of
Education, Science and Training on HECS is republished in
'Nelson Hides Behind Sir Humphrey' at http://smh.com.au/
articles/2003/08/12/1060588393187.html. There's more on the
scandal in 'Nelson's Purge Escalates as the Education
Department Burns' at http://www.smh.com.au/articles/2003/
08/14/1060588517300.html.

Paddy Manning relied heavily on 'War on Non-profits: NGOs: What Do We Do About Them?' by Martin Mowbray in *Just Policy*, no. 30, July 2003; 'Redefining NGOs: The Emerging Debate' by Dr Ravi Tomar in the federal Parliamentary Library's Current Issues Brief no. 5 at http://www.aph.gov.au/library/pubs/CIB/2003-04/04cib05.htm#review; and 'Neo-liberal Think Tanks' by Philip Mendes in the *Journal of Australian Political Economy*, no. 51, June 2003.

John Anderson's words are quoted in Donald Horne's reflection 'John Anderson and Australian Civilisation', *Arena*, Feb.–March 2004. Mark Lyons's words are from his book *The Third Sector: The Contribution of Nonprofit and Cooperative Enterprises in Australia*, published by Allen & Unwin, 2001. The Industry Commission's report *Charitable Organisations in Australia* was published in June 1995 and can be found at http://www.pc.gov.au/ic/inquiry/45charit/finalreport/45charit.pdf. The survey of attitudes to NGOs, by Edelman Public Relations Worldwide, was reported in the *Australian Financial Review* on 3 November 2000. Details of the Australian National University's Australian Election Study are at http://aussa.anu.edu.au/ausElectionStudy.htm. The quote from Eric Sidoti is from his 'Australian Democracy: Challenging the Rise of Contemporary Authoritarianism', based on a 17 August 2003 seminar address, and is at http://www.hrca.org.au/CCJP.htm. Information about the ACF is sourced from an interview with Don Henry; for the environment movement's response to the Costello charities proposal see the joint submission at http://www.acfonline.org.au/docs/general/00489.pdf. The Charities Definition Inquiry report by Fitzgerald, Gonski and Sheppard is at http://www.cdi.gov.au/html/report.htm. Details of Peter Costello's draft charities legislation and his inquiry into the definition of charities are in 'Charitable Free Speech on Endangered List!' at http://www.smh.com.au/

articles/2003/07/30/1059480394375.html, 'Costello's Free
Speech Record' at http://www.smh.com.au/articles/2003/
07/30/1059480399575.html and 'Costello Spin Exposed on
Charity Free Speech Clampdown' at http://www.smh.com.au/
articles/2003/07/31/1059480469952.html. The Board of
Taxation website is at http://www.taxboard.gov.au/content/.
The *Australian Financial Review*'s editorial on Costello's draft
charities bill ran on 1 August 2003. Senator John Cherry's
interview on ABC Radio's *AM* on 30 July 2003 is at http://
www.abc.net.au/am/content/2003/s913151.htm. Peter
Costello's response to the claims by critics is at http://
www.treasurer.gov.au/tsr/content/pressreleases/2003/
066.asp?pf=1</a> and in 'Real Charities Need not Worry',
published in the *Australian Financial Review* on 19 August 2003.
Deborah Snow's interview with Peter Costello, 'The Deputy's
Dilemma', was published in SMH, 10 January 2004. The
'Prime Minister's Community Business Partnership' website
is at http://www.partnership.zip.com.au/. Details of the Prime
Minister's Not For Profit Council of Australia can be found at
http://www.smithfamily.com.au/content.cfm?randid=593721.
Adele Horin's piece 'Alarm at Non-profit Newcomer' was
published in SMH, 8 November 2003. See also her 'More
Intimidation as the "Hear No Evil" Regime Targets NGOs',
published in SMH on 30 August 2003. Details of the NGO
round-table were reported by Michael Cave in 'Non-profit
Groups Link up to Present a United Front', *Australian Financial
Review*, 26 June 2002. See also http://www.philanthropy.org.au/
factsheets/7-05-03-nonprof.htm. For more information on
Canada's Voluntary Sector Initiative see http://www.vsi-isbc.ca/
eng/index.cfm and for the UK's Charity Commission see http://
www.charity-commission.gov.uk/. Details on the funding of
Gary Johns's Fulbright Professional Award are in an answer by
Senator Robert Hill to a question on notice by Greens Senator

Bob Brown, given on 7 October 2003, at http://parlinfoweb.
aph.gov.au/piweb/view_document.aspx?id=914337&table=.
For more information see http://www.fulbright.com.au/nav/
05frame.htm. Dennis Shanahan's 'Howard Tightens Screws
on Charities', the first news of the IPA's consultancy, was
published in the *Weekend Australian* of 2–3 August 2003.
Nicholson and Hughes's *Sunday Age* quote is from 'Attack
on Covert Project for IPA' at http://www.theage.com.au/
articles/2003/08/09/1060360555284.html. A transcript of
'NGOs Watching NGOs', ABC Radio National producer Stan
Correy's report for *Background Briefing* of 28 March 2004, is at
http://www.abc.net.au/rn/talks/bbing/stories/s1078182.htm.
The website of the Institute of Public Affairs is at http://
www.ipa.org.au/. A list of the IPA's media commentary is at
http://www.ipa.org.au/Media/mediaisslist.htm. The IPA's
'NGO Watch' is at http://www.ipa.org.au/Units/NGOWatch/
ngowatch.html. The IPA's October 2003 submission to the
Board of Taxation's review of the draft charities bill is at http://
www.ipa.org.au/Speechesandsubmssns/ipacharitiessub.pdf.
And see also http://www.disinfopedia.org/wiki.phtml?title=
Institute_of_Public_Affairs. Details on the decline in IPA
funding and the resignation of certain companies and directors
were drawn from the IPA's annual reports for the financial years
1990–2002 inclusive, obtained through ASIC, and from an
investigative piece on think tank funding by Brad Norington,
'The Deep Pockets Behind Deep Thought', published in SMH
on 12 August 2003, which also contains Nahan's commitment
to publish IPA's donors in his 2002–03 annual report.
Information on American donors to the IPA was obtained
from http://www.mediatransparency.org/search_results/
info_on_any_recipient.php?recipientID=598. Thanks to
Webdiarist Philip Gomes for information on the Bradley and
Orin foundations. Johns's speech to the American Enterprise

Institute, 'The NGO Challenge: Whose Democracy Is
It Anyway?', is at http://www.aei.org/docLib/20030630_
johns.pdf. Full event materials from the joint American
Enterprise Institute–Institute of Public Affairs conference
at which Johns spoke are at http://www.aei.org/events/
eventID.329,filter.all/event_detail.asp; the conference was
entitled 'We're Not from the Government, but We're Here
to Help You Nongovernmental Organizations: The Growing
Power of an Unelected Few' and held on 11 June 2003. The
American Enterprise Institute's NGO Watch website is at
http://www.ngowatch.org/. The Andrew Natsios quote and
other ideas were drawn from a speech given by Andrew
Hewett, Executive Director of Oxfam Community Aid Abroad,
at the Public Right to Know conference of the Australian
Centre for Independent Journalism at the University of Sydney
on 17 October 2003.

Paddy Manning wishes to thank Andrew Hewett and James
Ensor, Martin Mowbray, Senator John Cherry, Don Henry,
Marsali McKinnon, Robert Manne, Stephen Jolly, Keith Moor,
Nick Poletti, Patrick Earle and a couple of individuals who
prefer to remain anonymous.

Chapter 15: Democracy v. the Beast

Tim Dunlop's Hanson piece was published on 28 August 2003
in his 'Road to Surfdom' weblog at http://
www.roadtosurfdom.com and republished, with his permission,
in Webdiary on 1 September 2003 in 'Pauline Hanson's Gift to
Democracy' at http://www.smh.com.au/articles/2003/09/01/
1062268515520.html. For Pauline Hanson's maiden speech
refer to Hansard at http://www.aph.gov.au/hansard/index.htm.
Howard's refugee mantra was 'formalised' at the Liberal Party's
Sydney election campaign launch in October 2001; my account
of the launch, where Howard first used the phrase 'We will

decide', is in 'Howard's Australia' at http://www.smh.com.au/
articles/2003/11/26/1069522662977.html. The history of
Howard and Abbott's attitude to Hanson is in 'Unmasked
Howard Gets Amnesia on Hanson' at http://www.smh.com.au/
articles/2003/08/29/1062050665430.html. For Howard's early
position on Hanson, see especially 'Hanson Still Dividing
Liberals', by Gerard Henderson, *The Age*, 2 September 2003,
at http://www.theage.com.au/articles/2003/09/01/
1062403447717.html. Dick Morris's *The New Prince:
Machiavelli Updated for the 21st Century* was published by
Renaissance Books, 1999. Kim Beazley's 1983 commendation
of new disclosure laws is from Hansard; Abbott's explanation of
why the laws don't apply to his trust is from a 5 September
2003 interview with the author (see Chapter 16). The transcript
of a groundbreaking story by Ross Coulthart after the 1998
Queensland election, 'Pauline Hanson and the Media', is at
http://sunday.ninemsn.com.au/sunday/cover_stories/transcript_
240.asp. Tony Abbott's quote about the tactical shift, and the
one later in the chapter about the new trust, was in his chapter
for the book *Two Nations: The Causes and Effects of the Rise of the
One Nation Party in Australia*, published by Bookman, 1998.
The Brisbane opinion poll referred to was for the *Sunday Mail*
and taken twenty-four hours after Hanson was released; it
showed 30 per cent would have awarded her their primary vote
for a Senate position. Terry Sharples now insists his cross-
examination answer 'No, he didn't' was due to him
misconstruing the question as relating to funds for the
injunction only; he nevertheless later pursued Abbott for 'costs'
reimbursement. Deborah Snow's original feature of 11 March
2000 did not publish the phrase 'you have perjured yourself' in
Abbott's description to her of his response to Sharples' cross-
examination. His full response, first revealed by Snow in
'Abbott in New Tangle over Sharples Claim' for SMH,

30 August 2003, is at http://www.smh.com.au/articles/2003/08/
29/1062050664908.html. The judgement in the Sharples civil
action (Sharples v. O'Shea) can be viewed via the Macquarie
University Law website at http://www.law.mq.edu.au/Units/
law309/sharples.htm. The Queensland Supreme Court ruling
quashing Hanson's conviction can be viewed at http://
www.austlii.edu.au/au/cases/qld/QCA/2003/488.html.
Hanson's first three interviews after her release from jail are in
'Hanson's First Words: Three Transcripts' at http://
www.smh.com.au/articles/2003/11/07/1068013386611.html.
Hanson's final quotes are from the exclusive interview with the
Australian's David Nason in which she announced her
retirement, as reported on 15 and 16 January in that newspaper.

Chapter 16: Australians for Honest Politicians

Webdiary posts on the Hanson–Abbott–AEC affair commence
with 'Mother of the Nation in Jail, It's Father in Charge' on
21 August 2003, at http://www.smh.com.au/articles/2003/08/
21/1061434978164.html. Webdiarist quotes, references and the
trajectory of my investigation as described can be cross-checked
and sourced in the Abbott fund archive at http://
www.smh.com.au/news/opinion/webdiary/abbott/. For more
on Wilson Tuckey see 'Will Howard Convict Tuckey After
Excusing Himself?' at http://www.smh.com.au/articles/2003/
08/19/1061261157036.html and 'Judging Tuckey's Fitness for
Office' at http://www.smh.com.au/articles/2003/08/20/
1061261204583.html. The Howard–Honan affair is reported in
'Howard Meets Honan: You Be the Judge Whether He Lied
About It' at http://www.smh.com.au/articles/2003/08/12/
1060588384214.html. The full transcript of the Abbott–Kerry
O'Brien interview is at http://www.abc.net.au/7.30/content/
2003/s933489.htm. Jack Robertson's review of the interview is in
'The ABC of Journalistic Precision' at http://www.smh.com.au/

articles/2003/08/28/1062028274721.html. John Howard's
27 August 2003 doorstop comments on Abbott and the purpose
of the AHPT fund were made in Sydney, and are at http://
www.pm.gov.au/news/interviews/Interview458.html. Peter
Costello's comments on the law versus the ballot box were
made at a press conference on 2 September 2003. Dr Graeme
Orr's comments were published in 'Memo to AEC: Why not
Let the Courts Decide Abbott Slush Fund Secrets?' in Webdiary
on 16 September 2003 and can be read in full at http://
www.smh.com.au/articles/2003/09/15/1063478123244.html.
Dr Orr is a Senior Lecturer at Griffith University's School of
Law; his Ph.D was on electoral bribery. The Australian
Electoral Act may be viewed via the AEC website at http://
www.aec.gov.au/. For Beazley's comments see Hansard at http://
www.aph.gov.au/hansard/index.htm. Joo-Cheong Tham is an
Associate Lecturer at the School of Law and Legal Studies, La
Trobe University; *Realising Democracy: Electoral Law in
Australia*, which was co-edited and introduced by Dr Graeme
Orr and to which Tham contributed the chapter 'Campaign
Finance Reform in Australia: Some Reasons for Reform', is
published by the Federation Press, 2003. The BEACON
(Byron Environmental and Conservation Organisation
Incorporated) press release calling for an ALP 'quote' for equal
access to Premier Carr as granted to developer Becton can be
seen at http://www.byronenvironmentcentre.asn.au/
becton.htm#quote. Tony Abbott's full letter to the AEC and
its response were published in 'AEC Pulls up Its Socks, Starts
Serving the People' in Webdiary on 4 September 2003 at http://
www.smh.com.au/articles/2003/09/04/1062548971030.html;
copies were kindly forwarded by the *Australian Financial
Review*'s Canberra bureau chief, Tony Walker, to whom Abbott
had released them. *The Age*'s Michael Gordon revealed Trevor
Kennedy as a donor on 30 August 2003 in 'Abbott Donor:

I Gave Gladly', which can be seen at http://www.theage.com.au/
articles/2003/08/29/1062050672319.html. For the Clough
details see 'Abbott's Slush Fund Zoo: The Western Australian
Connection' at http://www.smh.com.au/articles/2003/09/18/
1063625155054.html; Senator Andrew Murray was quoted the
same day by Mike Seccombe in SMH article 'Tricks of the
Trade' at http://www.smh.com.au/articles/2003/08/29/
1062050672552.html. The AEC charter is at http://
www.aec.gov.au/_content/what/about/goals.htm. For full
Webdiarist quotes and interview transcripts see my online
archives (see beginning of Notes for this chapter). Abbott's
10 September 2003 fax, published in 'Dear Margo . . . Tony
Abbott Writes' in Webdiary, is at http://www.smh.com.au/
articles/2003/09/11/1063191493352.html. On Abbott and
future disclosure see, for example, his interview with Channel
Seven's *Sunday Sunrise* program, 7 September 2003: 'If the
AEC was to change its mind and ask me to disclose the donors
I certainly will be happy to do so.' For a fuller background on
the AEC's Andy Becker, see my Webdiary piece 'Meet Andy
Becker, Your Fearless Honest Politics Enforcer' at http://
www.smh.com.au/articles/2003/09/19/1063625212259.html.

Chapter 17: Ever More Democratic
Harry Heidelberg's columns are at http://smh.com.au/news/
opinion/webdiary/heidelberg/. Carmen Lawrence's education
piece, 'A Fair Go Education System: The Advantages for
All of Us', is at http://www.smh.com.au/articles/2003/09/
29/1064817581627.html. Harry's response, 'Waking up to
Strange Bedfellows: A Dirty Capitalist's Lament', is at http://
smh.com.au/articles/2003/10/07/1065292572906.html. Harry's
first piece on ethics, 'My Ethics', is at http://smh.com.au/
articles/2002/09/10/1031608245090.html. Before the Iraq
war he wrote pro-war pieces, which included 'Yes, It Really Is

About Getting the Weapons' at http://smh.com.au/articles/
2003/01/22/1042911432299.html and 'Anti-war Nostalgia:
Baby Boomers Strike Again' at http://smh.com.au/articles/
2003/01/17/1042520766722.html. His change of mind is
recorded in 'Bush and Howard the Living Dead as Our
Democracies Awaken' at http://smh.com.au/articles/2003/
09/15/1063478112123.html and 'Harry's Protest' at http://
smh.com.au/articles/2004/03/21/1079823239594.html. His
diaspora pieces include 'What to Make of the Australian
Diaspora' at http://smh.com.au/articles/2003/01/13/
1041990218079.html and 'We Expats: Our Needs, Our
Connection with Home' at http://smh.com.au/articles/2003/
11/04/1067708209254.html. His first piece on Dean was 'Will
Howard Beat Bush?' at http://smh.com.au/articles/2003/08/04/
1059849331236.html. The happiness and democracy *Economist*
articles, 'Something to Be Proud Of', 12 February 2004, and
'Happiness Is a Warm Vote', 15 April 2004, are at http://
www.economist.com (payment required).

Chapter 18: Democrazy: Ten Ideas for Change
The Stephanie Dowrick quote is the title of her address to the
Adelaide Festival of Ideas on 12 July 2003; her website is at
http://www.stephaniedowrick.com/. The John Ralston Saul
quote is from an interview in the University of Alberta's *Express
News*, 21 September 2001, and can be found at http://
www.expressnews.ualberta.ca/expressnews/articles/
news.cfm?p_ID=1040. Gara LaMarche's words are from his talk
to the University of California at Irvine, 28 January 2004,
entitled 'Suppose We Had a Real Democracy in the United
States?: A Time for Imagination', and is at http://www.soros.org/
resources/articles_publications/articles/irvine_20040204. The
Beazley quote is from Hansard and is at http://www.aph.gov.au/
hansard/index.htm; John Menadue's words are from his article

'Insiders, Spin Doctors and Dog-whistlers' in the *Australian Financial Review* on 12 December 2003. Webdiary published Mark Latham's democracy speech in 'Putting Meat on the Bones of Latham's "New Politics"' at http://www.smh.com.au/articles/2004/03/23/1079939638012.html. Michael Hessenthaler's email, 'Abbott Slush: Your Ideas', is at http://www.smh.com.au/articles/2003/09/13/1063341817396.html. Andrew Bolt quoted the ONA report in a *Sun-Herald* article on 23 June 2003, describing it as 'the only secret report that Wilkie ever wrote about Iraq'. (Wilkie later confirmed that the report Bolt had quoted was highly classified; to receive such an intelligence document without authorisation is a crime under Section 79 of the Crime Act. Howard denied unequivocally that his office leaked the material; Alexander Downer has said only that he will 'fully co-operate with the police'.) George Williams is Director of the Gilbert and Tobin Centre of Public Law, University of New South Wales; see his *A Bill of Rights for Australia*, University of New South Wales Press, 2000. Carmen Lawrence's 'Ideas to Save Our Withering Democracy' is at http://www.smh.com.au/articles/2003/08/07/1060145791873.html. Cameron Andrews' piece is in 'Rekindling Liberalism: A Beginning' at http://www.smh.com.au/articles/2003/08/15/1060871763525.html; Syd Hickman's Reid Group launch speech, on 19 August 2003 at NSW Parliament House, is in 'Can Liberalism Fight Back?' at http://www.smh.com.au/articles/2003/08/19/1061261148724.html; and at http://reidgroup.org. For direct democracy in Switzerland see http://www.admin.ch/ch/e/pore/index.html, http://www.swisspolitics.org/en/links/index.php?page=links&catid=9&linktopcat=demokratie and http://www.swissinfo.org/sen/swissinfo.html?siteSect=570&sid=1294806. More on Patricia Karvelas and Michael Costa is in 'Hey Joh: Costa's the New Demon Along the Watchtower' at http://www.smh.com.au/articles/2002/11/14/1037080844929.html.

Further Reading

I read these books while writing this one.

Barker, Geoffrey, *Sexing It Up: Iraq, Intelligence and Australia*, University of New South Wales Press, 2003

Barns, Greg, *What's Wrong with the Liberal Party?*, Cambridge University Press, 2003

Clarke, Lowen, *How Media and Advertising Are Killing You: Unhook and Live!*, Glen Ormond and Goodaay, 1987

Funnell, Warwick, *Government by Fiat: The Retreat from Responsibility*, University of New South Wales Press, 2001

Gaita, Raimond (ed.), *Why the War Was Wrong*, Text Publishing, 2003

Glover, Dennis, *Orwell's Australia: From Cold War to Culture Wars*, Scribe Publications, 2003

Griffen-Foley, Bridget, *Party Games: Australian Politicians and the Media from War to Dismissal*, Text Publishing, 2003

Keating, Michael, Wanna, John and Weller, Patrick (eds), *Institutions on the Edge?: Capacity for Governance*, Allen & Unwin, 2000

Lumby, Catharine and Probyn, Elspeth (eds), *Remote Control: New Media, New Ethics*, Cambridge University Press, 2003

Orr, Graeme, Mercurio, Bryan and Williams, George (eds), *Realising Democracy: Electoral Law in Australia*, Federation Press, 2003

Postman, Neil, *Amusing Ourselves to Death*, Methuen, 1987

Rosenbaum, Ron, *Explaining Hitler*, Random House, 1998

Saul, John Ralston, *On Equilibrium*, Penguin, 2001

Sawer, Marian, *The Ethical State?: Social Liberalism in Australia*, Melbourne University Press, 2003

Sawer, Marian and Zappala, Gianni (eds), *Speaking for the People: Representation in Australian Politics*, Melbourne University Press, 2001

Scheer, Christopher, Scheer, Robert and Chaudhry, Lakshmi, *The Five Biggest Lies Bush Told Us About Iraq*, Allen & Unwin, 2003

Spritzler, John, *The People as Enemy: The Leader's Hidden Agenda in World War II*, Black Rose Books, 2003

Internet activism sites

The following websites associated with themes covered in *Not Happy, John!* may be of interest and practical assistance.

Democracy and Australia

http://www.aph.gov.org
> Official website of Parliament House.

http://aec.gov.au
> Website of the Australian Electoral Commission.

http://www.zmag.org/asiawatch/australasiawatch.htm
> US-based political website, with a collection of Australian content and activist sites.

http://www.sydneypeace.com/
> An active, innovative group on Sydney's North Shore focused on peace and democracy in Australia. Includes a draft charter for a democratic Australia.

http://www.nowwethepeople.org/
> Australian activism and discussion to put the people back into politics.

http://www.cbaa.org.au/
> Australia's community broadcasting website.

http://acid.green.net.au/acidgrn.htm
> The independent directory of Australian community groups.

http://www.aidwatch.org.au/
> Aidwatch is a 'not for profit activist organisation monitoring and campaigning on Australian overseas aid and trade policies and programs'.

http://www.spareroomsforrefugees.com/
> Information on Australia's refugee policies and the ways in which individuals and groups can become involved in campaigns to hold our government accountable.

http://www.onlineopinion.com.au/
> E-journal on political, social and economic issues from various political perspectives.

http://www.roadtosurfdom.com/
> Washington-based Tim Dunlop is Australian born and his weblog is one of the best sources of news and views on the Australian and American political scene.

http://www.ozprospect.org/

> Progressive Australian think tank engaged in major issues of the day, including immigration, the US–Australia free trade deal, and social policy.

Democracy and the Middle East

www.robert-fisk.com

> Collection of the UK *Independent*'s Beirut-based journalist's writings.

http://www.gush-shalom.org/english/

> Israel's most committed peace movement.

http://www.haaretzdaily.com/

> Israel's liberal daily newspaper.

http://www.zmag.org/weluser.htm

> US-based political website, frequently discussing Middle East politics.

http://www.palsolidarity.org/

> International solidarity movement, committed to Palestinian human rights.

http://www.tikkun.org/

> US-based progressive Jewish magazine and movement.

http://www.counterpunch.com/

> US-based political newsletter, frequently discussing Israel–Palestine.

http://www.miftah.org/

> Palestinian human rights group, led by Hanan Ashrawi.

http://www.womenforpalestine.com/020403v2/index.htm

> Australian-based group dedicated to peace in the Middle East.

http://www.arabmediawatch.com/

> UK-based group highlighting anti-Arab bias in the media.

http://www.normanfinkelstein.com/

> Home page of writer and historian Norman Finkelstein.

http://pluto.huji.ac.il/~mskimmer/

> Home page of Baruch Kimmerling.

http://www.spf.arts.usyd.edu.au/index.html

> Home page of the Sydney Peace Foundation.

http://www.jewishvoiceforpeace.org/

> US-based progressive group dedicated to Middle East peace.

http://www.memri.org/
> US-based Middle East Media Research Institute, translating and
> covering media from across the Arab world.

http://www.jao.org.au/
> Australian-based Jews Against the Occupation.

Democracy and globalisation: general

www.moveon.org
> Aiming to 'bring ordinary people into politics', the site is one of the
> most prominent in the progressive US movement. Active in the
> anti-war movement, cross-media campaigns and rights advocacy.

http://blog.deanforamerica.com/
> Howard Dean's US presidential ambition has choked, but his
> weblog is an innovative idea connecting ordinary citizens to the
> political system.

http://rightweb.irc-online.org./
> US-based advocacy group informing people of the business,
> corporate, educational and political connections between
> conservative groups and big business in America.

http://campaigndesk.org/
> *Columbia Journalism Review*'s daily weblog on the US presidential
> campaign, with links to news and analysis of all the major players.

http://wef.blogs.com/editors/
> Weblog featuring contributions from the world's best newspapers
> and insight into the decisions of the world's major media players.

http://www.prwatch.org/index.html
> US-based Center for Media Democracy's website featuring
> analysis and exposes on political, business and media spin
> throughout the world, but primarily in the US.

http://bsd.mojones.com/cgi-bin/Database_search/db_search.
cgi?setup_file=links.setup&submit_search=yes&sort_by=8
> US-based *Mother Jones* magazine's list of progressive, activist and
> informative websites on issues of democracy, human rights,
> workers' rights and the environment.

http://www.rcfp.org/behindthehomefront/
> US-based 'daily chronicle of news in homeland security and
> military operations affecting newsgathering, access to information
> and the public's right to know'.

http://www.tom-watson.co.uk/

> Tom Watson was the first UK politician to utilise the interactive weblog and 'talk' to his constituents. Many other politicians in England have followed Watson's lead.

http://www.guardian.co.uk/online/comment/story/
0,12449,998732,00.html

> Comprehensive list of the UK's best political weblogs from the right, left and centre.

http://www.mediareform.net/index.php

> US-based national, non-partisan organisation working to inform people about crucial media debates, cross-media laws and the role of the media moguls. (Using FoI laws, this site obtained the first pictures of the coffins of American soldiers who had died in Iraq.)

http://www.thememoryhole.org/

> US-based website designed to source hidden, lost or retrieved files on issues of national importance, from government or business: 'The emphasis is on material that exposes things that we're not supposed to know (or that we're supposed to forget).'

http://www.publicintegrity.org/dtaweb/home.asp

> Based in Washington DC, the Center for Public Integrity, a non-profit, non-partisan, tax-exempt organisation, has a reputation for 'public service journalism' and aims to highlight ethical breaches in government and the media. See http://www.publicintegrity.org/dtaweb/list.asp?L1=10&L2=0&L3=0&L4=0&L5=0 for its aims: 'The mission of the Center for Public Integrity is to provide the American people with the findings of our investigations and analyses of public service, government accountability and ethics related issues.'

http://www.corporatecrimereporter.com/

> US-based legal print newsletter highlighting the corrupt connections between big business, government and the legal industry.

http://www.multinationalmonitor.org/

> US-based, 'the *Multinational Monitor* tracks corporate activity, especially in the Third World, focusing on the export of hazardous substances, worker health and safety, labor union issues and the environment'.

http://www.alternet.org/
    US-based progressive news and analysis.
http://www.thenation.com/
    Website of the *Nation*, legendary US-based progressive
    publication analysing politics and the media.
http://www.fair.org/
    US-based Fairness and Accuracy in Reporting website, detailing
    bias and misrepresentation in the media.
http://www.medialens.org
    UK-based media analysis and comment, 'correcting for the
    distorted vision of the corporate media'.
http://www.democracynow.org/
    US-based independent radio station broadcast across America
    (with worldwide web streaming available), featuring interviews,
    features and news on the burning issues of the day.
http://airamericaradio.com
    Progressive radio station in the US focusing on media and politics.

Index